Also by Robert F. Berkhofer, Jr.

SALVATION AND THE SAVAGE:
*An Analysis of Protestant Missions
and American Indian Response,
1787-1862*

A BEHAVIORAL APPROACH
TO HISTORICAL ANALYSIS

The White Man's Indian

THE
WHITE MAN'S
INDIAN

〜〜〜〜〜〜

Images of the American Indian
from Columbus to the Present

ROBERT F. BERKHOFER, JR.

ALFRED A. KNOPF   NEW YORK   1978

Copyright © 1978 by Robert F. Berkhofer, Jr.
All rights reserved under International and Pan-American Copyright Con-
ventions. Published in the United States by Alfred A. Knopf, Inc., New
York, and simultaneously in Canada by Random House of Canada Limited,
Toronto. Distributed by Random House, Inc., New York.

*Grateful acknowledgment is made to the following for permission
to reprint the illustrations in this book:*

The University of Michigan Library (Plates 1, 2, and 9)
The William L. Clements Library, University of Michigan (Plate 3)
*The Metropolitan Museum of Art, Gift of the Estate of James
Hazen Hyde, 1959 (Plate 4)*
*The Slide and Photograph Collection, History of Art Department,
University of Michigan (Plate 5)*
The National Collection of Fine Arts, Smithsonian Institution (Plate 6)
The Architect of the Capitol, Washington, D.C. (Plates 7 and 8)
*The Newberry Library, Edward E. Ayer Collection,
Chicago, Illinois (Plate 10)*
Keep America Beautiful, Inc. (Plate 11)

*Grateful acknowledgment is made to the following for permission
to reprint previously published material:*

The Hakluyt Society, London: from The Journal of Christopher Columbus,
translated by C. Jane, revised and annotated by L. A. Vigneras.

Harper & Row, Inc.: from Charles Gibson, editor,
The Spanish Tradition in America *(New York: Harper & Row, 1968).*

Library of Congress Cataloging in Publication Data

Berkhofer, Robert F., Jr. [date]
The white man's Indian.

Includes bibliographical references and index.
1. Indians of North America—Public opinion.
2. Public opinion—United States. 3. United States—
Civilization—Indian influences. I. Title.
E98.P99B47   1978   301.15'43'9700497   77-15568
ISBN 0-394-48485-1

Manufactured in the United States of America
FIRST EDITION

For Mary E. Young

Contents

Illustrations

Plates follow page 138.

Acknowledgments

THOSE FRIENDS who have commented upon some or all of this book as manuscript deserve to be thanked as much as the authors I have cited in the footnotes. They have saved me from embarrassing slips in fields and topics that are outside my training or knowledge. If I have at times forgotten or twisted their advice in my eagerness to present a thesis, I hope they will forgive me. The work is dedicated to Mary E. Young for her understanding criticism of this as well as others of my books. James Axtell, Robert Bieder, Paul Conkin, Charles Gibson, Lee Goerner, John King, Alfonso Ortiz, George Stocking, George Mosse, and Stephen Tonsor all have improved this volume in small and large ways. My wife, Genevieve, performed the important function of listener as well as editor. James Hennessey, Raymond Boryczka, and Michael Pfeiffer helped as research assistants. Angus Cameron waited patiently for the author to finish the manuscript and had faith the wait was worthwhile.

Portions of the manuscript or its ideas were discussed with the fellows at the Center for the History of the American Indian at the Newberry Library over several years. I owe thanks to James Tracy for the opportunity to present the overall thesis for criticism at a colloquium on the Noble Savage at the University of Minnesota. To William Sturtevant and Wilcomb Washburn, respectively editor-in-chief of the *Handbook of North American Indians*, and editor of the volume on Indian-White relations to be issued by the Smithsonian Institution, I owe appreciation not only for reading my original drafts of some of the manuscript but also for permission to use some of the material originally commissioned for the *Handbook*. Parts Two and Three and half of Part One are greatly expanded versions of the article on White conceptions of the Indian that will appear in the Indian-White relations volume.

Today an author must not only rely on friends for criticism but also on institutions for support. The Folger Library and the National Endowment for the Humanities provided fellowships for research and writing, and the Universities of Wisconsin and Michigan gave grants-in-aid for research assistance.

Preface

WHITE INTEREST in the American Indian surges and ebbs with the tides of history. While White fascination with things Indian never entirely fades, it has easily discernible high and low points. Recently, Americans went through another period of great interest. Real and imitation Indian jewelry festooned the arms and necks of White American men and women, while bedspreads, towels, and tablecloths decorated with supposed Indian motifs adorned their homes. Books by and about Indians made the best-seller lists, and Indian heroes appeared upon movie and television screens. Authentic and fake Indians emerged in mass-media advertisements to sell everything from breakfast cereals to ecology. Newspapers and magazines carried exposés of the Indians' plight, and Indian leaders gained attention for the problems of their people through Red Power slogans and tactics. Doctoral students in American literature and history as well as anthropology produced increasing numbers of dissertations upon the image and reality of Indian life in the present and the past, while history and English departments hastily instituted courses in Indian history and literature to bolster their declining enrollments through capitalizing upon the latest interest of college students.

Just as surely as in the past, this fascination with things Indian will recede. Clearance sales of Indian jewelry and household furnishings have already come and gone. Books about Indians gather on the remainder tables. Red Power slogans have lost their power to excite middle-class liberals to larger contributions. Indian leaders search for new ways to capture the attention of the American public as its interest in political change disappears with the altered economic outlook in the United States. The appearance of numerous doctoral dissertations and monographs on a topic usually marks the end, not the high point, of a fad.

This book seeks not so much to explain the fluctuating White interest in the Indian as to present the implications of the ideas and imagery used by Whites to understand the peoples they call Indians. If history is a series of questions put to the past by the present, then one of the goals of this book is to query why we think about the Indian the way we do today. Through examining how the White image of the Indian developed over time, I seek to illumine contemporary understanding of Indians as people. By suggesting the continuity as well as the changing uses of the idea and imagery of the Indian, this book also hopes to influence our future understanding of the first Americans. If the last goal seems too weighty for an essay, then this book at least offers perspective upon the many other books that have issued forth so profusely in recent times. Such perspective comes from the book's continuing focus upon how present assumptions shape the study of the Indian of the past as much as how today's ideas about the first Americans derive from yesteryear's. Indeed, the chief intellectual object of this book is to exemplify as well as to explicate the constant interaction between the past and present in molding current understanding of the Indian and therefore in turn the changing comprehension of past understandings as well. In other words, I try to treat current conceptions of the Indian in the same relativistic manner as I do those of the past.

In fact, the immediate stimulus for my own volume comes precisely from the stances on these very points by those many other books and articles flowing so swiftly from the presses today. The initial draft of parts of this book began as an assignment for the new multi-volume *Handbook of North American Indians* to be published by the Smithsonian Institution. At the request of Wilcomb Washburn, the editor of the volume on the history of Indian-White relations, I prepared a long article on White conceptions of the Indian from Columbus to the present. In the course of surveying the voluminous secondary literature from the several disciplines that I considered relevant to the topic, I was constantly struck by how often scholars seemed oblivious of research germane to their topics in other disciplines or how frequently they presented conclusions and themes about a historic period without being aware of similar patterns holding for another era.

In reaction to this state of the scholarly literature, my own book stresses the themes common to the idea and imagery of the Indian over time and across physical and intellectual space. If I err in overemphasizing the persistence of the basic White conception of the Indian over time at the expense of subtle and not so subtle discontinuities, the reader may attribute it to my attempt to provide a perspective across historic periods usually compartmented in modern scholarly niches. If I overstress the essential coherence of the basic imagery and evaluations among White individuals and groups at the cost of variations upon those fundamentals held by sundry occupations, religions, and nationalities, the reader may ascribe it to my eagerness to call attention to the common elements of the perceptual constructs and conceptual categories among various White societies and classes. If ideas seem disembodied from the social groups holding them, however, this results as much from lacunae in the literature as from my proclivity to concentrate on the quintessential patterns of White understanding of the first Americans. If the overall story I present of such White understanding of the Indian over time is not encyclopedic but episodic and even provincial at times, it comes from my concern for presenting the core of the story as well as from my own limitations of scholarship. In short, this book is shaped by my reading of the secondary literature and subsequent desire to compensate for what I felt was understressed in that scholarship as a result of modern disciplinary specialization and focus.

In the end, this book essays to synthesize the diverse and compartmented nature of previous scholarship by concentrating upon the general themes that constitute the heart of White understanding of the Indian in the past and the present. The aim of this book is therefore as ambitious as its accomplishment may be modest. If it calls the attention of general readers to the metaphysics of White Indian-understanding, to paraphrase the now famous words of Herman Melville, and offers a unified perspective to scholars of diverse disciplines and specializations, then the book will have served its author's purposes.

As with images of other races and minorities, the essence of the White image of the Indian has been the definition of Native Americans in fact and fancy as a separate and single other. Whether evaluated as noble or ignoble, whether seen as exotic or degraded, the Indian as an image was always alien to the White. In the metaphysics of race and minority relations, such a dichotomy between the "we" and the "they" is common. Thus the tendency for Whites to understand and evaluate Native Americans as others was not unique in the history of cultural and racial contact of Europeans and their descendants. Nor were the Native Americans unique in being the objects of such categorization. Just as Black Africans became "Negro" others and Red Americans "Indian" others to Whites, so had other ethnic groups become alien others to still other societies and cultures throughout history. The paradigm of polarity that lies at the heart of minority and race relations assumes uniqueness for the Whites as classifiers and for Native Americans as the classified only through the content of specific imagery and the context of a particular history and space. In the end, to understand the White image of the Indian is to understand White societies and intellectual premises over time more than the diversity of Native Americans. Although the social and cultural attributes of Native Americans influenced the conception of them by Whites, it is ultimately to the history of White values and ideas that we must turn for the basic conceptual categories, classificatory schema, explanatory frameworks, and moral criteria by which past and present Whites perceived, observed, evaluated, and interpreted Native Americans, whether as literary and artistic images, as subjects of scientific curiosity, or as objects of philanthropy and policy. As fundamental White ways of looking at themselves changed, so too did their ways of conceiving of Indians. Since the description, interpretation, explanation, and manipulation of the Indian as image and person were and are inextricably combined in White minds, the scholarly understanding of past and present White images becomes but the latest phase of a centuries-old White effort to understand themselves through understanding Native Americans and vice versa.

To write of the overall history of White Indian imagery and conceptions from Columbus to the present not only demands rigorous selectivity of focus and subject matter, as the reader will discover, but also reliance upon the published work and friendly advice of many other scholars. This book is truly dependent upon the authors cited in the notes, for they often directed me to topics and fields where I knew little and needed their valuable guidance. My first thanks must therefore go to the many authors listed in the notes. Since I have profited from their scholarship, I have tried to indicate for my readers the most recent or most comprehensive works on the many topics upon which I touch in this volume. In other words, the notes are meant to provide a comprehensive bibliography of the subject either directly through what I have listed or indirectly through those authors I cite as useful guides to the vast bodies of literature available upon the concerns of this book.

For this preface to serve its function of informing the reader of what is to follow and why, it must end upon a technical note. I have followed the policy of the new *Handbook of North American In-*

dians in capitalizing *White* whenever the word refers to the ethnic group, so as to make my usage consistent with *Red* and *Black* as comparable terms. A few spelling practices of the sixteenth and seventeenth centuries, as well as some typographical and punctuation conventions of that period, have been modernized for the sake of the modern reader if they did not hurt the meaning or context of the quotation. Whenever possible I have employed English translations of the early French and Spanish authors I quote that were contemporary to their own times, for I feel that these preserve much better the flavor and prejudice of that time rather than the often racially "sanitized" translations of our own day. Finally, I have employed the phrase *Native American(s)* to refer to the actual peoples designated by the term *Indian(s)*, which I reserve almost exclusively for the White image of those persons. My reason for this seemingly fastidious but arbitrary distinction should become abundantly clear as the reader proceeds through the pages that follow.

Less clear may be my use of *idea, image,* and *stereotype* in light of today's custom in scholarly writing. For someone less a relativist than I, the words might clearly be distinguished respectively as concept, concept plus emotion, and a rigid and oversimplified, even inaccurate, conception or image. But such well-defined distinctions presume a much clearer differentiation between other people's intellectual constructs and the knowledge of reality than I am able to offer in the following pages. Thus I mean by *image* the more literal, even pictorial, representation people had of the Indian in their minds, and *stereotype* designates any image we today no longer find accurate in light of our knowledge. To me an *idea* is a conceptual category. Thus the three words meld into one another far more in my writing than is usual today, but I think the history that follows shows why I take this stance in regard to the *Indian* as a collective and general conception.

Robert F. Berkhofer, Jr.

Ann Arbor, Michigan
May 1977

The White Man's Indian

PART ONE

~~~~~~~~

The Idea of the Indian: Invention and Perpetuation

Since the original inhabitants of the Western Hemisphere neither called themselves by a single term nor understood themselves as a collectivity, the idea and the image of the Indian must be a White conception. Native Americans were and are real, but the *Indian* was a White invention and still remains largely a White image, if not stereotype. According to a modern view of the matter, the idea of the *Indian* or Indians *in general* is a White image or stereotype because it does not square with present-day conceptions of how those peoples called Indians lived and saw themselves. The first residents of the Americas were by modern estimates divided into at least two thousand cultures and more societies, practiced a multiplicity of customs and lifestyles, held an enormous variety of values and beliefs, spoke numerous languages mutually unintelligible to the many speakers, and did not conceive of themselves as a single people—if they knew about each other at all. By classifying all these many peoples as *Indians*, Whites categorized the variety of cultures and societies as a single entity for the purposes of description and analysis, thereby neglecting or playing down the social and cultural diversity of Native Americans then—and now—for the convenience of simplified understanding. To the extent that this conception denies or misrepresents the social, linguistic, cultural, and other differences among the peoples so labeled, it lapses into stereotype. Whether as conception or as stereotype, however, the idea of the Indian has created a reality in its own image as a result of the power of the Whites and the response of Native Americans.

If the term *Indian* and the images and conceptual categories that go along with that collective designation for Native Americans are White inventions, then the first question becomes one already old in 1646 when an unnamed tribesman asked the Massachusetts missionary John Eliot: "Why do you call us Indians?" The first task of this book becomes therefore the study of the origins of the terminology and imagery for the collective *Indian* among those European nations most powerful in the colonization of the Western Hemisphere: Spain, France, and England. That the term survives into the present, evokes imagery and emotion yet today, and constitutes an intellectual classification of Native Americans in our own time raises the second major question: Why has the idea of *Indian* persisted for so many centuries? This problem is considered in general in the second half of this part as prelude to the histories of various aspects of White thinking and policy.

The Spanish Legacy of Name and Imagery

WHAT WHITES CALLED THE DISCOVERY of the New World and its inhabitants was, of course, part of the new economic and intellectual world of Western Europe at the time. The rising spirit of nationalism and the emergence of nation-states in that area spurred exploration of the non-European world and divided the rest of the globe into national spheres of colonization. The new printing press disseminated information about the new-found lands and expanded educated Europeans' knowledge of other peoples and their ways of life. But, if Europeans added a fourth part, America, to the traditional tripartite division of the inhabited world, they comprehended that New World and its peoples in terms of their own familiar conceptual categories and values, as can be seen in the terminology and overall images in first the Spanish and then the French and English accounts and travel literature.[1]

The specific term *Indian* as a general designation for the inhabitants of North and South America in addition to some Asians stems from the erroneous geography of Christopher Columbus. Under the impression he had landed among the islands off Asia, he called the peoples he met *los Indios*. Although he quite self-consciously gave new names to islands upon his first voyage, his application of the term *Indios* seems to have been almost casual. The word was introduced to the public in the offhand manner of an aside through his oft-reprinted letter of 1493.[2] Regardless of whether Columbus thought he had landed among the East Indies or among islands near Japan or even elsewhere near the Asian continent, he would probably have used the same all-embracing term for the natives, because *India* stood as a synonym for all of Asia east of the river Indus at the time and *Indies* was the broadest designation available for all of the area he claimed under royal patent.[3] Even after subsequent explorations corrected Columbus's error in geography, the Spanish continued to employ *Indios* for all peoples of the New World, including the Aztec and Inca societies. As Gonzalo Fernández de Oviedo y Valdés explained to his readers in *De la natural hystoria de las Indias* (1526), the general term was *Indians* "for so caule wee all nations of the new founde lands."[4] The word continues in Spanish usage today and still includes the Filipinos as well. From the Spanish term came eventually the French *Indien*, the German *Indianer*, the English *Indian*, and similar words in other European languages for the New World inhabitant.

Not only was the general word a Spanish legacy to Europe but so was the basic imagery of the Indian. Until the latter half of the sixteenth century what educated Europeans knew of the geography and inhabitants of the Americas came mainly from Spanish sources, for the initial White explorations and settlement of the Western Hemisphere were conducted under the auspices of that nation. Collections of travel accounts and chronicles of Spanish discoveries appeared as early as the first decade of the 1500s, but the first comprehensive and authoritative collection of travel literature, compiled by Giovanni Battista Ramusio under the title *Delle navigationi et viaggi* and published in three massive volumes in Venice, did not appear until the 1550s.[5] In the third volume, which is devoted to the New World, all of the extracts and journals are of Spanish origin except for the voyages of Verrazano and Cartier for the French monarch. Likewise, the first translated materials on the Americas published by Richard Eden for the English in the same decade drew largely upon Spanish accounts except for those of some Italians exploring for other countries.[6]

The initial image of the Indian, like the word itself, came from the pen of Columbus. Although neither Columbus nor the converted Jew he took along to act as translator understood the language of the islanders they encountered on the first voyage, the Admiral of the Ocean Sea described with confidence in his widely published letter of 1493 the lifestyles of those peoples he called *Indians:*

> The people of this island and of all the other islands which I have found and of which I have information, all go naked, men and women, as their mothers bore them, although some of the women cover a single place with the leaf of a plant or with a net of cotton which they make for the purpose. They have no iron or steel or weapons, nor are they fitted to use them. This is not because they are not well built and of handsome stature, but because they are very marvellously timorous. . . . It is true that, after they have been reassured and have lost this fear, they are so guileless and so generous with all that they possess, that no one would believe it who has not seen it. They refuse nothing that they possess, if it be asked of them; on the contrary, they invite any one to share it and display as much love as if they would give their hearts. They are content with whatever trifle of whatever kind that may be given to them, whether it be of value or valueless. . . .
>
> They do not hold any creed nor are they idolaters; but they all believe that power and good are in the heavens and were very firmly convinced that I, with these ships and men, came from the heavens, and in this belief they everywhere received me after they had mastered their fear. This belief is not the result of ignorance, for they are, on the contrary, of a very acute intelligence and they are men who navigate all those seas, so that it is amazing how good an account they give of everything. It is because they have never seen people clothed or ships of such a kind. . . .
>
> In all these islands, I saw no great diversity in the appearance of the people or in their manners and language. On the contrary, they all understand one another, which is a very curious thing. . . .
>
> In all these islands, it seems to me that all men are content with one woman, and to their chief or king they give as many as twenty. It appears to me that the women work more than do the men. I have not been able to learn if they hold private property; it seemed to me to be that all took a share in whatever any one had, especially of eatable things.[7]

How Columbus ascertained the religious values and property customs of the islanders must be left to his imagination, but the description he gave of the Arawak tribespeople was the first in a long succession of such images of the Indian as lacking in European accomplishments but pleasant withal.

In contrast to this favorable view of Indians, he also provided the first of the bad images as well:

> In these islands I have so far found no human monstrosities, as many expected, but on the contrary the whole population is very well formed. . . . Thus I have found no monsters, nor had a report of any, except in an island "Carib," which is the second at the coming into the Indies, and which is inhabited by a people who are regarded in all the islands as very fierce and who eat human flesh. They have many canoes with which they range through all the islands of India and pillage and take whatever they can. They are no more malformed than are the others, except that they have the custom of wearing their hair long like women, and they use bows and arrows of the same cane stems, with a small piece of wood at the end, owing to their lack of iron which they do not possess. They are ferocious among these other people who are cowardly to an excessive degree, but I make no more account of them than of the rest.[8]

From this hearsay but accurate description of the Caribbean cannibals came the line of savage images of the Indian as not only hostile but depraved.

As important in establishing the early conception and imagery of the Indian was an oft-reprinted tract of Amerigo Vespucci, after whom the continents of the New World were named. In the tract that gained him this distinction, the Florentine merchant who sailed for both Spain and Portugal summarized his experiences with the natives of Brazil. Although modern scholars question the authenticity of some of the navigations chronicled in Vespucci's *Mundus Novus*, published around 1504–1505, it provided European readers with the most detailed ethnography of New World peoples since Columbus.[9] Furthermore, this pamphlet reinforced and enhanced the ambivalent images of the Indian in the minds of educated Europeans at the time, for its publication was even more widespread than Columbus's letter and its description of Indian customs was far more detailed and vivid. So influential was this description at the time that it deserves quotation at length to convey both its flavor and its impact upon the European imagination:

> First then as to the people. We found in those parts such a multitude of people as nobody could enumerate (as we read in the Apocalypse), a race I say gentle and amenable. All of both sexes go about naked, covering no part of their bodies; and just as they spring from their mothers' wombs so they go until death. They have indeed large

square-built bodies, well formed and proportioned, and in color verging upon reddish. This I think has come to them, because, going about naked, they are colored by the sun. They have, too, hair plentiful and black. In their gait and when playing their games they are agile and dignified. They are comely, too, of countenance which they nevertheless themselves destroy; for they bore their cheeks, lips, noses and ears. Nor think those holes small or that they have one only. For some I have seen having in a single face seven borings any one of which was capable of holding a plum. They stop up these holes of theirs with blue stones, bits of marble, very beautiful crystals of alabaster, very white bones, and other things artificially prepared according to their customs. But if you could see a thing so unwonted and monstrous, that is to say a man having in his cheeks and lips alone seven stones some of which are a span and a half in length, you would not be without wonder. For I frequently observed and discovered that seven such stones weighed sixteen ounces, aside from the fact that in their ears, each perforated with three holes, they have other stones dangling on rings; and this usage applies to the men alone. For women do not bore their faces, but their ears only. They have another custom, very shameful and beyond all human belief. For their women, being very lustful, cause the private parts of their husbands to swell up to such a huge size that they appear deformed and disgusting; and this is accomplished by a certain device of theirs, the biting of certain poisonous animals. And in consequence of this many lose their organs which break through lack of attention, and they remain eunuchs. They have no cloth either of wool, linen or cotton, since they need it not; neither do they have goods of their own, but all things are held in common. They live together without king, without government, and each is his own master. They marry as many wives as they please; and son cohabits with mother, brother with sister, male cousin with female, and any man with the first woman he meets. They dissolve their marriages as often as they please, and observe no sort of law with respect to them. Beyond the fact that they have no church, no religion and are not idolaters, what more can I say? They live according to nature, and may be called Epicureans rather than Stoics. There are no merchants among their number, nor is there barter. The nations wage war upon one another without art or order. The elders by means of certain harangues of theirs bend the youths to their will and inflame them to wars in which they cruelly kill one another, and those whom they bring home captives from war they preserve, not to spare their lives, but that they may be slain for food; for they eat one another, the victors the vanquished, and among other kinds of meat human flesh is a common article of diet with them. Nay be the more assured of this fact because the father has already been seen to eat children and wife, and

I knew a man whom I also spoke to who was reputed to have eaten more than three hundred human bodies. And I likewise remained twenty-seven days in a certain city where I saw salted human flesh suspended from beams between the houses, just as with us it is the custom to hang bacon and pork. I say further: they themselves wonder why we do not eat our enemies and do not use as food their flesh which they say is most savory. Their weapons are bows and arrows, and when they advance to war they cover no part of their bodies for the sake of protection, so like beasts are they in this matter. We endeavored to the extent of our power to dissuade them and persuade them to desist from these depraved customs, and they did promise us that they would leave off. The women as I have said go about naked and are very libidinous; yet they have bodies which are tolerably beautiful and cleanly. Nor are they so unsightly as one perchance might imagine; for, inasmuch as they are plump, their ugliness is the less apparent, which indeed is for the most part concealed by the excellence of their bodily structure. It was to us a matter of astonishment that none was to be seen among them who had a flabby breast, and those who had borne children were not to be distinguished from virgins by the shape and shrinking of the womb; and in the other parts of the body similar things were seen of which in the interest of modesty I make no mention. When they had the opportunity of copulating with Christians, urged by excessive lust, they defiled and prostituted themselves. They live one hundred and fifty years, and rarely fall ill, and if they do fall victims to any disease, they cure themselves with certain roots and herbs. These are the most noteworthy things I know about them.[10]

The influence of Vespucci's vivid characterization may be seen in the first pictorial all-Indian scene and the first known description of Indians published in the English language. Although naked people appeared as Indians in the woodcuts illustrating the letters of Columbus and Vespucci (see Plate 1), the first picture depicting the domestic life of the Indians as such was produced in Augsburg or Nuremberg around 1505.[11] Supposedly of the Tupinamba or Guarani of Brazil, the scene graphically portrayed the vice most sensational and horrifying in European eyes—cannibalism—as an everyday Indian way of life (see Plate 2). Native life as portrayed in the picture fits the first brief mention of *Armenica*, or America, in English. Published some time between 1511 and 1522, the text was taken from a Dutch pamphlet of the period:

the people of this lande have no kynge nor lorde nor theyr god [.]
But all thinges is comune/ this people goeth all naked But the men

and women have on theyr heed/ necke/ Armes/ Knees/ and fete all
with feders bounden for there bewtynes and sayrenes. These folke
lyven lyke bestes without any resonablenes and the wymen be also
as comon. And the men hath conversacyon with the wymen/ who
that they ben or who they fyrst mete/ is she his syster/ his mother/
his daughter/ or any other kyndred. And the wymen be very hoote
and dysposed to lecherdnes. And they ete also on[e] another[.]
The man eteth his wyfe[,] his chylderne/ as we also have seen and
they hange also the bodyes or persons fleeshe in the smoke/ as men
do with swynes fleshe. And that lande is ryght full of folke/ for they
lyve commonly. iii. C.[300] yere and more as with sykeness they dye
nat/ they take much fysshe for they can goen under water and
fe[t]che so the fisshes out of the water. And they werre also on[e]
upon a nother/ for the olde men brynge the yonge men therto/
that they gather a great company therto of towe partyes/ and come
the on[e] ayene the other to the felde or bateyll/ and flee on[e] the
other with great hepes. And nowe holdeth the fylde/ they take the
other prysoners And they brynge them to deth and ete them/ and
as the dede is eten then sley they the rest. And they been eten also/
or otherwyse lyve they longer tymes and many yeres more than
other people for they have costly sypces and rotes/ where they them
selfe recover with/ and hele them as they be seke.[12]

With the new printing press purveying such images in print and
picture, the idea of the Indian as different from the European quickly
developed in the minds of Europeans even before they knew for sure
that these people did not live off Asia.

As the Spanish empire extended over the American continents
and Europeans came to understand that these new-found lands were
indeed a New World, the Spanish observations amplified what was
known of the diversity of the aboriginal inhabitants of the Western Hemisphere but did not change the fundamental conception of the
Indian. The basic themes that would dominate so much of White
thinking on Native Americans for the next few centuries were well
developed in the literature on the Spanish conquest and settlement of
the Americas. Using the twin criteria of Christianity and "civilization," Spaniards found the Indian wanting in a long list of attributes:
letters, laws, government, clothing, arts, trade, agriculture, marriage,
morals, metal goods, and above all religion. Judgments upon these
failures might be kind and sympathetic or harsh and hostile, but no
one argued that the Indian was as good as the European in this early
period. Neither discovery that the new-found lands constituted a
whole new world nor the conquest of the Aztec and Inca civilizations

altered the basic understanding of the *Indian* as a generic conception for the inhabitants of the Americas. Knowledge of Aztec and Inca achievements in art and agriculture and in social and political organization added to the concrete information about the diversity of peoples but did not transform the overall conception of the *Indian*.[13] If the Aztecs, for example, possessed sophisticated governmental, agricultural, and social systems, so too they practiced a religion that appeared to Spanish eyes as the very worship of the Devil, with its emphasis on human sacrifice.[14] Indians might, therefore, have the wrong or no religion, have misguided or no government, in addition to other negative qualities attributed to the stereotype, but they always stood in Christian error and deficient in civilization according to Spanish standards of measurement.

Under this impression, no wonder Spaniards debated what means were necessary to bring the Indian in line with their ideals of Christian civilization according to European criteria. Was the nature of the Indian so bestial as to demand force and ultimately enslavement to accomplish his conversion to Christ and Spanish ways, or was the Indian sufficiently rational and human to achieve these goals through peace and example alone? The Dominican friar Bartolomé de Las Casas, appalled by the cruelty, the suffering, and the deaths that accompanied Spanish exploitation of the natives, became the most vigorous publicist and lobbyist for the side favoring peaceful means and Indian freedom. In his arguments he portrayed the Indian as essentially virtuous:

> God created these simple people without evil and without guile. They are the most obedient and faithful to their natural lords and to the Christians whom they serve. They are the most submissive, patient, peaceful, and virtuous. Nor are they quarrelsome, rancorous, querulous, or vengeful. Moreover they are more delicate than princes and die easily from work or illness. They neither possess nor desire to possess worldly wealth. Surely these people would be the most blessed in the world if only they worshipped the true God.[15]

Las Casas' opponent in the great formal debate on the matter in 1550 at Valladolid, Juan Ginés de Sepúlveda, delineated Indian character in quite different terms as he sought to justify Spanish conquest and enslavement of Native Americans:

> Now compare their [the Spanish] gifts of prudence, talent, magnanimity, temperance, humanity, and religion with those little men (*homunculos*) in whom you will scarcely find traces of hu-

manity; who not only lack culture but do not even know how to write, who keep no records of their history except certain obscure and vague reminiscences of some things put down in certain pictures, and who do not have written laws but only barbarous institutions and customs. But if you deal with the virtues, if you look for temperance or meekness, what can you expect from men who were involved in every kind of intemperance and wicked lust and who used to eat human flesh? And don't think that before the arrival of the Christians they were living in quiet and the Saturnian peace of the poets. On the contrary they were making war continuously and ferociously against each other with such rage that they considered their victory worthless if they did not satisfy their monstrous hunger with the flesh of their enemies, an inhumanity which in them is so much more monstrous since they are so distant from the unconquered and wild Scythians, who also fed on human flesh, for these Indians are so cowardly and timid, that they scarcely withstand the appearance of our soldiers and often many thousands of them have given ground, fleeing like women before a very few Spaniards, who did not even number a hundred.[16]

Brave or meek, the Indian stood condemned in Sepúlveda's words.

The significance of these two opposing conclusions, employing two disparate images, lies not in their contrast alone but in what they show about Spanish conceptions of Indian as a general category. Although Las Casas tried to differentiate orders of barbarians among Native Americans, both he and Sepúlveda, like other Spaniards, viewed all peoples of the Western Hemisphere as a collective entity when they used the term *Indios*.

French and English Terms and Images

TO WHAT EXTENT THESE CONCEPTIONS bequeathed by the Spanish to other Europeans became the preconceptions of the French and English in their subsequent contact with Native Americans is difficult to tell. Even without such advance information, the French and the English would have approached the New World's inhabitants with the same basic values and orientations as had the Spanish. Thus, whether they were or were not influenced by Spanish reports, French and English explorers saw Native Americans in light of the Christianity and civilization they knew and valued and therefore made the same comparisons as had the Spanish adventurers and settlers earlier. That such judgments had to be the outcome of contact between the French and English with the Indians was further assured by the type of native societies and cultures the representatives of those two nations encountered.[17] No Aztec or Inca civilizations awaited discovery and exploitation in the areas claimed by the two countries. Rather than peoples with complex social and governmental organizations, the explorers of those two nations met "wilder" Indians, and so perhaps the denomination of these peoples as *sauvage* in French and *savage* in English seemed more appropriate to early explorers from those two countries. Certainly this impression led to Jacques Cartier's conclusion upon the natives of the Gaspé Basin he encountered in 1534: "These men may very well and truely be called wilde, because there is no poorer people in the world."[18]

Sixteenth-century Frenchmen, Italians, and Englishmen generally employed a variant of the Latin *silvaticus*, meaning a forest inhabitant or man of the woods, for the Indian as the earlier spellings of *saulvage*, *salvaticho*, and *salvage* show so well in each of the respective languages. English usage switched from *savage* to *Indian* as the general term for Native Americans in the seventeenth century, but the French continued to use *sauvage* as the preferred word into the nineteenth century.[19] The original image behind this terminology probably derives from the ancient one associated with the "wild man," or *wilder Mann* in Germany. According to medieval legend and art, the wild man was a hairy, naked, club-wielding child of nature who existed halfway between humanity and animality. Lacking civilized knowledge or will, he lived a life of bestial self-fulfillment, directed by instinct, and ignorant of God and morality. Isolated from other humans in woods, caves, and clefts, he hunted animals or gathered plants for his food. He was strong of physique, lustful of women, and degraded of origin. As the chief historian of the image suggests:

> Wildness meant more in the Middle Ages than the shrunken significance of the term would indicate today. The word implied everything that eluded Christian norms and the established framework of Christian society, referring to what was uncanny, unruly, raw, unpredictable, foreign, uncultured, and uncultivated. It in-

cluded the unfamiliar as well as the unintelligible. Just as the wilderness is the background against which medieval society is delineated, so wildness in the widest sense is the background of God's lucid order of creation. Man in his unreconstructed state, faraway nations, and savage creatures at home thus came to share the same essential quality.[20]

French and English explorers, like Columbus, were therefore both surprised and not surprised by the lifestyles they encountered when compared to what they expected of "wild" strangers. For the French, the dictionary definition of *sauvage* came to be that of André Thévet's description of the Tupinamba: "a marvelously strange wild and brutish people, without faith, without law, without religion and without civility."[21] In fact, these are almost exactly the words used in the great *Encyclopédie* of the eighteenth century to describe the *sauvage:* "peuples barbares qui vivent sans loix, sans police, sans religion, & qui n'ont point d'habitation fixe."[22] According to the author of this definition, a large part of America was still peopled with savages who were ferocious and ate human flesh but who lived in natural liberty because they lacked civilized institutions.

English usage mixed both *savage* and *Indian* in the travel accounts and letters of the sixteenth and early seventeenth centuries. Information about the Western Hemisphere and its inhabitants first became available in any quantity in English through the translations of Richard Eden in the 1550s. In these translated texts and the marginal notations upon them, Eden uniformly employed *Indians* for *Indios.*[23] The more famous Richard Hakluyt the Younger in his great *The Principal Navigations, Voyages, Traffiques, and Discoveries of the English Nation*, published in 1598–1600, also uses *Indians* for *Indios* in the Spanish accounts he includes but "wild men" for the *sauvaiges* of Jacques Cartier's journals. Moreover, in his marginal notations he invariably writes *savages* regardless of the original word in the text.[24] He shares this preference for *savage* with many of the early English adventurers in their denomination of the natives of Roanoke, Virginia, New England, and northward.[25] Many other explorers, however, did select more neutral terms, like *inhabitant*, to describe the Native Americans they met in the sixteenth century,[26] but no English explorer's account used *Indians* until the seventeenth century.

The officers of the Virginia Company in London wrote of *natives* in their instructions to governors of that colony, but the recipients of those letters and the Englishmen resident in Virginia talked most frequently of *Indians* and less often of *infidels* and *savages* in reply, even though they were well aware of the various tribes among whom they lived, as the famed Captain John Smith's writings show.[27] The same mingling of general terms for Native Americans and specific names and understanding of individual tribes can be found in the writings of the Pilgrims and Puritans during the first decades of their plantations in New England.[28]

What Englishmen called Native Americans and how they understood them after a few decades of settlement was summarized by Roger Williams in a brief analysis of nomenclature in *A Key Into the Language of America; Or, An Help to the Language of the Natives in That Part of America Called New-England* (1643). Under the heading "By what names are they distinguished," he divided terminology into two sorts:

> First, those of the *English* giving: as *Natives, Salvages, Indians, Wild-men,* (so the *Dutch* call them *Wilden*) *Abergeny men, Pagans, Barbarians, Heathen.*
> Secondly, their *Names,* which they give themselves.
> I cannot observe that they ever had (before the comming of the *English, French* or *Dutch* amongst them) any *Names* to difference *themselves* from strangers, for they knew none. . . .
> They have often asked mee, why we call them *Indians*[,] *Natives,* &c. And understanding the reason, they will call themselves *Indians,* in opposition to *English,* &c.[29]

Although few Englishmen possessed the linguistic skill or the toleration of the founder of Rhode Island, his summary of European terms seems accurate in light of the publications and manuscripts of the time. For Englishmen as for other Europeans, the use of general terms for Native Americans coexisted with knowledge of specific differences among the peoples so denominated. Williams's list also suggests that Native Americans themselves needed new general terms to designate the peoples invading their lands and to differentiate themselves from those strangers just as much as the Europeans did in the contact process.

Less used than *Indian* and *savage* but still prevalent among early English synonyms for Native Americans, as Williams's little catalog indicates, were the terms *infidel, heathen,* and *barbarian*. Both *infidel* and *heathen* were based upon religious criteria and derive from ancient Jewish and early Christian distinctions between themselves and other peoples. In fact, at the time of the initial English colonization of the New World, the word *nation* still retained its older meaning of a people or race usually heathen as well as the more modern meaning of a country or kingdom. In brief, the term designated a foreign people of another religion or culture as well as the territory they occupied.[30] Given the ambiguity of the word at the time and the nationalistic outlook emerging then, small surprise that Englishmen applied *nation* to what later was called a *tribe*. The latter term did not replace the former until well into the nineteenth century. The older usage is perhaps best known today in the references to the League of the Iroquois as the Five Nations, but then the term was used widely for individual tribes as well as for other confederacies in the colonial and early national period of the United States. *Barbarian* contrasted, of course, with one who was civilized and stemmed from the ancient Greeks' prejudice against peoples whose languages sounded a babble to them. By the sixteenth century, *barbarian* and *heathen* had come to be used almost interchangeably in English usage, for civility and Christianity were presumed necessarily and therefore inextricably associated.[31]

Just as all these terms indicate that the French and the English like the Spaniards compared their own societies and cultures with those of the Native Americans, so they too, like their rivals to the south, created basically favorable and unfavorable images of the Indian. What the French concluded from these images of the good and bad *sauvage* is told in pages 12–22.[32] How the English moved from supposedly factual descriptions of the Native Americans to the symbolism of the Indian can be traced briefly from Richard Hakluyt to Thomas Hobbes and John Locke.[33]

The English discoveries of the last quarter of the sixteenth century could be followed easily by that country's readers from the accounts reprinted or published for the first time in the various compendia of Richard Hakluyt the Younger. In the folio pages of the third volume of his last and greatest collection, *The Principal Navigations, Voyages, Traffiques, and Discoveries of the English Nation* (1598–1600), appeared the usual opposing descriptions of the inhabitants of the New World. Of the English accounts he printed, perhaps no person provided a more discouraging view of the Americans than Dionyse Settle in his discussion of Innuik Eskimo eating habits. After an account reeking with his disgust for their custom of eating meat raw, he concludes: "What knowledge they have of God, or what Idoll they adore, we have no perfect intelligence, I thinke them rather

Anthropophagi, or devourers of mans flesh than other wise: for that there is no flesh or fish which they find dead (smell it neverso filthily) but they eate it, as they finde it without any other dressing. A loathesome thing, either to the beholders or hearers."[34] From this same man comes the remarkable tale of the capture of an old woman during a skirmish with the Eskimos: "The old wretch, whom divers of our saylers supposed to be eyther a devill, or a witch, had her buskins plucked off, to see if she were cloven footed, and for her ugly hew and deformity we let her goe."[35]

In this case, preconception seemed to have created image, and image in turn became fact. From Hakluyt, the diligent reader could also obtain a most favorable view of the Indian. Now well known through modern quotation are the phrases of Arthur Barlowe, who sailed in 1584 under the auspices of Sir Walter Raleigh to reconnoiter his patron's grant from the Queen. He sums up his first impression of the natives of Roanoke Island after his initial reception as "very handsome, and goodly people, and in their behavior as mannerly and civil, as any of Europe." After a banquet, he again comments: "We were entertained with all love, and kindnes, and with as much bountie, after their manner, as they could possibly devise." Although he noted that the Indian peoples maintain an extremely ferocious warfare among themselves, he depreciated any fears of hostilities from these natives because: "for a more kinde and loving people, there can not be found in the world, as farre as we have hitherto had triall."[36] No wonder Barlowe concluded: "Wee found the people most gentle, loving, and faithful, void of all guile, and treason, and such as lived after the manner of the golden age."[37]

From Raleigh's attempt to establish a colony upon the Carolina coast come some of the best "scientific" descriptions of Native Americans in the sixteenth century.[38] Accompanying the expedition that founded the Roanoke colony were the artist John White, who provided detailed drawings of the flora and fauna of the area, and the mathematician Thomas Hariot, who gave an elaborate description "of the commodities there found . . . and of the nature and manners of the naturall inhabitants" in his *A Briefe and True Report of the New Found Land of Virginia.* Hariot assured his fellow Englishmen that the natives of the proposed colony were easily intimidated by White arms and valor, that their towns and fighting strength were small, and that they were in awe of English artifacts and skills. In short, the natives were readily available for English colonization and exploitation, to tell which was his purpose in writing the pamphlet. Published originally in 1588 and included by Hakluyt in his travel collections, it was reissued in 1590 by the Flemish engraver and publisher Theodor de Bry at the behest of Hakluyt as the first volume in his great illustrated series of *Grand Voyages to America*. Now Englishmen and other Europeans could see pictures of Indians as well as read the accompanying ethnography of Hariot. Under the hands of De Bry's engravers, the portraits and posture of the Carolina Indians became more classical in pose and composition than the more accurate water-colors of John White, from which the engravers worked (Plate 3). In pictures and in Latin, German, French, and English, Europeans could judge for themselves the appearance, the clothing, the government, the religion, the manner of fishing and making boats, and the burial customs of the Carolina natives. These neoclassical Indians were thought such fit illustrations of the Indian in general that the De Bry plates subsequently adorned Captain John Smith's *The Generall Historie of Virginia, New-England and the Summer Isles* (1624) and even appeared in slightly modified form as late as 1705 in Robert Beverly's *History and Present State of Virginia*. Thus the heritage of the lost colony of Roanoke and the legendary Virginia Dare proved to be of two sorts: one, the peril of colony making in the new land; and two, the classical portrait of the Indian in the colonial period.[39]

By the time of the founding of Jamestown in 1607, therefore, the English, whether as promoters of colonization, founders of the Virginia Company, or as adventurers to the new colony, all thought they knew what Indians were like, how they looked and behaved, and what could be expected from them. Small wonder their expectations were fulfilled. Did these images even predetermine their actions in early encounters? Their terminology and descriptions all indicate that the English saw Indians according to the twin criteria of Christianity and civilization. The Native Americans of the Jamestown area also probably had some images of the Whites from previous contact or at least hearsay from the Roanoke colony. Perhaps in this way both sides exhibited behavior that confirmed previous stereotypes of each other.[40]

Once again one of the first impressions was of hospitality, but as English adventurers and Indian leaders competed over land and power cautious cooperation turned to outright conflict. As one gentleman observed as early as 1607: "The [native] people used our men well untill they found they begann to plant & fortefye, Then they fell to skyrmishing & kylled 3 of our people."[41] The most informative and certainly the most voluminous reports on the numerous tribes of the Jamestown area came from the pen of Captain John Smith. In his many self-advertisements he tells of how he adopted a policy of striking fear into the native population in order to coerce their respect and their help in colony building. Although predisposed to see the bad side of Indian character and custom, Smith nevertheless presented an ambiguous picture of the Indian to his readers. If, on the one hand, they appeared "inconstant in everie thing, but what feare constraineth them to keepe," they also were "craftie, timorous, quicke of apprehension & very ingenuous."[42] While Smith carefully differentiated the various tribes in contact with the English on the James, he characterized them all as Indians in his description and therefore perpetuated the general category in English minds at the same time as he presented the dual evaluation of that category.[43]

How both images served the needs of the English may be seen in the pamphlet of Alexander Whitaker, a minister in Henrico, Virginia, who urged his fellow countrymen to support the philanthropic impulse in the colony for both base and high motives in his *Goode Newes from Virginia* (1613). To prove the natives needed conversion, he resorted to the image of the bad Indian:

> . . . let the miserable condition of these naked slaves of the divell move you to compassion toward them. They acknowledge that there is a great good God, but know him not, having the eyes of their understanding as yet blinded: wherefore they serve the divell for feare, after a most base manner, sacrificing sometimes (as I have heere heard) their own Children to him. . . . Their priests . . . are no other but such as our English witches are. They live naked in bodie, as if their shame of their sinne deserved no covering: Their names are as naked as their bodie: They esteem it a virtue to lie, deceive and steale as their master the divell teacheth to them.

On the other hand, to prove them capable of conversion, Whitaker stressed the favorable aspects of Indian character and custom:

> But if any of us should misdoubt that this barbarous people is uncapable of such heavenly mysteries, let such men know that they are farre mistaken in the nature of these men, for the promise of God, which is without respect to persons, made as well to unwise men after the flesh, as to the wise, &c. let us not thinke that these men are so simple as some have supposed them: for they are of bodie lustie, strong, and very nimble: They are a very understand-

ing generation, quick of apprehension, suddaine in their dispatches, subtile in their dealings, exquisite in their inventions, and industrious in their labour.

In fact, their government appears a model for their condition:

> Finally there is a civill government amongst them which they strictly observe, and shew thereby that the law of Nature dwelleth in them: for they have a rude kinde of Common-wealth, and rough government, wherein they both honor and obey Kings, Parents, and Governours, both greater and lesse, they observe the limits of their owne possessions, and incroach not upon their neighbours dwellings. Murther is a capitall crime scarce heard among them: adultery is most severely punished, and so are their other offences.[44]

The missionary concluded such glimmerings of reason and governance encouraged the English to hope for their conversion, while their savage condition demanded it. In brief, he used both images of the Indian to substantiate his argument for the prayers and particularly the generosity of the English people in the enterprise to bring these heathen under the command of Christ.

The continued conflict over land and power as the early English settlements expanded in Virginia culminated in what the Whites called the massacre of 1622 led by Opechancanough, the successor to Powhatan. The bloody devastation of the infant colony prompted one poet to pen perhaps the darkest picture of Indian character in his demand for revenge upon the murderers of supposedly innocent women and children:

> . . . *let these [lines] excite*
> *Your military judgments to give light*
> *In safe securing of the residue*
> *Or extirpation of theat Indian crewe.*
>   *For, but consider what those Creatures are,*
> *(I cannot call them men) no Character*
> *of God in them: Soules drown'd in flesh and blood;*
> *Rooted in Evill, and oppos'd in Good;*
> *Errors of nature, of inhumane Birth,*
> *The very dregs, garbage, and spanne of Earth;*
> *Who ne're (I think) were mention'd with those creatures*
> ADAM *gave names to in their several natures;*
> *But such as coming of a later Brood,*
> *(Not sav'd in th' Arke) but since the generall Flood*

Sprung up like vermine of an earthy slime,
And so have held b' intrusion to this time:
 If these (I say) be but Consider'd well
(Father'd by Sathan, and the sonnes of hell,)
What feare or pittie were it, or what sin,
(the rather since with us they thus begin)
To quite their Slaughter, leaving not a Creature
That may restore such shame of Men, and Nature.[45]

So enraged was this poet over what he considered the perfidy of the Virginia natives that he lapsed into heresy to express his anger, for in depicting the savage character of the Indians he denied God's creation of all human beings in a single act at one time.

More orthodox in theology but equally uncomplimentary in judgment and vehemence were the words of Samuel Purchas in reaction to the massacre. In his first collection of travel accounts, *Purchas his Pilgrimage or Relations of the World*, the successor to Hakluyt in ambition if not in influence presented a less unfavorable picture of the Indian than he did in his magnum opus, *Hakluytus Posthumus or Purchas His Pilgrimes*, issued in four volumes in 1625. There in a discourse arguing for the benefits of Virginia settlement, he summarized his judgment of the natives:

> On the other side considering so good a Countrey, so bad a people, having little of humanitie but shape, ignorant of Civilitie, of Arts, of Religion; more brutish than the beasts they hunt, more wild and unmanly then that unmanned wild countrey, which they range rather then inhabite; captivated also to Satans tyranny in foolish pieties, mad impieties, wicked idlenesse, busie and bloudy wickednesse.[46]

The massacre of 1622 may have escalated English rhetoric, but the basic imagery had long been set in Virginia by White experiences previous to settlement as well as the actual contact during the early years of the colony. Subsequent English experience would only prove what they already knew about the good and bad qualities of Indian character and life. Tribes might differ and specific knowledge would increase about native individuals and groups, but the meaning of the Indian was beyond such knowledge.

The impact of the dual imagery upon the minds of educated Englishmen can be seen in their uses by that nation's two greatest philosophers of the seventeenth century. In discussing the fundamen-

tals of government in 1651, Thomas Hobbes thought the state of
nature clearly undesirable:

> In such condition, there is no place for Industry; because the
> fruit thereof is uncertain; and consequently no Culture of the Earth;
> no Navigation, nor use of the commodities that may be imported by
> Sea; no commodious Building; no Instruments of moving, and re-
> moving, such things as require much force; no Knowledge of the
> face of the Earth; no account of Time; no Arts; no Letters; no So-
> ciety; and which is worst of all, continuall feare, and danger of vio-
> lent death; And the life of man, solitary, poore, nasty, brutish, and
> short.

For proof that such horrible conditions could actually exist, he
pointed to evidence all his readers knew already:

> It may peradventure be thought, there was never such a
> time, nor condition of warre as this; and I believe it was never gen-
> erally so, over all the world: but there are many places where they
> so live now. For the savage people in many places of *America*, ex-
> cept the government of small Families, the concord whereof de-
> pendeth on naturall lust, have no government at all; and live at this
> day in that brutish manner, as I said before.[47]

For John Locke "in the beginning all the World was *America*"
also, but he contradicted Hobbes in equating the state of nature with
the state of war, for men could live in reason and peace without
government as the Europeans knew it.[48] That the two eminent English philosophers believed the Indian proved their opposing cases
shows the ambivalence of the imagery as well as the implications of
using a general name for all Native Americans regardless of what
Whites knew of the social and cultural diversity among the inhabitants of the Western Hemisphere. In the books of Hobbes and Locke
the Indian had moved from the contrasting descriptions of explorers
and settlers to the ideological polemics of social philosophers.

Significance of *Indian* as a General Category and Conception

FROM THE VERY BEGINNING of White penetration of the Western Hemisphere, Europeans realized that it was inhabited by peoples divided among themselves. Even Columbus on his first voyage distinguished between peaceful and hostile Indians on the basis of cannibalism and military ardor. Subsequent Spanish explorers, conquerors, and writers noted the differences among the many Indian societies of the New World, especially between the Aztec and Inca civilizations and other peoples. Both French and English explorers remarked the contrasts between the Eskimos and other peoples to the south of them. Early English adventurers into Virginia spoke of *Indians, savages,* and *infidels* in one breath at the same time as they carefully studied the various alliances and specific characteristics of the tribes around Jamestown. The ability to differentiate one tribe from another only increased as White knowledge accumulated over time, but the general term *Indian* or a synonym continued to coexist with—and in spite of—such information. If Whites understood the many differences among Native American peoples, why did they persist in using the general designations, which required the lumping together of all Native Americans as a collective entity? The answer to this question reveals much about later as well as early White images of Native Americans.

Increased knowledge of the fundamental differences among peoples of the world also seemed to promote Europeans' recognition of the similarities among themselves. In other words, exploration and expansion overseas resulted from and reinforced nationalism at the same time that it promoted an overall collective vision of a Europe in contradistinction to the rest of the world. The transition in thinking can perhaps be seen best in the increasing use of "Europe" for self-reference during the fifteenth and sixteenth centuries in preference to the older "Christendom." Another indication would be the new word *continent* to characterize the emerging geographical notions of collective physical self-definition of Europeanness in contrast to other peoples broadly conceived.[49] Humanist scholars endowed the old image of mythical Europa with new secular characteristics in tune with their times and what they considered her place in history. The basic attributes ascribed to continents showed most vividly in the symbolic pictures applied to title pages and to maps, but the same meaning lay behind the more prosaic written descriptions and discourses on the peoples of the world. Europeans portrayed their own continent in terms of intellectual, cultural, military, and political superiority, for Europa was usually pictured wearing a crown, armed with guns, holding orb and scepter, and handling or surrounded by scientific instruments, pallets, books, and Christian symbols. While Asia was richly dressed, rarely did she possess superior signs of power, learning, or religion. America and Africa appeared naked, and the former usually wore a feathered headdress and carried a bow and arrow. Europe, in brief, represented civilization and Christianity and learning confronting nature in America (see Plate 4).[50]

The general terms *heathen, barbarian, pagan, savage,* and even *Indian* revealed these criteria of judgment at the same time that they validated the use of collective terms for the peoples of other continents. The European takeover of the New World proved to Europeans, at least, their own superiority and confirmed the reliability of the classification of peoples by continents. Common concepts combined with successful conquest reinforced the general impression of the deficiency of primitives everywhere and validated the continuation of the general conception and the glossing over of the growing knowledge of specific social and cultural differences among New World peoples. Even among themselves and the peoples they had long known well, Europeans correlated whole nationalities with uniform moral and intellectual attributes; it should be no surprise that they should stereotype the new peoples they met elsewhere. If Shakespeare had his Caliban to symbolize New World savagery, he also had his Shylock, his Othello, as well as his Irishmen, Turks, Italians, and others to appeal to his audiences' preconceptions.[51]

Part of this stereotyping of national as well as continental characteristics must be ascribed to the confusion among the realms of culture and biology, nation and race prevalent then and until recently in Western thought. Lifestyles, bloodlines, and national boundaries were all mixed together in White analysis of humankind. Until social heritage and biological heredity were separated in the twentieth century, national character, racialism, and culture were confused and therefore blended together, whether of nations or of continents. Although as time passed the relations among environment, biology, and culture might be seen as dynamic, with each being the cause as well as the effect of the others, their confusion due to imprecise delineation and misunderstanding of the mechanism of transmission meant that race and national character studies were the same thing until very recent times. Nations, races, and cultures were all basically seen as one interchangeable category for the understanding of peoples, and individuals were usually judged as members of their collectivity rather than as different, separate humans. Therefore, general terms embracing stereotyped characteristics made sense to Whites and could exist alongside knowledge of specific societies with individual characteristics or of individuals with varying qualities.

One important consequence of this style of thought was the continuance of the general term *Indian*. The use of the general term demanded a definition, and this definition was provided by moral qualities as well as by description of customs. In short, character and culture were united into one summary judgment. The definition and characterization of *Indian* as a general term constitutes the subject proper of this book as opposed to the history of the evolution of images and conceptions of specific tribes. The basic question to be asked of such overall White Indian imagery and conception is not, therefore, why its invention in the first place but why its continuance, or perpetuation, for so many succeeding centuries? To what extent do these old approaches to the *Indian* still constitute the chief White views of Native Americans even today?

Persisting Fundamental Images and Themes

THE CENTURIES-LONG CONFUSION and melding of what seem to us fundamentally different, even incorrect, ways of understanding human societies account for several persistent practices found throughout the history of White interpretation of Native Americans as Indians: (1) generalizing from one tribe's society and culture to all Indians, (2) conceiving of Indians in terms of their deficiencies according to White ideals rather than in terms of their own various cultures, and (3) using moral evaluation as description of Indians.[52]

Not only does the general term *Indian* continue from Columbus to the present day, but so also does the tendency to speak of one tribe as exemplary of all Indians and conversely to comprehend a specific tribe according to the characteristics ascribed to all Indians. That almost no account in the sixteenth century portrays systematically or completely the customs and beliefs of any one tribe probably results from the newness of the encounter and the feeling that all Indians possessed the same basic qualities.[53] Although eyewitness accounts and discourses by those who had lived among Native Americans in the seventeenth and eighteenth centuries often describe in detail the lives of a specific tribe or tribes, they also in the end generalize from this knowledge to all Indians. The famous reporters on Native American cultures in the colonial period of the United States, for example, invariably treated their tribe(s) as similar enough to all other Indians in customs and beliefs to serve as illustrations of that race in thought and deed.[54] Even in the century that saw the rise of professional anthropology, most social scientists as well as their White countrymen continued to speak and write as if a specific tribe and all Indians were interchangeable for the purposes of description and understanding of fundamental cultural dynamics and social organization.[55] Today, most Whites who use the word *Indian* have little idea of specific tribal peoples or individual Native Americans to render their usage much more than an abstraction, if not a stereotype. Even White writers on the history of White images of the Indian tend to treat all Native American cultures as a single Indian one for the purposes of analyzing the validity of White stereotypes.[56]

Another persistent theme in White imagery is the tendency to describe Indian life in terms of its lack of White ways rather than being described positively from within the framework of the specific culture under consideration. Therefore, tribal Americans were usually described not as they were in their own eyes but from the viewpoint of outsiders, who often failed to understand their ideas or customs. Images of the Indian, accordingly, were (and are) usually what he was not or had not in White terms, rather than in terms of individual tribal cultures and social systems as modern anthropologists aim to do.[57] This negative prototype of the deficient Indian began with Columbus but continues into the present as any history of the White education of Native Americans reveals. To this day such education is still too often treated as philanthropy to the "culturally deprived" Indian.[58]

Description by deficiency all too readily led to characterization by evaluation, and so most of the White studies of Indian culture(s) were (and are) also examinations of Indian moral character. Later White understanding of the Indian, like that of earlier explorers and settlers, expressed moral judgments upon lifestyles as well as presented their description, or mixed ideology with ethnography, to use modern terms. Ethnographic description according to modern standards could not truly be separated from ideology and moral judgment until *both* cultural pluralism and moral relativism were accepted as ideals. Not until well into the twentieth century did such acceptance become general among intellectuals, and even then only a few Whites truly practiced the two ideals in their outlook on Native Americans. Thus eyewitness description prior to this century and so much still in our time combines moral evaluation with ethnographic detail, and moral judgments all too frequently passed for science in the past according to present-day understanding. If ideology was fused with ethnography in firsthand sources, then those images held by Whites who never had experience with Native Americans were usually little more than stereotype and moral judgment.

Whether describing physical appearance or character, manners or morality, economy or dress, housing or sexual habits, government or religion, Whites overwhelmingly measured the Indian as a general category against those beliefs, values, or institutions they most cherished in themselves at the time. For this reason, many commentators on the history of White Indian imagery see Europeans and Americans as using counterimages of themselves to describe Indians and the counterimages of Indians to describe themselves.[59] Such a negative reference group could be used to define White identity[60] or to prove White superiority over the worst fears of their own depravity. If the Puritans, for example, could project their own sins upon people they called savages, then the extermination of the Indian became a cleansing of those sins from their own midst as well as the destruction of a feared enemy.[61]

Since White views of Indians are inextricably bound up with the evaluation of their own society and culture, then ambivalence of Europeans and Americans over the worth of their own customs and civilization would show up in their appraisal of Indian life. Even with the image of the Indian as a reverse or negative model of White life, two different conclusions about the quality of Indian existence can be drawn. That Indians lacked certain or all aspects of White civilization could be viewed as bad or good depending upon the observer's feelings about his own society and the use to which he wanted to put the image. In line with this possibility, commentators upon the history of White imagery of the Indian have found two fundamental but contradictory conceptions of Indian culture.[62]

In general and at the risk of oversimplifying some four centuries of imagery, the good Indian appears friendly, courteous, and hospitable to the initial invaders of his lands and to all Whites so long as the latter honored the obligations presumed to be mutually entered into with the tribe. Along with handsomeness of physique and physiognomy went great stamina and endurance. Modest in attitude if not always in dress, the noble Indian exhibited great calm and dignity in bearing, conversation, and even under torture. Brave in combat, he was tender in love for family and children. Pride in himself and independence of other persons combined with a plain existence and wholesome enjoyment of nature's gifts. According to this version, the Indian, in short, lived a life of liberty, simplicity, and innocence.

On the other side, a list of almost contradictory traits emerged of the bad Indian in White eyes. Nakedness and lechery, passion and vanity led to lives of polygamy and sexual promiscuity among themselves and constant warfare and fiendish revenge against their enemies. When habits and customs were not brutal they appeared loathsome to Whites. Cannibalism and human sacrifice were the worst sins, but cruelty to captives and incessant warfare ranked not far behind in the estimation of Whites. Filthy surroundings, inadequate cooking, and certain items of diet repulsive to White taste tended to confirm a low opinion of Indian life. Indolence rather than industry, improvidence in the face of scarcity, thievery and treachery added to the list of traits on this side. Concluding the bad version of the Indian were the power of superstition represented by the "conjurers" and "medicine men," the hard slavery of women and the laziness of men, and even timidity or defeat in the face of White advances and weaponry. Thus this list substituted license for liberty, a harsh lot for simplicity, and dissimulation and deceit for innocence.

Along with the persistence of the dual image of good and bad but general deficiency overall went a curious timelessness in defining the Indian proper. In spite of centuries of contact and the changed conditions of Native American lives, Whites picture the "real" Indian as the one before contact or during the early period of that contact. That Whites of earlier centuries should see the Indian as without history makes sense given their lack of knowledge about the past of

Native American peoples and the shortness of their encounter. That later Whites should harbor the same assumption seems surprising given the discoveries of archeology and the changed condition of the tribes as the result of White contact and policy. Yet most Whites still conceive of the "real" Indian as the aborigine he once was, or as they imagine he once was, rather than as he is now. White Europeans and Americans expect even at present to see an Indian out of the forest or a Wild West show rather than on farm or in city, and far too many anthropologists still present this image by describing aboriginal cultures in what they call the "ethnographic present,"[63] or as if tribes live today as they once did. Present-day historians of the United States, likewise, omit the Indian entirely after the colonial period or the last battles on the Plains for the same reason. If Whites do not conceive of themselves still living as Anglo-Saxons, Gauls, or Teutons, then why should they expect Indians to be unchanged from aboriginal times, Native Americans ask of their White peers?[64]

If Whites of the early period of contact invented the Indian as a conception and provided its fundamental meaning through imagery, why did later generations perpetuate that conception and imagery without basic alteration although Native Americans changed? The answer to this question must be sought partially in the very contrast presumed between Red and White society that gave rise to the idea of the Indian in the first place. Since Whites primarily understood the Indian as an antithesis to themselves, then civilization and Indianness as they defined them would forever be opposites. Only civilization had history and dynamics in this view, so therefore Indianness must be conceived of as ahistorical and static. If the Indian changed through the adoption of civilization as defined by Whites, then he was no longer truly Indian according to the image, because the Indian was judged by what Whites were not. Change toward what Whites were made him ipso facto less Indian.

The history of White-Indian contact increasingly proved to Whites, particularly in the late eighteenth and nineteenth centuries, that civilization and Indianness were inherently incompatible and verified the initial conception that gave rise to the imagery. Death through disease and warfare decimated the aboriginal population in the face of White advance and gave rise by the time of the American Revolution to the idea of the vanishing race. If Whites regarded the Indian as a threat to life and morals when alive, they regarded him with nostalgia upon his demise—or when that threat was safely past.

Indians who remained alive and who resisted adoption of civilization appeared to accept White vices instead of virtues and so became those imperfect creatures, the degraded or reservation Indian. If there is a third major White image of the Indian, then this degraded, often drunken, Indian constitutes the essence of that understanding. Living neither as an assimilated White nor an Indian of the classic image, and therefore neither noble nor wildly savage but always scorned, the degraded Indian exhibited the vices of both societies in the opinion of White observers. Degenerate and poverty-stricken, these unfortunates were presumed to be outcasts from their own race, who exhibited the worse qualities of Indian character with none of its redeeming features. Since White commentators pitied when they did not scorn this degenerate Indian, the image carried the same unfavorable evaluation overall as the bad or ignoble Indian.

Complete assimilation would have meant the total disappearance of Indianness. If one adds to these images the conceptions of progress and evolution, then one arrives at the fundamental premises behind much of White understanding of the Indian from about the middle of the eighteenth century to very recent times. Under these conceptions civilization was destined to triumph over savagery, and so the Indian was to disappear either through death or through assimilation into the larger, more progressive White society. For White Americans during this long period of time, the only good Indian was indeed a dead Indian—whether through warfare or through assimilation.[65] Nineteenth-century frontiersmen acted upon this premise; missionaries and philanthropists tried to cope with the fact. In the twentieth century anthropologists rushed to salvage ethnography from the last living members left over from the ethnographic present, and historians treated Indians as "dead" after early contact with Whites. In these ways modern Native Americans and their contemporary lifestyles have largely disappeared from the White imagination—unless modern Indian activism reverses this historic trend for longer than the recurring but transitory White enthusiasm for things Indian.

That the White image of the Indian is doubly timeless in its assumption of the atemporality of Indian life and its enduring judgment of deficiency does not mean that the imagery as a whole does not have its own history. The problem is how to show both the continuity and the changes in the imagery. Ideally such a history would embody both (1) what changed, what persisted, and why, and (2) what images were held by whom, when, where, and why. On the whole, scholars of the topic attempt only one or the other of these approaches and adopt quite different strategies in doing so. One group traces the imagery in the cultural context and intellectual history of a nation or of Western civilization. The other group examines the socioeconomic forces and vested interests of White individuals and groups. To oversimplify somewhat, the first group of scholars sees the imagery as a reflection of White cultures and as the primary explanation of White behavior vis-à-vis Native Americans, while the second group understands the imagery to be dependent upon the political and economic relationships prevailing in White societies at various times. Usually the former concentrates upon imagery and ideas, and the latter emphasizes policy and actual behavior toward Native Americans. As a result of these differences in attention and explanation, nowhere does one find a comprehensive history of White imagery.[66]

If the remarkable thing about the idea of the Indian is not its invention but its persistence and perpetuation, then the task of this book becomes one of delineating that continuity in spite of seeming changes in intellectual and political currents and alterations in social and economic institutions. Accordingly, Part Two searches beneath the "scientific" conception of the Indian as it moves from premises in Christian cosmogony to modern anthropology for the familiar imagery. Part Three examines the persistence of the dual imagery of the Indian in imaginative and ideological literature and art despite changing intellectual and political climates. The last part turns to the continuing use of the basic Indian imagery to justify White public and private policies and actual dealings with Native Americans as political regimes altered and economic institutions changed.

PART TWO

From Religion
to Anthropology:
The Genealogy of the
Scientific Image of the Indian

WHAT WE CALL THE SCIENTIFIC or anthropological image of the Indian is fundamental to modern White understanding of Native Americans. To trace completely the genealogy of that image involves nothing less than telling the entire story of changes in the basic intellectual orientations of Western civilization. Such larger intellectual currents as the decline of religion, the rise of secularism and the scientific outlook, and changing moral and political ideology deeply influenced the evolving scientific image of the Indian. So did European and American economic, social, and political trends over five centuries. To separate certain images as "scientific" in contradistinction to others during most of these five centuries violates the intellectual context of past times by imposing modern disciplinary and occupational specialization upon intellectual and social categories of previous thinkers.[1] Nevertheless, we can trace ideas about Indian origins and culture regardless of occupational and disciplinary context back into the centuries before such thoughts were specifically labeled natural or social science, religion or philosophy, with the care we exercise today.

For this rather selective survey of the genealogy of the scientific image, we will concentrate on some of the formal efforts by White Europeans and Americans to understand Native Americans in relation to the human race as a whole and to Whites in particular by con-

centrating on the role of the Indian in formal explanations for the
diversity of human beings and their geographical distribution. How
have Whites accounted for the origins of Indians and their location in
the Western Hemisphere? How did they explain the differences observed in appearance, customs, language, and social organization between Indians and themselves? Were the differences observed inherent and immutable or relative and changeable? How should the
Indian be ranked in relation to other societies known to Euro-Ameri-
cans? Although the European discovery and increasing knowledge of
Indians and other non-White peoples produced and motivated these
questions, the history of the answers indicates that the Indian, like
other non-Whites, more often than not proved to White thinkers
what they presumed to be true in the first place rather than upsetting
old theories and their long-established intellectual foundations. The
Indian was an integral part of the development of what we call
anthropology but certainly cannot be said to have determined the
basic changes in that discipline's orientation over time as much as did
the larger intellectual currents of the various centuries.[2] Moreover,
Indians, in general, were never considered as low in the hierarchy of
races as the Blacks, but they were consistently ranked lower than
Whites in formal, "scientific" thought until recently, just as they
were in general White thinking.[3]

Christian Cosmogony and the Problem of Indian Origins

THE PROBLEM OF THE ORIGINS of peoples in the Americas attracted
only subsidiary attention at best in the first two centuries or so of
European interest in the Indian, but the discussion of the problem
revealed the explicit premises and the assumptions of the religious
world view that governed the basic White understanding of Native
Americans during the period. For the orthodox believer, the Christian
cosmogony that explained the origin and history of all humankind
also had to explain the Indians' presence and state of society in the
Western Hemisphere. It even determined—or allowed—the questions

that could be asked once Europeans realized that the lands discovered by Columbus constituted not part of Asia but a whole new world inhabited by peoples and animals unknown, or at least unmentioned, in the Scriptures and classical authors. How came these previously unknown peoples to be in the Americas, given the story told in Genesis of Adam and Eve first peopling the Earth after their expulsion from the Garden of Eden and a repeopling of the planet from the children of Noah after the Flood? If Native Americans were unknown to Biblical and classical authorities, were they a part of the human race at all? If so, from what branch had they sprung? Whence came they to the Western Hemisphere and by what means? In short, how could Christians reconcile their traditional explanation for the distribution and variety of peoples with the new challenge posed by the Indian presence in the New World?[4]

The challenge appeared not very great, if the relative lack of writing on the subject during the first two centuries of contact is any indication. Fear of heresy might have muted possible bold speculation, but more likely belief in the validity of the Biblical explanation, with the scholarly glosses upon it that appeared, was sufficient to satisfy almost everyone except a few skeptics.[5] For the sake of consistency, orthodox Christian thinkers had to grant the Indians souls and humanness, because scriptural history posited God's creation of all humankind in a single act at one time at a specific spot. This monogenetic explanation therefore assumed all people were of one blood and possessed but one inheritance. Hence all people were once physically, ethnically, and socially homogeneous. Thus the problem became how to trace the Indians back to Adam and Eve through the Old World peoples known to be descended from them, for naturally in the Europocentric view of history the Old World was the original one and the New World with its peoples was the one that required explanation.

Such a scriptural solution to the problem of origins demanded efforts to plug up the loopholes left by the Mosaic account. If diversity of religions, languages, lifestyles, and colors posed the basic question of origins, then the similarity of words, manners, or customs seemed to provide the answers many thinkers sought. Through comparison of a few cultural affinities in word usage, dress, religious rites, or other cultural traits, commentators linked Indians with most of the cultures known previously to Westerners from Old World antiquity: to ancient Greeks, Scythians, Tartars, Spaniards, Hebrews, or even the peoples of Atlantis, and then to the Biblical Hebrews. Of these choices the ancient Hebrews proved most popular in the hopes of connecting Native Americans to the Ten Lost Tribes. Most thinkers on the topic, however, rejected these speculations in favor of a migration from the Old World to the New over some land bridge, probably from Asia. First proposed by José de Acosta in 1590 in his *Natural and Moral History of the Indies,* this approach to the problem rejected accidental cultural similarities as spurious and eliminated the major puzzle of devising a method of transporting the people from the Old to the New World.

Migrations across a land bridge or across oceans might solve how the Indians got to America but it did not explain how they developed so differently from other peoples. In other words, the problem of reconciling cultural diversity with Biblical chronology and history remained for the monogenetic account. If God had created humankind in a single act at one time and place, then not only did all peoples descend from one ancestor but they also at one time possessed one culture and belonged to one society as well. Moreover, the multiplicity of languages, societies, and cultures that sprang from the original homogeneity must be contained within the relatively short time span scholars of that era had calculated from the genealogy of the Old Testament. If God had created man at some time between 6000 and 4000 B.C., as was generally accepted, then how had all the puzzling diversity taken place in the few short millennia subsequently? The Bible provided dual catastrophes caused by divine intervention as a fundamental solution to the puzzle. The theory traced the differences among races and nations back to the post-Flood migrations of Noah's three sons and their progeny to various parts of the globe and explained the multiplicity of languages by the confusion of tongues that resulted from the fall of the Tower of Babel.

Barring further special providence and even accepting the theory of migrations, how could scholars account for so much striking diversity in such a short time? The major line of reasoning in this period, and the one most congruent with the classical humanist's conceptions of a Greek and Roman Golden Age as well as with the orthodox Christian's conception of monogenesis, pictured the continuing degeneration of human beings after the expulsion from the Garden of Eden to the present. For those orthodox and humanist thinkers who discussed degeneration, differences in languages and customs as well as the presence of heathenism and idolatry derived from the universal and continuing decay of the original knowledge of God and society from the time of Eden and the Golden Age. Diffusion of customs like cultural changes over time had led to decline not progress, corruption not advancement, and all the while to greater societal diversity. The strain of pessimism in Renaissance thought conceived temporal change of the human condition as cyclical at best and usually bleak and therefore made degeneration seem a viable explanation for social and cultural differences among peoples.

Accordingly, Indians were portrayed as corrupt copies of the Jewish or other high civilizations of the past or, at worst, the very agents of Satan's own degeneracy. As Cotton Mather phrased it: the savages were "doleful creatures who were the veriest ruines of mankind, which were found on the earth."[6] Although some Indians still had vestiges of natural religion or even inklings of the true faith, they had lost the bulk of what they and other peoples must once have known and practiced. While such vestiges enabled scholars to trace their origins back to the Old World, they did not redeem the Indian from his degenerate if not savage state. As even the otherwise sympathetic Roger Williams summarized the religion of the tribes he knew: "the wandring Generations of *Adams* lost posteritie, having lost the true and living God their maker, have created out of the nothing of their owne inventions many false and fained Gods and Creators."[7]

A minor line of reasoning at the time focused upon the effects of climate and physical environment to explain the varieties of lifestyles, but this hypothesis was not generally accepted until the eighteenth century, when new assumptions about social process provided a revitalized context for applying this old theme in Western thought to Native Americans.[8] Naturally, the Christian world view and the cosmogony that lay at its base formed the limits of most White thinking long beyond the 1680s, the decade conventionally said to begin the Age of Reason or the Enlightenment, but about that time thinkers critical of traditional religious and political beliefs gave a new twist to old thoughts sufficient to justify many later scholars in claiming that the modern social sciences began then. Certainly, the intellectual currents of the so-called Enlightenment provided additional assumptions and ways of looking at the Indian for many thinkers of that era—to the extent that they thought about the Indian at all.

For the overwhelming majority of Whites who remained orthodox Christians, however, these new thoughts and those of succeeding centuries had to be grafted onto or reconciled with the traditional scriptural history or be rejected. Degeneration therefore remained a powerful analytical tool in White discussions of the Indian well into the nineteenth century for the orthodox, scholar and non-scholar alike, even for those persons called the founders of modern American ethnography.[9] Moreover, the basic idea of degeneracy became fused with later interpretations of the Indian through the doctrines of environmentalism, progress, evolutionism, and racism to explain the decline of Native Americans from alcohol, disease, and general deterioration in the face of White contact. In that sense, the idea of Indian degeneracy and decay extended far beyond its religious origins of the Renaissance period to become entwined in and with the very foundations of modern social scientific thinking.

In fact, the whole Christian interpretation of human diversity in general and Indian origins and differences in particular influenced the fundamental assumptions of the scientific image of the Indian for centuries to come. So long as secular or scientific explanations of human social and cultural variations postulated a single origin for all peoples, then the Christian assumption of a monogenetic origin may be said to have continued its influence. Insofar as White scholars presume the fundamental unity of all humans in psyche and intelligence, then the Christian belief in the brotherhood of all God's souls left its impression on the subsequent social sciences. In these basic outlooks the Christian parenthood of the social scientific image of the Indian becomes apparent.[10]

Environmentalism and the Varieties of the Human Species in Enlightenment Thought

THE EFFECT OF PHYSICAL ENVIRONMENT as an explanation of human social and cultural diversity goes back at least to the ancient Greeks, but as a way of analyzing the place of the American Indians among the races of man it was particularly characteristic of Enlightenment thought. Environmental explanation of Indian life originated in Europe, but this approach particularly appealed to thinkers in the newly founded United States. Grounded upon basic biological and psychological theories of the period, it seemed to account for racial diversity in terms of the liberal social ideals of the time as well as its scientific knowledge.[11]

Although many Enlightenment thinkers criticized and even repudiated various aspects of the Christian world view, they shared with more orthodox brethren many of the basic assumptions of that outlook. Thinkers still measured the age of the earth and mankind's existence upon it by the relatively short time span of the Old Testament, even if they questioned the literal truth of the account given in Genesis. Almost all thinkers continued to postulate the monogenetic origins of humanity, and therefore they also accepted the unity of mankind as fundamental corollary—though the phraseology may have changed from the unity of souls under God to the unity of the species and a common human nature. They also conceived of the universe as ordered and probably designed, and they stressed final causes and the teleological interpretation of events in their own way as much as men of the earlier period. The universe was no accident nor was it governed by chance, in the opinion of the philosophers no less than the churchmen. What was new in the application of these fundamental assumptions in the Enlightenment was the belief in the power of human understanding unaided by divine revelation—even the authority of the ancients—to comprehend the universe and the effort to substitute natural for supernatural explanation of the workings of that universe. Nature was conceived of as a system of causes and effects subject to universal laws that could be known to and through reason in terms of their immutability, regularity, and universality. Such a view of natural laws presumed a universe relatively fixed and unchanging throughout time, certainly not one subject to sudden transformative changes whether by catastrophes, accidents, or miracles, except for its creation in the first place.[12]

The ever-increasing information about the multiplicity of plants and animals as well as the diversity of human beings in all parts of the world made the reconciliation between the ideal of an ordered universe and the knowledge of a diverse one a particularly acute problem for eighteenth-century natural history. That is why the classification by Carl von Linné—better known to history as Carolus Linnaeus—of all of the earth's living creatures into one system seemed an intellectual feat rivaling the great Newton's. His *Systema Naturae*, first published in 1735, classified all life, including human, according to its appearance, habits, relations to each other, and uses. Although all known specimens of the human race were counted as a single species, *Homo sapiens*, which stood at the head of the long list of fauna and flora, it was divided into five or six varieties. Besides the four standard divisions of Americans, Europeans, Asians, and Africans, Linnaeus included feral and monstrous peoples, the latter two referring to the wild men and the deformed and unusual persons to whom he found references in classical or travel literature. *Homo sapiens Americanus* was essentially the traditional White image of the Indian as can be seen in the elaborated description of that variety of humankind contained in the later editions:

> reddish, choleric, erect
> *Hair* black, straight, thick; *Nostrils* wide; *Face* freckled; *Chin* beardless
> *Persevering*, content, free
> *Paints* himself with skillful red lines
> *Governed* by custom

In contrast, White Europeans exhibited an easygoing, active, ingenious nature, wore tailored clothing, and were governed by laws. Under the variety *monstrosus* he did include the slant-headed Indians said to live in Canada and the tall, lazy Patagonians of myth.[13]

The implications for the White, especially American, understanding of the Indian as one variety of all humankind classified as a single *species* can be seen in the technical definition of these two terms as used then. A convenient summary can be found in Noah Webster's first edition of his *American Dictionary* in 1828 under *species:*

> In zoology, a collection of organized beings derived from one common parentage by natural generation, characterized by one particular form, liable to vary from the influence of circumstances only within certain narrow limits. These accidental and limited variations are *varieties*. Different races from the same parents are called *varieties*.[14]

Generally, men of the time assumed in accordance with their fundamental cosmology that species were fixed for all time, immutable, with little or no possibility of transforming from one to another, for they really knew of no mechanism whereby mutation could occur. Varieties, on the other hand, could and did change from their initial creation, and so an explanation had to be found to account for such differences as occurred among the human species. Environmentalism became the preferred explanation used at the time. To the extent that the psychology of that era presumed mental processes a function of the environment, particularly in the form of Lockean sensationalism, then this approach reinforced the tendency to an environmental interpretation of human diversity.

The basic contentions of environmentalism were stated succinctly in the conclusion to Samuel Stanhope Smith's *An Essay on the Causes of the Variety of Complexion and Figure in the Human Species:*

> . . . when the whole human race is known to compose only one species, this confusion and uncertainty is removed, and the science of human nature, in all its relations, becomes susceptible of system. The principles of morals rest on sure and immutable foundations. Its unity I have endeavored to confirm by explaining the causes of the variety. Of these, the first I have shown to be *climate*, by which is meant, not so much the latitude of a country from the equator, as the degree of heat and cold, which often depends on a great variety of other circumstances. The next is the *state of society*, which may augment or correct the influence of climate, and is itself a separate and independent cause of many conspicuous distinctions among mankind. These causes may be infinitely varied in degree; and their effects may be diversified by various combinations. And in the continual migrations of mankind, these effects may be still further modified, by changes which have antecedently taken place in a prior climate, and a prior state of society.[15]

Indians therefore were products both of their social and physical environment in the confused mixture of character and circumstance that constituted environmental theory at the time, and their variation from other races must be explained by environmental factors and not by some inherently different nature due to separate creation as Smith reminds the reader in a special appendix devoted to "The Natural Bravery and Fortitude of the American Indians":

> The indian of North-America presents to us man completely savage, but obliged by the nature of the forest which he inhabits, and the variable temperature of the heaven under which he lives, as well as by the enemies with which he is surrounded, to employ both courage and address, for his subsistence and his defence. He is of savages, therefore, the most noble, in whom the unaided powers of human nature appear with greater dignity than among those rude tribes who either approach nearer to the equator, or farther removed towards the poles.[16]

Thus did the minister and president of the College of New Jersey hope to refute polygenism through use of standard Indian imagery and the environmental theory of the time.

This definition of species and the explanation of the varieties of humankind preserved the monogenetic interpretation so beloved of Christian and non-Christian alike of the period while it also accounted for the obvious racial differences so engraved upon the White imagination of the time. Under this theory all men were created equal by their Creator and the variations were explainable purely by natural causes. As Jefferson's friend, the Philadelphia doctor and scientist Benjamin Rush, succinctly summarized it all: "Human nature is the same in all Ages and Countries; and all differences we perceive in its characters in respect to Virtue and Vice, Knowledge and Ignorance, may be accounted for from Climate, Country, Degrees of Civilization, from Government, or other accidental causes."[17] Thus the Indian was declared equal in potential to Whites by reason of birth if not circumstances by many American thinkers from the 1780s to 1830 or so, even if he was not treated that way in policy or philanthropy. As Jefferson declared, "I believe the Indian then in body and mind equal to the White man," although his actions implied something else.[18]

Jefferson's vigorous declaration of Indian equality was in reaction to the eighteenth-century debate over the advantages and disadvantages to the world of the discovery of the Americas, for the logic of environmentalism could lead to arguments for the inequality as well as the equality of men. The other great naturalist of the eighteenth century, Comte de Buffon, started the environmental phase of the dispute in his various writings about the deficiency of animals native to the Americas and the degeneration of those introduced by the Europeans. He concluded that the smaller size and the fewer species of the indigenous animals and the degeneration of the imported animals was due to the insalubrious physical environment of the Western Hemisphere. The peoples native to the Americas were no exception to his hypothesis of deficiency as he cataloged the faults of New World inhabitants according to the list of bad Indian traits:

> For, though the American savage be nearly of the same stature with men in polished societies, yet this is not sufficient exception to the general contraction of animated Nature throughout the whole Continent. In the savage, the organs of generation are small and feeble. He has no hair, no beard, no ardour for the female. Though nimbler than the European, because more accustomed to running, his strength is not so great. His sensations are less acute; and yet he is

more cowardly and timid. He has no vivacity, no activity of mind. The activity of the body is not so much an exercise of spontaneous motion, as a necessary action produced by want. Destroy his appetite for victuals and drink, and you will at once annihilate the active principle of all his movements; he remains, in stupid repose, on his limbs or couch for whole days. It is easy to discover the cause of the scattered life of the savages, and of their estrangement from society. They have been refused the most precious spark of Nature's fire. They have no ardour for women, and, of course, no love of mankind. Unacquainted with the most lively and most tender of attachments, their other sensations of this nature are cold and languid. Their love to parents and children is extremely weak. The bonds of the most intimate of all societies, that of the same family, are feeble; and one family has no attachment to another. Hence no union, no republic, no social state, can take place among the morality of their manners. Their heart is frozen, their society cold, and their empire cruel. They regard their females as servants destined to labour, or as beasts of burden, whom they load unmercifully with the produce of their hunting, and oblige without pity or gratitude, to perform labors which often exceed their strength. They have few children, and pay less attention to them. Every thing must be referred to the first cause: They are indifferent because they are weak; and this indifference to sex is the original strain which disgraces Nature, prevents her from expanding, and, by destroying the germs of life, cuts the root of society.[19]

Other thinkers inimical to the idea of the good or Noble Savage in Europe picked up and amplified these thoughts and soon reached the inevitable conclusion that if European animals introduced into the Western Hemisphere degenerated so too would European peoples. Thus Americans, intellectuals in particular, defended their own enlightenment and the possibility of progress of their newly independent country by denying the facts adduced by the polemicists preaching degeneration. In doing so, they naturally had to prove the Indian at least equal in potential to the White man if indeed not in present accomplishments, and so Jefferson, for one, offered a point-by-point refutation of Buffon's and others' calumnies against the New World's flora and fauna, including Native Americans, in his only published book, *Notes on the State of Virginia* (1785, 1787).[20] Although Jefferson subscribed to the equality of all men in their original creation and to the potentiality of the Indian in particular, he graded peoples on a scale of superiority and inferiority as did his American and European counterparts.[21] In order to achieve such a ranking, however, they had to turn to principles other than those of environmentalism. Debate over the merits of the New World and the status of its inhabitants continued well into the nineteenth century as did the theory of environmentalism, but their significance in the scientific discussion of the Indian was superseded by theories of evolution and racism by the 1850s.

The Idea of Progress
and the State of Savagery
in the History of Mankind

THE MODERN VERSION of the idea of progress received its initial formulation during the Enlightenment. European thinkers in the seventeenth and eighteenth centuries, excited by the accomplishments of their countrymen in science, art, discovery and conquest, the commercial and agricultural revolutions, and the settlement of the New World, increasingly pointed out the possibility of human progress. Some few philosophers even postulated its inevitability. Insofar as Native Americans like other alien peoples figured in the history of European expansion over the world, their conquest seemed to justify to Europeans their understanding of history as progressive and their superiority to other peoples. Although information about Indians and other peoples contributed to the cosmopolitan goals and knowledge of the new science of mankind sought by thinkers of the period, such information did not shape the goals of that study, given its ethnocentric foundations.

European thinkers, impressed with their own accomplishments since the Renaissance, argued the idea of progress first in terms of the power of reason. If human nature was the same during all time, then the contribution of the moderns to learning and science appeared as great as that of the ancients; and indeed the achievements of Galileo, Newton, and others seemed to confirm this conclusion. Thanks to the passage of time, history favored the progress of the moderns over previous peoples because society accumulated knowledge over its life cycle. Basic man was what he had always been, but each generation stood on the shoulders of its predecessors in learning.

The progress of science, indeed, seemed to point to the best method whereby human progress could be both studied and advanced, for the philosophers mixed normative goals with their search for knowledge. Thinkers of the period thought that the scientific method applied to human beings necessitated assuming the commonness of human nature and the uniformity of the laws of human behavior over time. Thus the understanding of human institutions resulted equally well from the study of human social and cultural diversity in the past as from study in the present. What these social philosophers sought in both contemporary and past societies was the "natural" uniformities of human behavior as opposed to the accidental and unique events customarily chronicled in history.[22]

It is in the process of combining past and present into one history of all mankind that we find the interaction between the contribution of the Indian image to the study of man in this period and judgment on the Indians as a result of that study. Comparison among societies was the foundation of such a natural history of humanity, and the theoretical or conjectural history of the Enlightenment developed from four bodies of comparison: (1) between Europeans of modern times and the peoples of earlier times, (2) between modern Europeans and contemporaneous uncivilized societies, (3) between peoples of earlier times and modern uncivilized peoples, and (4) comparisons among the observable modern uncivilized themselves. The comparison between Europeans and peoples of classic times especially figured in the debate over the achievements of the moderns versus those of the ancients in the latter 1600s. Regardless of the side taken in this debate, the protagonists had to compare in detail the art, science, and other accomplishments of the Greeks and Romans with similar endeavors of their own times. In this dispute, the moderns positing progress depreciated the humanists' and neoclassicists' traditionally high valuation of Grecian and Roman institutions, especially in regard to the pagan religions, and thereby made possible the comparison of classic peoples and modern uncivilized societies.

In the other bodies of comparison the American Indian played a role, although often secondary.[23] As we have seen, comparison between Europeans and Native Americans was the very basis for the description and understanding of the Indian in the first place. Casual comparison of the Indians with ancient peoples occurred in most accounts of Indian beliefs and behavior as a device to make the unfamiliar known to readers and listeners in terms of the familiar found in the Bible, the classics, or other travel literature already known to the audience. The systematic analysis of parallel cultural traits and language was basic to the method of determining Indian origins at the time, as we have already said. Likewise, the systematic explication of correspondences between Indian customs and myths and those of the Greeks and Romans by French and English writers began shortly after settlement of North America by those nations. Marc Lescarbot, for example, devoted the entire sixth book of his *Histoire de la Nouvelle France* (1609) to the parallels found among Canadian Indians and the ancients. This book, which was so important for establishing the image of the Indian in the minds of French thinkers, was followed by *Jesuit Relations* and other books delineating these parallels. The trend to establish such correspondences between Indian, Roman, and Greek ways reached its most complete expression in 1724 with the publication of the Jesuit Joseph Lafitau's *Moeurs des sauvages Amériquains comparée aux moeurs des premiers temps*. By that date the various bodies of comparison had reached a point where Lafitau, as his title indicates, could employ the two different chronological groups of people to illuminate each other's cultures without fear of being accused of debasing the ancients. As he phrased his method:

> I was not content with knowing the nature of the savages and with learning of their customs and practices. I sought to find in these practices and customs vestiges of the most remote antiquity. I have read carefully those earliest authors who have dealt with the customs, laws, and usages of the peoples with whom they had some acquaintance. I have compared these customs, one with another, and I confess that while the ancient authors have given me support for several happy conjectures concerning the savages, the customs of the savages themselves have thrown much more light on the ancient authors.[24]

Included besides his chief interest in religion were analyses of governments, marriage, family, education, male and female occupations, techniques of hunting and fishing, burial customs, and language. The interest in religion, particularly, had produced by this time general collections of customs and treatises on comparative religions in which the American Indian at times figured.[25]

   The results of these bodies of comparison confirmed the fundamental assumptions that prompted them in the first place. The beliefs of earlier peoples and modern primitive peoples showed remarkable similarities; the beliefs and behavior of modern Europeans differed markedly from those of earlier peoples and contemporary primitives (except perhaps for some nations' peasantry and serfs). Entailed in these comparisons from the beginning and seemingly proven by the findings was the premise that the present conditions of primitive peoples could be taken to represent the early condition of present civilized societies. Conversely, the assumption that current savagery resembled past savagery in the history of mankind enabled philosophic students of human history to fill in the gaps in the evidence of the historical record. Under these rules, the missing history could be conjectured upon the basis of theory about what all peoples, presumed to have a common human nature, would do under the circumstances.

The history produced by these rules may not have been accurate, but no matter so long as it provided a plausible beginning point in time for the analysis of the history of human institutions. In this sense, the best history was not real history but an ideal or theoretical history that pointed out the normal, that is natural, development of humankind's behavior in contradistinction to what really happened. These rules and this goal made possible the many studies of the origins of social inequality, of the state, of the economy, of religion, and of other institutions produced by the philosophers. To the extent that the Indian image fit into the pattern being developed by a writer, then he employed Indian beliefs and customs to exemplify the earlier stages of human existence in his natural history of mankind, for as Edinburgh University professor Adam Ferguson wrote in 1767: "It is in their [the Indians'] present condition that we are to behold, as in a mirror, the features of our own progenitors."[26] Accordingly, the image of the good and bad Indian came to demonstrate what the life of man was like in the original state of nature.

In conjectural or theoretical history, the ranking of societies that was part of the comparative method became a theory of progression. By analogy between the life cycle of a human being and the history of the species, philosophers in the eighteenth century, especially in France and Scotland, produced a history of the sequence of stages of society that the race had passed through to reach the height of progress exemplified by Europe at the time. Just as a single person advanced from infancy through youth to reach adulthood, so all humankind had passed through savagery and barbarism before gaining civilization.

This idea was not new in the eighteenth century, for it can be found in the ancient writers, and Benjamin Keen discovered it in the discussions of Indians by the Spaniards Las Casas, Acosta, and Torquemada.[27] But the intellectual context that gave real meaning to such a sequence did not develop until the latter half of the eighteenth century. Only under assumptions of a common and constant human nature, the uniform workings of immutable laws in human affairs, and the abstraction of the natural from the accidental in history could thinkers of the time compare customs among widely divergent life-styles, range them into a series of gradations, and present them as the history of all human development and achievement. Out of this intellectual context in the eighteenth century came the new word *civilization* with its modern meaning.

Conjectural history traced the development of various human institutions as a whole or divided the total history of humankind into stages, epochs, or periods. In the latter case, the synthetic statement of the successive stages in human development constituted the progress version of the old genre of universal history, best known today from that period in the versions of Turgot and Condorcet.[28]

Whether such stages were grounded in the ability of the human intelligence as in the French school or on the modes of subsistence and the division of labor as in the Scottish school, the Indian ranked low or at the bottom of the scale. This theory of progress applied to the American Indian received extensive treatment in William Robertson's *History of America* published in 1777, a book particularly influential in the newly independent United States in shaping its leaders' comprehension of the Indian. He combined the environmentalism so prominent in the Scottish school with the idea of progress to delineate the history of the human mind as exemplified in the various stages of society. For the achievement of his goal, the life of Native Americans appeared particularly instructive:

> In America, man appears under the rudest form in which we can conceive him to subsist. We behold communities just beginning to unite, and may examine the sentiments and actions of human beings in the infancy of social life, while they feel but imperfectly the force of its ties, and have scarcely relinquished their native liberty. That state of primeval simplicity, which was known in our continent only by the fanciful description of poets, really existed in the other. The greater part of its inhabitants were strangers to industry and labour, ignorant of arts, and almost unacquainted with property, enjoying in common the blessings which flowed spontaneously from the bounty of nature.[29]

Except for the Aztec and Inca empires, Robertson thought all the Indian societies of the Americas so "rude" and so similar that they should be designated "savage." Although citizens of the new United

States debated the accuracy of Robertson's picture of the Indian, they accepted the Scottish school's version of progress just as they had its environmentalism. Thus Jefferson could both hold to the equality of the human species and yet rank Indians inferior in achievement and act accordingly in attitude and policy.[30]

Such thinking illustrates that men of the time were not moral relativists either in their judgments upon the ranking of societies or in their belief that historical knowledge proved the superiority of the European. They were absolute and ethnocentric both in their criteria of judgment, or the yardstick to measure progress, and in the proper outcome of mankind's history. They saw cultural diversity, but they did not really approve of it, a view held even among those who espoused primitivism.[31]

To have a theory of progress based upon the conception of natural law was not to have a natural law of progress in the eighteenth century. Thinkers of the period found the analogy between the life cycle of human beings and human societies too persuasive to be absolutely certain of the necessary inevitability of progress. Would not a society succumb to old age no matter how healthy it had once been, just like the human body? They lacked the faith of nineteenth-century thinkers, who, with the advances in biology, archeology, and physical anthropology, could strive to discover the very laws of progress itself.[32] In the United States students of the Indian continued with the older version of progress until the middle of the nineteenth century, when new intellectual currents provided new support for the old ideas.[33]

Evolutionism and Primitive Peoples in Nineteenth-Century Anthropology

THEORIES OF EVOLUTION dominated scientific thinking in the nineteenth century, and evolutionism became the foundation of one science after another as they differentiated and became specific disciplines during that century. What had often puzzled previous generations suddenly became explicable according to the natural laws of evolution. The formation of the solar system and the classes of stars represented stages in the evolution of the universe, according to the nebular hypothesis. Fossils figured prominently in the new sciences of geology and paleontology. In geology they allowed the dating of the various strata of the earth and proved its uniform formation over time. In turn, the stratigraphy in which fossils were found showed the changes occurring in organic life during past ages and permitted its arrangement into a developmental series in paleontology. In archeology, first the Stone, Bronze, and Iron ages were discovered, documented, and described, and then the Stone Age was divided into Paleolithic and Neolithic tools and times. Even in philology, the reconstruction of the evolution of language was carried forward through the systematic comparison of vocabularies and grammars.

The capstone of the evolutionary frame of mind was contributed by Charles Darwin in 1859 with his *On the Origin of Species by Means of Natural Selection, or the Preservation of Favoured Races in the Struggle for Life.* So important has his work been considered that his name and theory became synonymous in the popular mind with the idea of evolution itself. In historical perspective, his theory was but one of many theories of evolution during the century, and his accomplishment, though major, rested upon foundations built by others, just as his work stimulated others in both the natural and social sciences.[34]

The theories and findings of the many evolutionarily grounded sciences provided a whole new context for the study of humankind after the middle of the nineteenth century. What had been the speculation of a few in the eighteenth century became the accepted facts and beliefs of many thinkers in the succeeding century. Darwin and others had united man and nature; the relation between animals and people became less subject to disjuncture and more amenable to natural explanation. Species were no longer considered immutable; rather they changed over time, whether one preferred the theories of Lamarck or Darwin.[35]

With each new finding in geology, archeology, and biology, the beginning of the universe receded ever more distantly into the past. Biblical chronology no longer could contain the eons of time required for the slow transformations that took place in the history of the earth and the life upon it. Each science slowly but surely pushed back the Mosaic limits through the necessity of accounting for the initial formation of the earth, the slow cooling of it, the creation of its crust, and the evolution of the many life forms upon it. Increasingly thinkers, enthusiastically or reluctantly, concluded that the universe had been operating under uniform laws of constant change throughout time. The natural laws of the universe so beloved of the eighteenth century retained their uniformity, their regularity, and their stability in the succeeding century, but the timeless world of their operation was exchanged for a dynamic one to be comprehended best through evolutionary hypotheses.[36]

Such thinking in general had profound implications for the science of human societies and cultures during the last half of the nineteenth century and into the twentieth. Evolutionary advances in the natural sciences offered inspiration, theory, and method for the social sciences as they emerged during this period first as intellectual disciplines and then as academic specialties. To be scientific at this time was practically synonymous with evolutionary theory in the newly developing social as well as the natural sciences. Therefore the history of human customs and institutions came to be seen in the terms of genesis and growth, of transformations from step to step in a sequence of development. Both in social science and history, genealogy received scientific status through a genetic method of explanation using evolution. Societies and cultures were portrayed as slow accumulations obeying laws natural and evolutionary. Certainly the findings of archeology demonstrated that human society and culture did not form fully developed at one time but grew rather from slow beginnings just as had other elements of the universe. The destruction of the Biblical chronology gave the life and social sciences larger scope in which to trace the transformations of biology and society. The increased antiquity of man offered, in brief, a longer time span in which the conjectural historian could operate. If Darwin had demonstrated that human beings were the end product of a long process of evolution, could not the institutions and customs of civilization have developed from savagery in the same manner according to the same basic laws? In one way or another, Auguste Comte, Karl Marx, and Herbert Spencer, who popularized the term "evolution," were among the many social philosophers and intellectuals who attempted this task.

Evolutionism became the framework for the new anthropology, especially for the problems inherited from what had recently come to be called "ethnography" or "ethnology," through the application of the comparative method and conjectural history. The method remained fundamentally the same as developed by thinkers in the previous century, but in the hands of such men as Edward Tylor and John Lubbock in England and Lewis Henry Morgan in the United States it gained new authority and comprehensiveness for the treat-

ment of human culture and societies. What was new was the trend to
utilize more and better-authenticated data, but the basic assumptions
continued to be the same as earlier: uniformity of human mental
characteristics and abilities over space and time allowed the comparison of peoples regardless of geography or history; similarity of stages
in the course of cultural evolution of all peoples; and the use of
European standards and the idea of progress to measure the direction
and amount of development. All these assumptions in their new guise
of cultural and social evolution can be seen in the introduction to
Primitive Culture (1871) by Edward Tylor, the man who is usually
claimed to be the founder of modern anthropology, the inventor of
the word "culture" in its anthropological sense, and the person who
pronounced anthropology a new science. For example, he explains
there that his

> standard of reckoning progress and decline is not that of ideal good
> and evil, but of movement along a measured line from grade to grade
> of actual savagery, barbarism, and civilization. The thesis which I
> venture to sustain, within limits, is simply this, that the savage state
> in some measure represents an early condition of mankind, out of
> which the higher culture has gradually been developed or evolved,
> by processes still in regular operation as of old, the result showing
> that, on the whole, progress has far prevailed over the relapse.[37]

In short, he and his fellow anthropologists of the period took over the
eighteenth century's conceptual or logical relationships of a classificatory scheme embracing all coexisting and ancient peoples and made
it into the sequential relationship of a time series through analogy to
the transformism of organic growth.[38]

   The implications of the new evolutionary anthropology for the
scientific image of the Indian and the use of Native American ethnography in the newly emerging discipline can be traced most vividly in
the writings of Lewis Henry Morgan, said to be the "Tylor of American anthropology." In his *League of the Ho-dé-no-sau-nee, Iroquois,*
published in 1851 and often hailed as the first modern ethnographic
monograph, Morgan espoused a rather romantic aim: "To encourage
a kinder feeling towards the Indian, founded upon a truer knowledge
of his civil and domestic institutions, and of his capabilities for future
elevation, is the motive in which this work originated."[39] Although
he spoke of the Iroquois as representative of all Indians and presumed
the idea of progress and stages of development, he employed comparison only incidentally in his exposition of the tribes' familial and gov-

ernmental relations. The insight into kinship relations afforded by the Iroquois he extended to all *Systems of Consanguinity and Affinity of the Human Family*, published in 1871. Using kinship systems as clues to previous social organization, he reconstructed the conjectural history of the family and marriage. In addition to his research on American Indian tribes, he conducted the first systematic collection of questionnaires on a world-wide scale for his comparative analysis of this ethnological problem. His *Ancient Society, or Researches in the Lines of Human Progress from Savagery Through Barbarism to Civilization* (1877) espoused, as its title indicates, a full-fledged theory of social evolution, all proven by a wealth of ethnographic detail in the spirit of the new science of anthropology. In addition to the family, he traces the institutions of government, property, and technology through seven "ethnical periods"—lower, middle, and upper savagery; lower, middle, and upper barbarism; and civilization—differentiated according to technological innovation and economic development. As he measured the "ratio of human progress," the American Indians had advanced beyond the "zero" of lower savagery but had fallen far behind the superior Aryan and Semitic races. As he summarized their state:

> They commenced their career on the American continent in savagery; and, although possessed of inferior mental endowments, the body of them had emerged from savagery and attained the Lower Status of barbarism; whilst a portion of them, the Village Indians of North and South America had risen to the Middle Status. . . . While the Asiatic and European were waiting patiently for the boon of iron tools, the American Indian was drawing near to the possession of bronze, which stands next to iron in the order of time. During this period of arrested progress in the Eastern hemisphere, the American aborigines advanced themselves, not to the status in which they were found, but sufficiently near to reach it while the former was passing through the last period of barbarism, and the first four thousand years of civilization. It gives us a measure of time they had fallen behind the Aryan family in the race of progress: namely the duration of the Later Period of barbarism, to which the years of civilization must be added.[40]

Thus did Morgan place Native Americans as the collective entity Indian on the scale of evolutionary progress supposedly derived scientifically from the latest developments in geology, paleontology, biology, and archeology.

In both his respect for theory and his search for fact, Morgan, like Darwin, exemplified the best scientific procedure of the time. So impressed was Morgan with the necessity for the accumulation of masses of data for the scientific analysis of human history that he stressed the dire need to salvage anthropological information on Native Americans before it was too late. Combining his evolutionary approach with the traditional image of the collective Indian as a dying race, he pleaded with all his fellow White Americans who read his *Ancient Society* to direct themselves to this important task, because the American continent presented the last and best opportunity to study on such a large scale peoples from the ethnical period of barbarism.[41]

With the last of the great Indian wars out of the way in the United States, Morgan's plea was in tune with the wishes of the scientific community of the time as well as with the growing specialization of the American academic and professional worlds in the last quarter of the nineteenth century. The staffs of the new Bureau of American Ethnology, formed in the Smithsonian under the leadership of John Wesley Powell in 1879, and the new departments of anthropology in the museums and newly emerging large modern universities devoted their efforts to recording and collecting the ethnographic information and materials of the vanishing Indians.[42] Although much of the research of these new professional anthropologists was framed according to the evolutionary assumptions of the late nineteenth century—Powell, for example, hoped to organize the activities of his bureau along these lines—their findings tended increasingly to question the whole evolutionist approach in their field.[43] By the early decades of the twentieth century the older evolutionary anthropology was being successfully challenged by the modern conception of cultural pluralism and relativism.

Although the great evolutionary anthropologists of the nineteenth century used the term "culture," they thought of the concept in the singular and not the plural use of today. Infrequently did they try to see a culture as a whole from the inside; rather they were more interested in its place in conjectural history. Given their belief in progress, they ranked all societies, including those of the Native Americans, in hierarchical order according to ethnocentric criteria. Though Tylor and others thought of culture as the product of man alone and as extrasomatic, they were unclear on the mechanism of its transmission. So long as they confused culture and biology, they frequently had to adopt the racial characterization typical of their day to explain the diversity of human cultures, in spite of their uniformitarian and therefore egalitarian assumption of the psychic unity of all mankind.[44]

"Scientific" Racism and Human Diversity in Nineteenth-Century Social Sciences

MOST MODERN SCHOLARS DIFFERENTIATE between ethnocentrism and racism. To these scholars, ethnocentric judgment of one people's qualities by another in terms of the latter's own ideals and standards has prevailed from ancient times to the present among all peoples, but racism as a specific social doctrine is an invention of the European peoples in the modern period of their expansion around the world. According to this view, racism rests upon two basic assumptions: (1) the moral qualities of a human group are positively correlated with their physical characteristics, and (2) all humankind is divisible into superior and inferior stocks upon the basis of the first assumption. Racism, in other words, is an understanding of human diversity mainly or solely in terms of inherent racial differences (and the moral judgments thereon) and an explanation of that diversity entirely or mainly in terms of racial inheritances. While such a distinction between racism and ethnocentrism would seem correct in light of the modern clarity on the difference between social and biological inheritance, can the distinction be applied with historical validity to the period before the early decades of this century when culture and biology were still fused and therefore confused categories?[45]

Regardless of the answer to this question, we do know that, during the nineteenth century, several trends came together to provide in the minds of many European and American scholars a seemingly scientific foundation for the folk wisdom concerning the differences attributed to races. Such a science of race appears to us as a lack of understanding about the differences between culture and biology, but to many intellectuals of the period it promised a new stage in the development of ethnology, a new scientific specialization of the time. As part of this development, the word *race* replaced, or at least coexisted with, the word *nation* to designate a major division of humankind.[46]

Scientific racism accomplished the "biologization of history," to use Marvin Harris's expression, by equating the cultural hierarchy assumed under the idea of progress with the physical and mental differences popularly believed to exist among human groups. Certain counterassumptions about the common origin of the human species and the significance of the environment prevented most eighteenth-century thinkers from carrying racist thinking to its logical extreme as a science, but the growing belief in the polygenetic origins of human life, the transformation of the idea of progress into social and biological evolution, and the scientific study of comparative anatomy all persuaded most nineteenth- and early twentieth-century social scientists of the racial differences among nations and peoples and especially between the civilized and primitive peoples of the period.

Polygenetic (as opposed to monogenetic) explanation of human origins moved from a Christian heresy confined to a few brave thinkers in the seventeenth and even eighteenth centuries to a widely debated issue in the mid-nineteenth century. For the full-fledged scientific and scholarly polygenist of the period, human diversity resulted not from slow modifications wrought by varying rates of culture change or from contrasting environmental conditions but from innate differences among human beings existing from their original creation. Thus the differences among races stemmed from their primordial origin rather than subsequent history. Whether giving a Biblical or more secular explanation for these differences, the polygenist sought to classify the types of humankind as separate species, rather than tracing the cultural history of mankind as a single whole, as the key to understanding human diversity. Whereas the monogenist scientist and scholar presumed the unity of the human race as a single species in spite of seeming differentiation over time, the polygenist assumed the diversity of the human races resulted from originally separate species and the stability of those species throughout history. By the second half of the nineteenth century the influence of polygenetic thinking had spread far beyond its most ardent advocates to affect the views of even those who still espoused a more orthodox Christian view of human origins.[47]

Although still a minority opinion in the mid-century, the increasing influence of polygenetic assumptions pointed to the changing religious atmosphere and the coming divorce between religion and the scientific study of human origins. As evolution in all forms became increasingly acceptable to thinkers, most assumed that cultural evolution was parallel to biological evolution and maybe even part of it. Darwin himself used the cultural hierarchy of the social evolutionists to flesh out the story of human evolution in the absence of fossil evidence. Lastly, the use of comparative anatomy to study racial differences was supposed to offer a firm scientific basis for what so many thinkers had long assumed about the differences among various peoples.[48]

Before a science of race could start, however, the ready-made groupings of common knowledge had to be given scientific status through a classification system. The division of all humankind into a few races instead of many nations or peoples began in the last quarter of the seventeenth century with François Bernier and William Petty, but neither man singled out Native Americans as a separate race.[49] Although eighteenth-century classifiers differed on the number of races, they usually listed the American Indian as a separate race.[50] How the stereotype of the Indian entered the mainstream of scientific classification through Linnaeus's contribution has been shown in a preceding chapter. His confused mixture of geography, color, physique, customs, personality, and even the hoary theory of the four humors, as well as his Europocentric bias, indicates the state of scientific classification of the human species at that time.

Such gross comparisons of physical appearance, culture, and geography continued well into the next century, but some scholars as early as the late eighteenth century attempted to place the subject of race upon a more scientific basis through the detailed and quantified study of anatomy. The essential problem in raciology, or the supposedly scientific study of racial differences, was to find some sort of data to confirm the inferences based upon prejudice and casual observation. Attempts to pin down such verifiable attributes of race differences led repeatedly to a spectrum of variation instead of hard-and-fast differences among the races, and so the search for certain proof switched from one index to another, all the while adding to what came to be called physical anthropology.[51]

Although all parts of the human body underwent measurement, none received more anthropometric attention than the head, presumably as a result of its being the seat of the intellect and therefore the basis of social progress. Beginning in the late eighteenth century, scientists commenced measuring facial angles and cranium sizes in order to differentiate the races scientifically, but the fullest development of these activities came in the first half of the nineteenth century. Craniometry or craniology, the study of the size of the brain, shape of the skull, and the nature of the suture, reached its height with the invention of the cephalic index (length-breadth ratio) in Sweden and the treatises of the so-called American School in the mid-century.

In the United States the concern with craniology was part of the pro-slavery argument for the Black's inherent inferiority. Incidental to the measurement of Black and White skulls was the consideration of Indian anatomy. From the measurement of several hundred skulls, the leader of the American School, Samuel George Morton, and his disciples concluded that the skulls of various races ranged in size from a mean of 92 cubic inches for the modern Caucasian races to 79 cubic inches for the American races and 75 cubic inches for the Hottentots and Australian Bushmen. To them these measurements proved conclusively the superiority of the White over all other races. Under the section "Comparative Anatomy of Races" in the compendium issued by leading scholars of the school, significantly entitled *Types of Mankind: Or, Ethnological Researches* (1854), J. C. Nott summarizes the findings about the intellect of the various peoples inhabiting America:

> Intelligence, activity, ambition, progression, high anatomical development, characterize some races; stupidity, indolence, immobility, savagism, low anatomical development characterize others. Lofty civilization, in all cases, has been achieved solely by the "Caucasian" group. Mongolian races, save in the Chinese family, in no instance have reached beyond the degree of semi-civilization; while the Black races of Africa and Oceanica no less than the *Barbarous* tribes of America have remained in utter darkness for thousands of years. . . .
>
> Furthermore, certain savage types can neither be civilized or domesticated. The *Barbarous* races of America (excluding the Toltecs) although nearly as low in intellect as the Negro races, are essentially untameable. Not merely have all attempts to civilize them failed, but also every endeavor to enslave them. Our Indian tribes submit to extermination, rather than wear the yoke under which our Negro slaves fatten and multiply.
>
> It has been falsely asserted, that the *Choctaw* and *Cherokee* Indians have made great progress in civilization. I assert positively, after the most ample investigation of the facts, that the pure-blooded Indians are everywhere unchanged in their habits. Many white persons, settling among the above tribes, have intermarried with them; and all such trumpeted progress exists among these whites and their

mixed breeds alone. The pure-blooded savage still skulks untamed through the forest, or gallops athwart the prairie. Can any one call the name of a single pure Indian of the *Barbarous* tribes who—except in death, like a wild cat—has done anything worthy of remembrance?[52]

Such was the virulent racism given the patina of science through craniology by this school. This science was used to rationalize White American policies toward Indians as well as Blacks at the time.[53]

By the 1860s the cultural hierarchy of social progress had been fused with the racial hierarchy of physical anthropology, and Darwinian biology only seemed to confirm further the conventional wisdom. Ascent up the ladder of social evolution was closely linked to mental capacity, and mental capacity was presumed a function of brain or cranial size. Whether such differences were due to Lamarckian adaptation to physical environment, to the Darwinian struggle for survival, or to polygenetic primordial inheritance, the conclusion on all sides was the same: cumulative mind growth meant a better mentality as well as a difference in mentality. The lower races, therefore, not only possessed darker skins and bad manners but their organic equipment was inferior as well. The reason that white-skinned peoples ruled the world and epitomized civilization was not accidental, according to scientific racism, but an inevitable result of biological inheritance. Thus Darwin pointed out the implications of racial selection for the history of mankind, and Lewis Henry Morgan connected culture to heredity through the blood. That both men were confused about the mechanism of the transmission of cultural traits illustrates how the social evolutionists of the nineteenth century could be racists in attitude although their technical assumptions, as outlined in the previous chapter, theoretically excluded such a position.[54]

As a result of this confusion and these developments in the sciences, most social scientists in the last decades of the nineteenth and the early decades of the twentieth centuries were both evolutionists and racists from a modern viewpoint, although some of these social scientists thought of themselves as combating the arrant assumptions of the raciologists of their era who so glibly equated culture and biology through their own contrasting stress on cultural history and evolution. Thus, for their time, many scholars considered themselves less racist than their colleagues in the social sciences but appear equally dependent upon racialist assumptions according to present-day understanding of the relation between cultural variation and biological inheritance and endowment. What eighteenth-century scholars, therefore, usually ascribed to the progress of reason or social stages in the history of nations, late nineteenth- and early twentieth-century social scientists generally and ultimately attributed to mental capacity and biological superiority in the history of races.[55]

Evolution and raciology influenced the newly developing psychology, and in turn that new discipline's findings were taken to support racial differences. The most important phase of this history for our purposes was the study of instinct as the mental feature common to animals and humans once scientists accepted the continuity of the two under evolution. Since savages were presumed to be closest to the animal stage, they were also presumed, therefore, to be creatures of instinct who reacted simply, almost automatically, to environmental stimuli. Advanced races applied their ratiocinative powers to their situation and produced literatures, ethical religions, independent states, and, in their highest form, a constitutional government. Thus, once again, science confirmed the long-time stereotyped characterization of primitive peoples.

The use of racial psychology in combination with physical anthropology and evolution formed the basis of Daniel Brinton's five-fold classification of the human species into hereditary races in his *Races and Peoples: Lectures on the Science of Ethnography* (1890).[56] The eminent University of Pennsylvania professor of anthropology sought through his study of ethnography to "study the differences, physical and mental, between men *in masses,* and ascertain which of these differences are least variable and hence of most value in classifying the human species into its several varieties and types." Since it is the "psychical endowment of a tribe or a people which decides its luck in the fight of the world," he paid as much attention to the instincts governing man according to "ethnic psychology" as he did to what we call ethnography today. He gave the same old capsule summaries of psychological characteristics long associated with the racial stereotypes of various peoples. Confessing that all Indians looked alike, for "so marked is the unity of its type, so alike the physical and mental traits of its members from the Arctic to the Antarctic latitudes, that I cannot divide it any other way than geographically," he devoted a chapter of thirty pages to the usual stereotyped materials on Native Americans in a confusion of race, physical structure, and culture.

Such confusion of categories from our viewpoint also marked

many of the contributions in the early pages of the *American Anthropologist*, founded in 1889, and in the work of the newly organized institutions fostering anthropological research in the late nineteenth century. In fact, remnants of such thought even showed up in the first *Handbook of American Indians North of Mexico* (issued by the Bureau of American Ethnology in two large volumes in 1907–1910) in the articles written by Aleš Hrdlička under the headings "Anatomy" (vol. 1, pp. 53–56) and "Physiology" (vol. 2, pp. 238–40) and J. N. B. Hewitt under "Mythology" (vol. 1, pp. 964–72).[57] So influential was ethnic psychology that, even though he was a Tuscarora himself Hewitt several times throughout his article referred to the "inchoate" reasoning or thought embodied in "savage" mythology.

Scientific racism continued into the early decades of the twentieth century as part of the social scientific mainstream in the United States, but new currents arose during this same period that gained command of the social disciplines by the 1930s in favor of the idea of cultural pluralism and provided a new context for the conceptions of culture and cultural relativity. The new mental testing in the early decades reinforced racist interpretations of inherent mental differences, and this trend reached its zenith with the analysis of the notorious Alpha and Beta tests administered to American soldiers in World War One. At the same time that racism was receiving this new scientific infusion, the rediscovery of Mendelian genetics, the lack of success in attempts to specify the exact nature of the so-called "primitive mind," and the failure of physical anthropology to provide absolutely certain indexes for racial differentiation all raised questions about the scientific status of raciology as an approach to human diversity. Accompanying this trend was the rise of cultural anthropology as an alternative way of looking at the problem of diversity and a changed intellectual context in the study of humankind, so that by the mid-twentieth century racism was discredited in science and considered merely a political and social ideology primarily espoused by those who would dominate other peoples for political or economic reasons.[58]

Cultural Anthropology and the Modern Conception of Indians

THE BASIC PRESUPPOSITIONS that govern the modern understanding of Native Americans as exemplified in the current teaching of anthropology can be traced back chiefly in the United States to Franz Boas and his students, although they were not the only social scientists developing new conceptions about human diversity. Boas, trained in Germany as a physicist and a geographer, switched to anthropology as a result of his field experiences among Eskimos. He brought his attitudes toward empiricism and neo-Kantian philosophy to the definition of the discipline as he introduced it into the United States. As founder of the anthropology department at Columbia University, which offered the first comprehensive graduate program in the country, he was responsible for training the founders of many other new university departments being established in the early twentieth century. He and his students came to dominate the profession by the time of the First World War. Soon, other professional anthropologists in the United States followed Boas and his students in repudiating raciology and evolutionism and espousing the idea of culture as the way of understanding human diversity in lifestyles and as the foundation concept of their discipline. Since these scholars found it expedient to test their concepts among the American Indians, the modern scholarly understanding of Native Americans according to the fundamental tenets of cultural pluralism and relativism principally derives in the United States from the articles, monographs, popular books, and teaching of this so-called Boasian or "American" school.[59]

Boas's own fieldwork among the Eskimo and Northwest Coast tribes as well as his experiments in physical anthropology caused him to question the easy correlation of race, language, culture, and social organization that lay at the foundation of racial and evolutionary anthropology at the turn of the century. His own experience among native peoples and his study of Northwest Coast mythology convinced him that the so-called primitive mind operated in the same way as the so-called civilized mentality. His experiments and measurements in physical anthropology revealed no stable and consistent features attributable to race. His and his students' interest in the distribution of Indian languages, cultural traits, and tribal boundaries, likewise, showed no uniform correlation. Boas's mastery of all the fields of anthropology at the time and the work of his many students, therefore, led them to separate biological heredity from the social transmission of culture and to treat as problematical the connections among biology, the physical environment, cultural traits, language, and social organization. In other words, the Boasian school questioned and sought to test what most previous anthropologists had presumed as given.

Boasian anthropology particularly sought to replace the conjectural approach of evolutionary history with what its practitioners thought was a more scientific method based upon empirical research. Their own findings showed that the simple unilinear sequence so often presumed by evolutionism just did not hold for the tribes they studied. Different aspects of a culture changed at different rates and the various parts of a culture lacked the compatibility postulated by the evolutionists. Diffusion far more often accounted for similar culture traits among tribes than simple psychic unity and evolutionary necessity. Thus these scholars stressed actual history over conjectural history and saw the comparative method as superficial research that ripped cultural elements out of their context to fit a preconceived scheme. In their own research, as a result, they showed greater interest in the wholeness of a single culture than in comparisons across cultures, less interest in the ultimate origins of traits than in their present distribution, and preferred the mapping of cultures in the New World to the proving of a cross-societal taxonomy based upon evolution. This school, often spoken of as the "historical school" because of its preference for actual history over the conjectural kind and particularism over nomothetic laws, therefore abandoned the postulated uniformitarianism, stage theory, psychic unity as previously defined, and structural necessity fundamental to evolutionary anthropology in favor of the wholeness of a culture and the ramifications of the functional interdependence of its parts for human behavior and diversity.

Although the concept of culture in a modern anthropological sense did not prevail in the social sciences in the United States until the 1930s at the earliest,[60] the basic assumptions of relativism, pluralism, and functionalism that underlay it were abundantly foreshadowed in the works of Boas and his followers by the time of the

First World War.[61] The most important change was signaled in the switch from the singular to the plural usage of the word *culture*. In the singular, the word designated all of human culture considered as an entity and acted as a synonym for *civilization*, with its implied moral judgments derived from the hierarchical ranking of societies traditional to conjectural history. The plural, on the other hand, signified the stress on the diversity of cultures manifested by human groups and dropped a morally absolute ranking in favor of the moral relativism implied in the new phrase *cultural pluralism*.[62]

The aim of the Boasian anthropology, therefore, became the study of localized cultural traits shared by social groups or the life-style and beliefs of a single group. To get to know a culture from the "inside" demanded intensive investigation among the people studied so the anthropologist could get the "feel" of the culture. Ethnographic description in terms of the interrelationship of the parts of one culture instead of cross-cultural comparison to establish evolutionary sequence became the goal of American anthropology. Separated from the biological and environmental aspects of human life, culture became almost autonomous and not a little deterministic in its own right for some members of the American school, perhaps reaching its epitome in the claim by Alfred Kroeber that culture was a superorganic phenomenon.[63]

As applied to Native Americans, the Boasian approach meant intensive fieldwork among one or a few tribes and the classification of cultures according to areas of trait distribution. Boas himself concentrated upon the Northwest Coast tribes, while Clark Wissler and Robert Lowie studied primarily the Plains Indians, Alfred Kroeber the California Indians, and Paul Radin the Winnebago. In other words, they researched Native Americans as tribes and as cultures, not as *the* Indian (but always as they had once lived in the past and not as they lived when the anthropologist visited the tribe). Although the ethnography of a tribe can be traced back in American anthropology at least to Henry R. Schoolcraft or Lewis Henry Morgan, never before had tribes been studied so completely or so intensively for their own sake by so many anthropologists as in this period. Moreover, the anthropologists professed to study these tribes in light of a cultural relativity and pluralism that denied explicit or implicit judgments on the moral superiority of White civilization.

The product of this work was at first the mapping of various modes of subsistence, social organization, languages, customs, and beliefs according to their distribution in aboriginal America before

White contact changed native ways of life. In the hands of the American school, these maps of distribution led to the designation of culture areas by the ways of life considered most characteristic before the coming of White peoples, especially for the museum display of artifacts. To the extent that New World anthropology was presumed unable at that time to depend upon dated records of culture change and diffusion, Clark Wissler and others chose to infer the history of culture change from geographical distribution.[64]

The first general works on Native Americans incorporating the new anthropology of the American school were Clark Wissler's *The American Indian: An Introduction to the Anthropology of the New World* (1917) and *American Indian Life by Several of Its Students* edited by Elsie Clews Parsons (1922). After a survey of food areas, means of transportation, arts and artifacts, housing, social organization, property and marriage customs, religion and mythology—all described in the ethnographic present, Wissler classified all of the aboriginal social groups of the two continents into fifteen culture areas. After describing the archeological history, linguistic differences, and physical features of the various peoples, he analyzed the degree to which correlations existed among race, culture, language, and archeology, and in case after case he concluded there were no necessary associations other than historical accident.[65] The Parsons volume tried to make the same point through short fictional pieces chiefly written by Boas and his students. Over twenty scholars wrote intimately from firsthand knowledge gained through fieldwork in nearly two dozen tribes in order to persuade the general reader of the wholeness and psychological validity of each culture.

The history of anthropological theory in the United States and knowledge of tribal culture has increased greatly since the 1920s, but the basic presuppositions of cultural pluralism and relativism as established by Boas and his followers remain as fundamental to the new developments as they were to the American or historical school. To the extent that many in the American school came to understand culture as a holistic configuration as well as patterned, as a mental blueprint as well as behavioral manifestations, as historicist as well as historical, then it substituted the German meaning of the term *culture* for the traditional humanistic English one. Ruth Benedict presented these presuppositions to the general reader in her enormously popular *Patterns of Culture* (1934), which sold over a million copies in the thirty years after its publication. Through the description at length of three cultures, two of which were Native American (Zuñi and

Kwakiutl), she hoped to persuade her reader that the integrative holism of individual cultures was as important as their diversity and that the psychological sources of another culture were as valid as those of one's own. In arguing that one should not make a moral judgment upon the quality of another culture, she, in fact, criticized White American culture through her interpretations of the Dobu and Kwakiutl cultures.[66]

By positing the integrative wholeness of each and every culture, she and other anthropologists finally challenged the assumptions that so long had been the basis of the traditional White image of the Indian, scientific as well as lay. By asserting that each culture could only be described and understood in terms of itself as a total entity and not in relation to other cultures or, worse, to aspects of other cultures ripped from context, these anthropologists pulled the scientific rug out from under the long-time deficiency image of the Indian. In their stress upon cultural holism with its moral correlates of pluralism and relativism, they contradicted the description of the Indian as counter-image, condemned favorable and unfavorable evaluations under the guise of fact, and denied the ranking of tribal society as inferior to White all in favor of appreciating Native American cultures in their multiplicity and understanding Indians and their achievements in terms of themselves.

Thus the assumptions of modern social science finally replaced the assumptions of so many centuries with new ones, to create, in effect, a new scientific image of the Indian. The culmination of this particular conception of culture occurred in the history and analysis of the idea of culture itself by the noted anthropologists Alfred Kroeber and Clyde Kluckhohn in 1952.[67] By that time English social anthropology had come to the United States and even a new evolutionism was arising to challenge the dominant cultural anthropology of the Boasian school and to present new research findings on Native Americans.[68] Although these new developments in anthropology provided new ways of understanding Native American lifestyles before the Whites came to the Western Hemisphere, they did not repudiate the basic moral and intellectual assumption of the idea of culture itself: the pluralism and relativism of moral non-judgment on and non-hierarchical ranking of social groups. Even the new evolutionism did not seek to establish a unilinear sequence of inevitable social development as actual history nor did it question the moral relativism, or should we say the moral agnosticism, of cultural pluralism.[69]

In spite of all the changes in the anthropological profession's theoretical orientations and the increased accumulation of research on Native Americans during the first half of the twentieth century, anthropological monographs and texts continued mainly to describe Indian life in the timeless ethnographic present. Leading texts of the 1950s on Indians divided Native Americans into cultural areas and slighted the changes in lifestyles since aboriginal times, as if the only true Indian were a past one. To that extent, these books, so sophisticated in the new scientific approaches to Native Americans, still retained vestiges of the classic idea of the Indian. Even though Ruth Underhill subtitled her *Red Man's America* (1953), *A History of Indians in the United States*, she barely mentioned any of the major changes in Native American lifestyles over time.[70] Not until 1970 did such texts expand their historical treatment or were new texts produced that stressed actual tribal cultural changes from early migration and origins to the modern day[71]—although anthropological interest in Native American culture change under the rubric of acculturation studies had risen and fallen in the profession by that time.[72] Thus anthropologists finally admitted in their general texts that the Native American no longer existed as a timeless Indian about the same time that their fellow White Americans were being reminded of the same thing by Indian activist groups.

The first major text based wholly upon historical principles, *North American Indians in Historical Perspective*, explicitly recognized the new Indian nationalism and Red Power movement of the 1960s as the fifth and latest phase in the generalized history of Native Americans. Impressed by the seeming renascence of Indian political activity, the editors of the text presumed that the Native American as Indian not only had endured but would also continue to endure. Although Native Americans no longer lived as they did aboriginally, nevertheless they had only changed in order to survive as Indians. As one of the editors declared:

> Arguments about the future of the first Americans have commonly focused on two alternatives: should Indian culture and identity be "preserved" and ways found for Indians to support themselves "as Indians," or should Indians be helped to "assimilate" and become absorbed into the "mainstream of American life"? One thesis of this book is that these are not the only alternatives; that Indians have played a role in American history, and that they still have a role to play, neither as "museum pieces" nor as individuals lost in

the "melting pot," but as Indians of the twentieth century. Indian traditions have neither fossilized nor disappeared; Indian ways of to-day are not those of centuries ago but they are nonetheless Indian. Indian cultural traditions have continued to grow and change, and there has been constant integration of innovations into character-istically Indian ways and Indian views. Today there is a strong in-terest in defining these ways.[73]

As this statement suggests, anthropologists had switched their attention from the historical determinants of acculturation that had been the focus of so many in the profession in the 1950s to the methods by which tribal Americans had successfully resisted White acculturative forces and preserved their Indianness over the centuries and particularly in the present. This movement paralleled the switch in general American opinion from fixation on the Cold War in the decades after the Second World War to concern for minorities and the quality of domestic American life in the 1960s. And so modern anthropologists, like those of the past, reflect in their thinking the currents of their times.

To the extent that evolutionism and scientific racism can be viewed as ideologies justifying economic and cultural imperialism over colonial peoples at home or abroad, then the concept of culture in its modern anthropological definition should be seen as a human-istic reaction to contemporary industrial civilization. To deny one's own society as the best in a cultural hierarchy in favor of moral agnosticism and relativity is to question if not challenge the values of one's own society and certainly represents an expression of alienation. Like other intellectuals, many anthropologists came to see Indian societies as embracing a unified way of life often with values superior to those found in the fragmented culture of modern industrial life. Insofar as they portrayed Indian cultures as manifesting the whole-ness of man, the humanity of interpersonal relationships, and the in-tegrity of organic unity, these anthropologists, like writers, artists, and social philosophers of modern times, had abandoned the liberalism of the mid-nineteenth century for the liberalism of the mid-twentieth as their way of judging the presumably splintered culture of their own industrial society. Modern social scientists, no less than their scholarly forebears, therefore, understood Indians according to ideo-logical positions as well as scientific assumptions, and in that sense they like other members of their society studied other cultures ac-cording to the premises of their own.[74]

As the cultural conception of the Indian and the premises upon which it was based became the prevailing view of the modern scholarly community, other images of the Indian based upon assumptions and evaluations derived from older intellectual milieus, no matter how popular among the general public, became characterized by scholars and social scientists as unscientific or stereotyped, even racist. In other words, the new scientific image of the Indian became the normative standard by which other imagery was judged. Thus, as in the past, the present scientific understanding of the Indian combines normative and descriptive dimensions into one fused intellectual construct and serves ideological as well as scientific purposes. While to scholars of the future this image may appear as biased and mythical as those we see in the past, at present it is our fundamental reality. How long it will continue to fit the times, however, remains to be seen.

PART THREE

Imagery in Literature, Art, and Philosophy: The *Indian* in White Imagination and Ideology

F OR MOST WHITES throughout the past five centuries, the Indian of imagination and ideology has been as real, perhaps more real, than the Native American of actual existence and contact. As pre-conception became conception and conception became fact, the Indian was used for the ends of argument, art, and entertainment by White painters, philosophers, poets, novelists, and movie makers among many. Although each succeeding generation presumed its imagery based more upon the Native American of observation and report, the Indian of imagination and ideology continued to be derived as much from the polemical and creative needs of Whites as from what they heard and read of actual Native Americans or even at times experienced. Although modern artists and writers assume their own imagery to be more in line with "reality" than that of their predecessors, they employ the imagery for much the same reasons and often with the same results as those persons of the past they so often scorn as uninformed, fanciful, or hypocritical. As a consequence, one finds less of a cumulative development in the genealogy of the imagery, for the basic images of the good and bad Indian persist from the era of Columbus up to the present without substantial modification or variation. The continuity results from the relationship between moral evaluation and sensibility and the acceptance or critique of White civilization that so often forms the motive for the Indian of imagination and ideology in the first place.

European Primitivism, the Noble Savage, and the American Indian

PRIMITIVISM AND MILLENNIALISM are opposite sides of the same coin of human aspiration for a way of life dramatically opposite in complexity and organization from the present. While millennialism looks to the future coming of utopia, primitivism dreams of a paradise on earth that does or did prove that an alternative to the present age could exist. By the time of the Renaissance, the Judeo-Christian and Greco-Roman traditions of Eden and Arcadia, or Paradise and the Golden Age, had combined in a myth of lands lying far away to the west or long ago in the past whose citizens dwelt in an ideal(ized) landscape and gentle climate in harmony with nature and reason. Usually without property, injustice, or kings, and often without work or war, these fortunate people possessed just those virtues so many commentators found lacking in their own times: sexual innocence, equality of condition and status, peaceful simplicity, healthful and handsome bodies, and vigorous minds unsullied by the wiles, complexities, and sophistication of modern civilization. In short, primitivism postulated people dwelling in nature according to nature, existing free of history's burdens and the social complexity felt by Europeans in the modern period, and offering hope to mankind at the same time that they constituted a powerful counter-example to existing European civilization.[1]

The primitivist tradition influenced the Renaissance explorers' perceptions of the native peoples they encountered. The Fortunate or Blessed Isles, the location of the Garden of Eden, and other versions of the earthly paradise, long presumed to exist somewhere in the West, naturally colored early observations of peoples who seemed to live in gentle climes without the culture or social organization of the Europeans.[2] Columbus on his first voyage described the Arawaks according to primitivist conventions when he noted the absence of iron and steel, their nakedness, their lack of private property, their timidity in warfare, their handsome physique, sharp wit, and generous hospitality. On his third voyage, he pondered whether he had truly discovered the fabled "site of terrestrial Paradise" and even named a spot Paradise Valley.[3] The search of Ponce de León and his countrymen for the Fountain of Youth perhaps portrays most vividly Spanish faith in the legends of a Western paradise.

English and French explorers later found similar examples of the Golden Age still lived on earth among the Indians they met. As mentioned earlier, Arthur Barlowe on a voyage of reconnaissance for Walter Raleigh depicted the North Carolina natives in just such tones in 1584: "We found the people most gentle, loving, and faithful, void of all guile and treason and such as lived after the manner of the Golden Age. The earth bringeth forth all things in abundance as in the first creation, without toil or labor."[4] Marc Lescarbot, who had lived in Acadia for a year in the first decade of the 1600s, looked back upon his Canadian experience as truly arcadian when he wrote his *History of New France.*

The primitivist tradition did not create the favorable version of the Indian; rather it shaped the vocabulary and the imagery the explorers and settlers used to describe their actual experience in the New World and the lifestyles they observed among its peoples.[5] In turn, the accounts of explorers, missionaries, and other early travelers and settlers seemed to provide the factual basis and therefore a validation for the primitivistic faith of many subsequent European writers. What these written accounts suggested to the European imagination was portrayed by the artist in André Thévet's *Cosmographie,* published in 1575, and the engravings in Theodor de Bry's editions in 1590 and 1591 of Thomas Hariot's *A Briefe and True Report of the New Found Land of Virginia* and Jacques Le Moyne de Morgues' *Brevis narratio eorum quae in Florida Americae provincia.* Likened to classic statues in poses and garb, these images of noble Indians became standard illustrations for texts about Native Americans for two centuries (see Plate 3).[6]

As information about the inhabitants of the New World became better known in the Old, Native Americans entered the literary and imaginative works of European writers, particularly the French. In this way the American Indian became part of the *bon sauvage* or Noble Savage tradition so long an accompaniment of the Golden Age or paradisaical mythology of Western civilization. First the natives discovered and conquered by the Spanish and then those invaded by the French and English joined the *bon éthiopien, bon oriental,* and *bon nègre* as a convention for enunciating the hopes and desires of European authors or for criticizing the institutions and customs of their own society, or in providing new imagery for the intellectual, literary, and artistic styles of the day. Whether the Indians north of Mexico were ever as influential in this tradition as those of Brazil and the Antilles or of the Inca and Aztec empires is difficult to say, because most European authors used the Indian generically for their purposes. Only after French and English exploration and settlement proceeded in the seventeenth century, however, could the European imagination be stimulated by accounts other than Spanish in origin, and the noble Huron and Iroquois and other tribesmen north of Mexico join their literary colleagues, the wise princes of the Inca and Aztec realms and the good Indians of Brazil and the Antilles.[7]

That the Indians north of Mexico came to loom large in the French image of the Noble Savage must be ascribed mainly to the voluminous *Relations* of the Jesuits. Published annually from 1632 to 1674 and sporadically before and after those years, the *Relations* from Canadian missions often provided flattering descriptions of Native Americans and their ways of life in order to gain contributions for missionary work from the faithful and to prove points against their Jansenist and atheistic opponents. To deny Jansenist and atheistic arguments about the lack of religion among Indians and as part of their own educational philosophy, the Jesuits had to prove the fundamental humaneness and natural theism of their charges through recourse to the "facts" in their *Relations*. Although the Jesuit missionaries generally found their Canadian charges more savage than noble, their allusions otherwise (usually to converts, though) provided the basis for eighteenth-century deists and philosophers to prove a beneficent state of nature as lived by the Hurons and other tribesmen of New France.[8]

Another tactic that ennobled the Indians of North America was the previously mentioned tendency of some French writers to compare the Indians of the New World with the ancient peoples of the Old. From Lescarbot's chapter in his *History of New France* in 1609 to Lafitau's book on the theme in 1724, the natives of New France were elevated in wisdom and status if not always in actual culture and custom by comparison to the highly regarded ancients. English travelers and settlers, on the other hand, provided little material on the happy Indian, with the exceptions of John Lawson, Cadwallader Colden, and James Adair.[9]

The transition from description of the American Indian as Noble

Savage to the use of the Noble American Indian as a critic of European society and culture is difficult to date, but scholars generally agree that most of the chief milestones occurred in France from the late sixteenth century to the late seventeenth century. Scholars usually credit Montaigne's synthesis of French and Spanish accounts of Mexican and South American Indians with French skepticism and humanism as the first full-length portrait of the Noble Savage as critic of contemporary European civilization and model of what men ought to, and could, be. In his *Apology for Raymond Saybond*, he used the many customs of Native Americans to show the diversity of moral beliefs and social practices that proved the cultural relativism he preached in his essay *On Cannibals*. He used the Brazilian cannibals to criticize French poverty and social inequality as well as to show the virtuous life of even such savages as those who devoured human flesh. He accused Europeans, at bottom, of even greater barbarity than the cannibals' mode of warfare and diet. In his essay *On Coaches* he condemned the torture and cruelty, the avarice for gold, and the debased examples Europeans introduced into the Aztec and Inca societies.[10] The transition was completed by the time Bishop Fénelon published *Aventures de Télémaque* in 1699 and Baron de Lahontan *Dialogues curieux entre l'auteur et un sauvage de bon sens qui a voyagé* in 1703. In *Télémaque* Fénelon depicts two states of ancient times, first to preach the ideal state as opposed to the France of Louis XIV and then to portray a state that was bad at first but then reformed. Basically, the book is a primitivistic appreciation of Huron life thinly disguised in ancient locale and garb. Lahontan openly presented the noble Huron, Adario, as a man of reason and sense and the Europeans as the real savages. Both men advocated a program of social and political reform for France in addition to praising the superior life of the noble Hurons. Rousseau, Voltaire, Diderot, and other famed philosophers of the eighteenth century had but to continue a tradition well established by their day of using the Noble Savage in general and the American Indian in particular for their critical moral and political purposes.[11]

The cult of the Noble Savage, especially as rational man, was far less developed outside of France, and what polemical and satirical use there was of the noble American Indian in England generally stemmed from French influence. Although Hobbes and Locke had already, in the seventeenth century, offered the Indian as example for their conception of the state of nature, the political and satirical use of the Native American mainly dates from the visit of the four kings, in

reality Mohawk chiefs, to England in 1710.[12] In that country, however, the rational savage soon merged with or was succeeded by the
sentimental savage as a precursor of romanticism. Neither the rational
nor the sentimental Indian ever achieved the popularity in England
that he did in France, perhaps because that country had already had
its revolution in the previous century.[13] In the English colonies the
literary and ideological use of the Noble Savage came on the scene
only during the Revolutionary era.[14]

The use of the Noble Savage, and the American Indian as part of
that convention, to criticize existing social institutions and to propose
reform reached its height with the *philosophes* of the Enlightenment.
Fundamental to their thinking was the dichotomy between nature
and convention. If what was natural was good, then what was civilized was artificial, hence decadent and certainly bad. Nature's plan,
moreover, was simple and therefore easily comprehended: if right
reason was universal and the instinct for good common to all humankind, then they must be found in the earliest and least sophisticated of
peoples as well as in the most civilized. In fact, primitive peoples
probably apprehended the laws of nature more clearly than civilized
man since they were less corrupted by the practices and prejudices of
civilization and more creatures of instincts considered natural. Man
was born good and equal but everywhere in modern Europe was
found chained by social convention and artificial civilization. Inquiries into the origins of man and the state of nature as exemplified
by contemporary primitives, therefore, not only served a philosophical purpose but also provided a critique of the social institutions inherited from an old regime. In the end, this use of the Noble Savage
and the primitivistic tradition was dedicated to the establishment of a
new social order consonant with the liberal ideals of the age. As a
result, the Noble Savage really pointed to the possibility of progress
by civilized man if left free and untrammeled by outworn institutions.[15]

When viewed in this manner, the life of the American Indian
offered a thoroughgoing critique of European social institutions and
cultural values. Whether employed in political and philosophical
treatise or play, novel, satirical essay, or imaginary voyage, the noble
American Indian scored specific points against religious beliefs and
institutions, the nature of education, the organization of government
and codes of laws, the prevalence of commerce and the organization
of the economy, the general social system and social inequality, and
the very complexity of life and corruption of civilized and sophisti-

cated customs in general. For deists Indian religion as they imagined it embraced the simple but cardinal principles of all religion: belief in a superior being, distinction between good and evil, and the expectation of rewards and punishment after death. Without the institutional structure of a complexly or corruptly organized church, the Indian managed to live according to a moral code far better than the European with his vaunted but hypocritical religion.[16] Rousseau was only one of many writers who thought of the noble Indian in regard to the reform of the educational system.[17] Likewise, the absence of intricate legal codes, of kings, and of authoritarian, hierarchical government among American Indians pointed to the overhauling of those legal and governmental institutions remaining in many European countries from the period before the rise of enlightened ideals of political rights and civil freedom. These writers followed a tradition old by their time in employing Indians as exemplars of the possibility of human freedom inherent in the state of nature.[18]

Useful as the American Indian was for these purposes, he took a minor position in comparison to other exotic peoples in the Noble Savage convention, and even in satirical and romantic uses by other critics and writers. Even when the Indian was employed, reference was more often to the natives of Latin America than to those in what is now the United States and Canada. The French critique of imperial administration and the treatment of colonial peoples, for example, condemned Spanish cruelty to the natives of Central and South America, not what was happening in New France or Louisiana.[19] Even when Indians are the nominal subject it is difficult to tell just how much a fictional or polemical savage is based upon information about actual Native Americans. Perhaps it is unimportant, because the general convention shaped the information somewhat in the first place and surely determined its later use by the poet, playwright, artist, or writer. Moreover, no philosopher or *littérateur* intended for his fellow citizens to adopt the lifestyles of the savages, noble or otherwise. Critical though the *philosophes* and authors may have been of European civilization, they merely wanted to reform it, not abandon it for the actual life of savagery they so often praised.[20]

By the end of the eighteenth century certain trends became clear in the history of the Noble Savage convention. To the extent that the Noble Savage was used as a polemical device to criticize European institutions of the period, then the supporters of those institutions felt compelled to attack the Noble Savage. Thus spokesmen for orthodox religion, established rulers, the contemporary social order, or the sophistication of civilized life all pointed out the brutish existence led by contemporary primitives in their defense of the status quo. The facts of savage life according to these supporters of existing institutions all pointed to conclusions quite the opposite of those drawn by the defenders of man's natural goodness and happiness in the state of nature. Whether it was Samuel Johnson favoring the civilized amenities,[21] a German encyclopedist defending religious orthodoxy,[22] or persons afraid of proposed political reforms, all could agree on the nastiness of man in his natural state as exemplified by existing primitive peoples. In fact, the whole dispute over the degeneracy of the American Indian must be viewed as an attack upon the Noble Savage idea and therefore as part of the larger struggle in the realm of ideas over the possibilities of political and social reform in the latter half of the eighteenth century.[23]

The American and French revolutions marked the turning point in the fate of the Noble Savage as a political device, for the two revolutions made concretely manifest what both sides to the argument over man's possibilities contended. Rather than referring to the somewhat hypothetical world of the Noble Savage and the state of nature, now both sides could point to the dramatic real world of the United States and France to document the benefits or tragedy of a new order. Thus the Noble Savage, although he continued to figure in literature and imaginative works, was displaced by the events of modern history in the arguments and polemics of social philosophers and political reformers.

Equally clear in the history of the Noble Savage convention by the end of the eighteenth century was the transformation of the literary primitive from a man of reason and good sense into a man of emotion and sensibility, in short, the romantic savage as opposed to an enlightened savage. Although the trend to the romantic savage culminated in the early nineteenth century, its beginnings must be traced far back into the Enlightenment. The romantic savage and the child of nature represent more a changing emphasis on old themes in a new intellectual context than a total repudiation of the basic idea of the Noble Savage of the eighteenth century, because a fundamentally romantic focus on the exotic and on the relation of man to nature was at the very center of primitivism from the beginning. The opposition of nature to the artificiality of civilization, the stress on the long ago and far away, and even the concern about impulse and instinct had long been an important side of primitivistic thinking. For example, the immediate emotional comprehension of the basic religious experience by the Noble Savage was grasped by the rationalists, as can be seen in the well-known words of Alexander Pope:

> *Lo, the poor Indian! whose untutor'd mind*
> *Sees God in clouds, or hears him in the wind;*
> *His soul proud Science never taught to stray*
> *Far as the solar walk or milky way;*
> *Yet simple nature to his hope has giv'n,*
> *Behind the cloud-topped hill, an humbler heav'n.*[24]

What was new in romanticism, however, was the conception of the primary task of the artist: to evoke feelings of compassion, sentimentalism, and romantic love as well as the lessons of nature, all enhanced through symbolism. Whereas the true Noble Savage of rationalism comprehended nature's laws through reason as well as instinct, the romantic savage depended upon passion and impulse alone for a direct apprehension of nature in all its picturesqueness, sublimity, and fecundity. Life like nature was or ought to be poetic in inspiration and experience. Social rules and conventions, like a formalistic appreciation of nature, were seen as a hindrance to the spontaneous experience of nature and of life in a direct and immediate way, a denial of the primacy of feeling. The romantic artist's task was to feel and imagine nature and life deeply and then to convey and evoke these feelings in his readers through his poetry, novels, and plays.[25]

The European use of the American Indian as a romantic Noble Savage culminated in Thomas Cooper in England and François-René de Chateaubriand in France. What had been in England a good adventure story of sentimental love amidst exotic scenery and American Indians reaches its height according to romantic conventions in the long poem by Cooper in 1809, *Gertrude of Wyoming*. The idyll of young love between two White youths on the Pennsylvania frontier tragically ends in the Wyoming Massacre of 1778. Throughout the poem, Outalissi, said to be an Oneida chief, manifests all the qualities beloved of romantic sensibilities: intense feeling alternating with stolidity, lofty virtues, and delicate emotions with the story set in an arcadian settlement amidst a sublime yet savage wilderness.[26] More profound in his employment of the conventions of primitivism in the romantic mode was Chateaubriand in *Atala, ou les amours de deux sauvages dans le désert* (1801). Originally planned as part of *Les Natchez*, Chateaubriand's projected epic of natural man, *Atala* was the story of romantic love between Chactas, the son of another

Outalissi (this time a Natchez chief), and the heroine of the novel's name, the Christianized daughter of a chief of the Muscogee tribe, said to be inveterate enemies of the Natchez. The picturesque landscape, the mysterious forest, the confrontation of civilized and savage virtues, and the melancholy of the emotions evoked all combined with the French image of the Indian to produce the epitome of romantic primitivism for generations of Europeans. *Atala* went through six editions the year of its publication and inspired a long line of artistic representations in the romantic vein of the heroine's death and other touching scenes from the book as well as encouraging other European writers to look to the American West for picturesque people and sublime nature (see Plate 5).[27]

Chateaubriand's accomplishment rested upon the French tendency, first popularized by Rousseau, to internalize the relation between nature and man and to combine the wildness of men in other places with the wildness within all men. Thus Cooper's Indian retains much of the traditional Noble Savage, but Chateaubriand's Indians embody the new. Whether new or old, however, the Noble Savage convention had just about run its course in European belles-lettres. But the romantic Noble Savage was to find a new home in the United States.

Puritanism, the Wilderness, and Savagery as Divine Metaphors

BELLES-LETTRES CAN hardly be said to have existed in the English North American colonies before thirteen of them revolted against the mother country. Before the mid-eighteenth century the English colonies on the mainland scarcely possessed the intellectual or material resources to support the presses, the men of letters, and the reading public for the higher forms of home-produced literature. The opening pages of literary histories of the United States discuss mainly the journals, chronicles, promotional tracts, sermons, and histories penned in the colonies rather than the poetry, novels, and plays upon which such history is usually grounded. New England far excelled other regions in the production of these latter literary genres, and it is primarily there that the imaginative transformation of the Native American from the Indian of contact into the Indian of symbol and myth took place during the colonial period of American cultural history. Both the reason for the outpouring of published works and the mythologizing of the Indian must be attributed to the Puritan beliefs of the region's writers.

For the Puritan the Indian as well as himself was part of the cosmic drama willed by God to reveal His sovereignty and His grace. The central theme of this drama was the eternal conflict between God and Satan, and the plot revolved about the salvation of some men who were to be born again to eternal bliss and the many who were unregenerate and therefore damned to hell. Puritans assumed God had purpose in each act, no matter how trivial in this larger drama, and that man was utterly dependent upon God's infinite mercy for his rebirth into salvation from Adam's sinfulness. The minutest as well as the greatest events came under the watchful governance of the Lord, and so happenings of the present, like those of the past, must be explained ultimately in terms of their original not their proximate causes according to their place in the cosmic drama. The whole of creation possessed meaning only in terms of God's purpose, and each event, trivial or great, displayed His secret will. Therefore, Puritans looked beyond mundane reality for suggestions of God's will and grace in relation to their own destiny. Daily events became for the devout Puritan, in short, symbols or metaphors of life's real meaning. Tragedy and happiness were part of God's plan for men as He willed the larger design of history, and untoward events were seen, therefore, as special providences through natural means to remind men to look to their sins and take remedy.

In this drama the Puritans saw themselves as the chosen of the Lord for the special purpose of bringing forth a New Zion, and those who fled from England to the shores of North America believed they had founded just such a holy commonwealth as God wished. The Native Americans, therefore, held meaning for Puritans in terms of the larger drama and the vision of their own place in it. Under these premises "the Indian" was but another tool of the Lord to help or hinder the future salvation as well as the earthly life of the Puritan. When the Indian helped the early settlers in New England, he became an agent of the Lord sent to succor the Puritan devout; when he fought or frightened the Puritans, he assumed the aspect of his master Satan and became one of his agents.[28]

The duty of the faithful Puritan historian of New England was to remember the Lord's mercies and recall the lessons of His visitations for evil-doing. The historian accomplished this goal by describing concrete events according to their place in the larger cosmic drama: no anecdote was too trivial to tell if relevant to God's plan, and no matter was too momentous to be omitted if its place in the cosmic drama was uncertain of interpretation. Devout Puritan historians moved back and forth easily between anecdote or happening and its implication for God's omnipotence and majesty in order to reveal fully the workings of Providence in history, for as Edward Johnson phrased the subtitle of his *History of New England* (1653), the true story was "The Wonder-Working Providence of Zion's Savior in New England." Although the providential interpretation of history was an ancient one, the New England Puritans presumed that they were God's most recently chosen people and therefore viewed their journeying to the New World as the latest phase of His plans for the preservation of the true religion rediscovered in the Reformation. They therefore assumed the founding and the history of their New Zion received the special attention of the Lord and deserved telling at length to point out to the world the true path to salvation. If the New England experience was the fulfillment of God's work to His *people*, then their history bore a special relation to those peoples they left in Europe and met in America.

When conceived of as the tale of a chosen people, the history of New Englanders naturally reminded the pious of the trials of the Israelites of old. Like the Old Testament Jews the Puritans fled a corrupt Egypt, in their case Anglican England, for the promised land, and like those ancient Israelites they too landed in the desert or wilderness, often spoken of as "howling" or "savage" and usually inhabited by Satan's agents.[29] As the self-conscious Puritan intellectual Cotton Mather phrased his task in *Magnalia Christi Americana* (1702):

> I write the *Wonders* of the CHRISTIAN RELIGION, flying from the Depravations of *Europe*, to the *American Strand*: And, assisted by the Holy Author of that *Religion*, I do, with all conscience of *Truth*, required therein by Him, who is the Truth itself, Report the *Wonderful Displays* of His Infinite Power, Wisdom, Goodness, and Faithfulness, wherewith His Divine Providence hath *Irradiated* an *Indian Wilderness*.[30]

The journey into the wilderness became as much a controlling metaphor for the story of the Puritans collectively as the spiritual pilgrimage formed the basis of the personal narrative, and the struggle between Puritans and Indians represented externally what the conflict between conscience and sin did internally. In fact, some modern commentators argue that the Puritans' image of the Indian was the projection of the fears and repressed desires in themselves upon the outsiders they encountered in America, and so the extermination of the Indian was part of the Puritan cleansing of sin from themselves.[31] Others see such imagery as mere cant designed to justify Puritan expropriation of native lands.[32]

Thus, in the histories written by Puritan divines and laymen alike, the Indian represents something larger than the actual Native Americans and their interactions with the New England saints. Hospitality and kindness represent not native friendliness and goodness but the Lord's mercy to His chosen people. William Bradford in his unpublished history of Plymouth Plantation, for example, writes of Squanto, whose crucial assistance to the Pilgrims enabled them to survive in the new environment, as "a spetiall instrument sent of God for their good beyond their expectation."[33] On the other hand, Indian character and lifestyle in general showed Native Americans to be in the clutches of Satan, for their souls in the wilderness were as unregenerate as their lands were uncultivated. And nowhere was their obeisance to his satanic majesty better exemplified in Puritan eyes than in "savage" warfare. They therefore expected the horrors of Indian warfare both because of the unregenerate state of the Indians who were trapped in the "snare of the Divell" and because God must from time to time send a scourge to chastise His chosen people in their pride and in their departure from His word. Thus the images of the good and bad Indian served the same didactic purposes for the Puritan imagination.

By the latter part of the seventeenth century devout Puritans eulogized the faith of the founding fathers of New England and lamented the lack of the same zeal in their descendants, and King Philip's War seemed to confirm the warnings of the godly about the imminent threat of a humbling experience sent by the Lord. The war gave vivid meaning to the jeremiads about the decline of Puritan piety, and both its coming and the hard-won victory were repeatedly used in sermon, history, and tract to point out the lessons for New England of God's punishments for the lax or the unrepentant, His infinite patience with His chosen people, and His great mercy in the end—for the victors at least.[34]

Among the spate of literature preaching this theme were the first captivity narratives published in New England. The lessons drawn from Indian capture by the minister's wife who published the first one of the genre in 1682 are revealed in its long title: *The Sovereignty and Goodness of God, Together, with the Faithfulness of His Promises Displayed; Being a Narrative of the Captivity and Restauration of Mrs. Mary Rowlandson. Commended by Her, to All that Desire to Know the Lords Doings to, and Dealings with Her. . . .* What made these lessons particularly vivid was the bringing of the larger forces of the Lord and Satan, Puritan and Savage into the microcosm of personal experience. To impress upon her readers the horrors of her ordeal, she resorted to the bad image of the Indian. She summarized in her preface the real nature of her captors as "Atheistical, proud, wild, cruel, barbarous, brutish, (in one word) diabolical Creatures . . . , the worse of heathen." She concluded that her own deliverance and the victory of her countrymen over the savages came only through "the strange providence of God, in turning things about when the Indians was at the highest, and the English at the lowest," because at long last the Christians through their tragedies had learned their sole hope for safety lay in submission to God's will and renewed faith in His grace and sovereignty.[35]

Ministers soon picked up this method of impressing the power of the Lord and the sinfulness of His people upon their listeners and readers both for its drama and its message. Increase Mather, for example, included a captivity narrative among his *Remarkable Providences* (1684) and his son Cotton, the great Puritan minister and intellectual, made plain the implications of capture by the Indians for all to read in his *Humiliations Follow'd with Deliverance* (1697). As these titles suggest, the image of the bad Indian was used by the Mathers and others to teach that these untoward events in the lives of New Englanders should be seen as God's warning for the state of their souls and that only He was the hope for redemption after capture by the savages in the wilderness. In the end the image of the bad Indian triumphed over that of the good one in the Puritan imagination, just as the Lord's forces in the end must overcome Satan's army in the cosmic drama in which both the Puritans and the Indians were actors.[36]

The evolution of the captivity narrative from the Puritan jeremiad into either the gothic novel or the commercial anthology by the last decade of the eighteenth century points to the future uses of Indian imagery in the American imagination. The best-seller status of the captivity narrative[37] led to the retention of its basic premise of the horrors Whites suffered under Indian "enslavement," but with a variation of style and intellectual thrust as the climate of opinion and literary fashions changed. Just as the implications and messages of the mid-sixteenth-century Spanish and seventeenth-century French narratives reflected their times and authors' world views, so those captivity accounts produced after the oft-called "classic" Puritan ones mirrored new interests and ideologies of the English colonists. As the successive wars between England and France continued during the eighteenth century, many of the English narratives emphasized the hated French and Catholic aegis behind the dreaded Indian warfare and atrocities. Moreover, a secular outlook increasingly replaced the religious orientation of the earlier New England tracts and sermons, and therefore the author-hero comes to escape more often through his own guile and effort than through divine assistance as earlier. Finally, American authors of the narratives followed the lead of the English writers of fake narratives in stressing stylistic embellishment and melodramatic action to capture the reading public's attention.

These twin trends of commercialism and literary self-consciousness culminated after the American Revolution in the first collection of captivity horrors issued in 1793 purely for commercial gain, the so-called Manheim anthology, and in Charles Brockden Brown's gothic novel, *Edgar Huntly: Or the Memoirs of a Sleepwalker* (1799), which sought to evoke the sublime by portraying the overwhelming emotion associated with savage capture by the Indians. From these works lead the dual paths of high and low cultural uses of the Indian in the nineteenth century. Brown's novel represented the search for an indigenous literature by White American authors in the newly independent United States; the Manheim anthology was the first of many such compilations of accounts in the next century, the best known and best edited of which was Samuel Drake's *Indian Captivities; Or Life in the Wigwam*, published in 1839. The blood-and-gore sensationalism of the commercially inspired and highly successful captivity narratives of the nineteenth century led directly to the dime novels and the later cowboy and Indian movies of popular culture.[38]

The Indian and the Rise of
an American Art and Literature

THE ONLY TIME the Indian figured prominently in the higher forms of American art and literature occurred between the War of 1812 and the Civil War as a result of two trends: cultural nationalism and romanticism. Belles-lettres arose in the United States after the Revolution and so in many ways the early history of American formal literature, and, for that matter, art too, is connected directly to the new nation's quest for a (high) cultural identity to match its political status. Newly founded periodicals urged American themes and materials in place of those inherited from abroad, and some editors and writers sought even an American style and language in their bid to declare intellectual independence from England. What began in the 1790s as scattered cries for the literary equivalent of what Americans felt were the glorious political and social achievements of the American republic reached a campaign after the second War for Independence, the War of 1812. In their search for American material the authors and artists of the day hit upon the American forest and the Indian as subjects fit for a new indigenous literature and art. Both the call for literary independence and the use of the Indian reached a height in the 1820s and the 1830s and declined in the decade before the Civil War. By that time the romantic movement, which had provided a basis for both literary independence and the use of the Indian as a proper literary subject, had waned also.[39]

If cultural nationalism prompted American authors and artists to turn to the Indian and the forest for subject matter, the importation of romanticism from Europe made possible the elevation of this subject matter to literary and artistic respectability. So long as the neoclassical perspective and subject matter of eighteenth-century rationalism dominated American letters, then the Indian was not really appropriate material for the American author seeking literary reputation at home and abroad. Romanticism came late to the United States, but its emphasis on indigenous traditions, folk customs, and the glorification of the national past dovetailed with the drive toward cultural nationalism in the newly independent nation. Against the universal standards and subjects of eighteenth-century neoclassicism, romantic writers posed the diversity of opinions and tastes of various peoples and stressed the variety of experience in different countries and regions.

Of central importance to the romanticist was emotion and intuition. The romantic writers and artists sought to evoke feeling and sentiment in their readers or viewers throughout the whole range of emotions. Fear, mystery, devotion, despair, exaltation, pity, sentiment —all were to flow from pen or brush onto paper or canvas and thence to the audience. One of the chief sources of inspiration for poet and novelist, painter and playwright alike was nature with its picturesque beauty and its sublime awesomeness. Other sources were the nostalgia aroused by ancient castles, moldering monuments, and old ruins from the past as well as the heroism inspired by old legends and histories of various peoples. For Americans no European author embraced these tendencies better than Sir Walter Scott with his stories of Scottish heroes of the past. His emphasis on regional traditions, rugged scenery, and nonliterary folk served as an important model for those Americans seeking to raise the Indian and the forest to literary respectability as proper themes for an American art and literature.[40]

Given romantic premises, then, both the noble and savage Indian made an ideal subject for American high culture. Whether American *littérateurs* looked to the past, to nature, or to exotic peoples in their country they found the Indian each time. Certainly the American forest possessed a grandeur, an expanse, and a wildness unknown to European nature, sublimer by far than the meek pastoral scenes across the Atlantic. Part of the wildness of the American forest came from the nature of its inhabitants and the horrors of Indian warfare. The tortures, vengeance, escapes, and ambushes of Indian warfare aroused a variety of emotions of the most romantic sort.

Compared to the future Americans envisaged for themselves, their past looked meager indeed for the artist and the author looking for ruins and ancient monuments. But the mysterious Indian mounds gained much attention at this time as the American equivalent of European ruins and castles. Perhaps, some American men of letters reasoned, these mounds showed the indigenous origins of the Indian and revealed a Golden Age in America in the distant past. Even when an American author looked to the short history of his own country, he found the Indian a prominent participant in the colonial struggle or even in the Revolution.

Certainly the Indians were an exotic folk with quaint customs, heroic acts, and alive to the impressions of nature surrounding them. Their language was filled with picturesque allusion and metaphor and their legends equaled the tales of Old World folk. Indian rhetoric had long existed as a kind of literature in the form of treaty proceedings, and Jefferson's version of Logan's famed speech was memorized from McGuffey readers by schoolchildren of the nineteenth century.[41] Perhaps the best-known publication of legends was the compilation of Ojibwa and other tribes' tales published by Henry Rowe School-craft as the *Algic Researches: Comprising Inquiries Respecting the Mental Characteristics of the North American Indian: First Series: Indian Tales and Legends* (2 volumes, 1839), which later served Longfellow as a source for his *The Song of Hiawatha*.

Most romantic of all was the impression of the Indian as rapidly passing away before the onslaught of civilization. The nostalgia and pity aroused by the dying race produced the best romantic sentiments and gave that sense of fleeting time beloved of romantic sensibilities. The tragedy of the dying Indian, especially as portrayed by the last living member of a tribe, became a staple of American literature, beginning with Philip Freneau's poems in the 1780s. It made its mark on world literature through James Fenimore Cooper's *The Last of the Mohicans* (1826), and inspired George Catlin to do his famed portraits of noble Indians on the plains and prairies before it was too late to capture on canvas a dying race. In short, whether Indians were portrayed as bad or as good, they were in romantic eyes a poetical people whose activities took place in a sublime landscape and whose fate aroused sentiment.

To pity truly the poor dying Indian, American authors and artists had to transform him from a bloodthirsty demon into a Noble Savage. That transformation occurred late in the United States compared to Europe. Except for a few examples among eighteenth-century accounts, the Noble Savage in the United States is really a nineteenth-century fashion.[42] Just as it has been said that the Europeans could easily ennoble the Indian because of their remoteness from savage warfare, so commentators have argued that American authors and artists of the Eastern United States only conceived of the Indian as noble after that section of the country had eliminated its Indian problem.[43] Even so, the number of truly Noble Savages in book or painting was relatively few and relegated to the far away or the long gone.

For the artist of the time the noble Red Man was to be found only in the still Wild West beyond the corruption of advancing White civilization. Fears of the imminent passing of the Red race prompted painters to hurry to capture the likenesses of these noble beings. The portraits of Charles Bird King, which became the color lithographs in Thomas McKenney and James Hall's *History of the Indian Tribes of North America, with Biographical Sketches and Anecdotes of the Principal Chiefs* (3 volumes, 1836–44); the Indian gallery painted by George Catlin that toured the United States and Europe during the 1830s and 1840s; and the paintings of Captain Seth Eastman, which were reproduced as illustrations in Henry Rowe Schoolcraft's *Historical and Statistical Information Respecting the History, Condition, and Prospects of the Indian Tribes of the United States* (6 volumes, 1851–57), all helped to popularize the supposed nobility of the wild Indian before the onslaught of civilization. As Catlin rhapsodized:

> Nature has nowhere presented more beautiful and lovely scenes, than those of the vast prairies of the West and of *man* and *beast* no nobler specimens than those who inhabit them—the *Indian* and the *buffalo*—joint and original tenants of the soil, and fugitives together from the approach of civilized man; they have fled to the great plains of the West, and there under an equal doom, they have taken up their last abode, where their race will expire and their bones will bleach together.[44]

How civilization destroyed the noble Indian, if it did not kill him, was graphically portrayed by Catlin in his dual portrait of the Assiniboin chief Wi-jún-jon before and after his visit to Washington (see Plate 6).

By reliance upon classic analogy and/or romantic conventions in painting, these and other artists ennobled the Indian on canvas during the beginning decades of American art at the same time that they thought they were only recording a fast-disappearing phase of history.[45] Just how much of these painters' canvases are ethnography and how much artistic convention and whether they are more realistic in portraying Indians than artists of previous centuries is still debated.[46] Much of what seems realistic is painted with a romantic style. Eventually the stalwart tribespeoples of the Plains became the quintessential American Indian in the eyes of the White citizens of the United States and elsewhere and even many Native Americans themselves. In replacing the long-standard pictorial image derived from the classical conventions started by the de Bry and others in the sixteenth century, the canvases of these romantic artists and visiting painters from Europe played an important, if not crucial, role.[47]

The authors of poems, plays, and novels generally conceived of the Indian as noble only before White contact or during the early stages of the encounter between the Red and White cultures. In short, they portrayed the Noble Savage as safely dead and historically past. Thus many famous Indians of the past were revived as noble figures in the literature influenced by cultural nationalism during the first half of the nineteenth century. The first Pocahontas and noble love reentered the American literary world in 1808 through James Nelson Barker's play *The Indian Princess; Or, La Belle Sauvage*.[48] Washington Irving first wrote an essay in 1814 challenging the traditional Puritan judgment on King Philip, which later appeared in his *Sketchbook* (1819).[49] Of the many works praising Philip as a Noble Savage, Lydia Maria Child's novel *Hobomek*, published in 1824, not only reversed the adverse opinions of Puritan historian William Hubbard on the Wampanoag chief but made him a proponent of toleration against Puritan intolerance. In the forty years the famous actor Edwin Forrest played the role of the chief in John A. Stone's play *Metamora, Or the Last of the Wampanoags*, first performed in 1829, American audiences wept over the hopeless cause of the freedom-loving Philip as he tried in vain to defend his homeland against the hostile New Englanders.

The high point of the tendency to romanticize the safely dead Indian was Henry Wadsworth Longfellow's long poem *The Song of Hiawatha*, published in 1855. Confusing an Iroquois hero with an Ojibwa deity, Longfellow placed his Indian Prometheus' noble deeds and love life in the picturesque forests before the coming of White people. He reinforced the antiquity of Hiawatha's time by selecting the meter and mood of an old legend. Even the Iroquois of Lewis Henry Morgan's *League of the Ho-dé-no-sau-nee, Iroquois* (1851) can be seen as part of this trend to romanticize a past golden age of Indian life prior to White contact. His description of the primitive democracy and utopian harmony of the League takes place outside the story of actual White-Iroquois relations and history.[50]

Just as Americans in their quest for literary independence and a cultural identity commensurate with their conception of the nation's glorious political and social achievements repudiated European models of civilization, so too did they disavow the Indian version of life as they imagined Native Americans lived it. The effort of holding a middle ground between European decadence and Indian savagery fostered a curious ambivalence in American writers and artists toward the frontier. Repudiation of overcivilized ways led to celebration of White pioneer individualism, but frontier White life ought not to degenerate into savage ways. The difficulty of maintaining this American position between European civilization and Indian savagery without slipping into either extreme accounts for the strange paradoxical admiration found in the art and literature of this period for the hunter as well as the farmer, the explorer as well as the cultivator, the adventurer as well as the settler, frontier solitude as well as pioneer social institutions. The resolution of this ambivalence constituted the chief creative problem for an American author or artist in the first half of the nineteenth century.

In the end, the battle between savagery and civilization, with glory for one race and tragedy for the other as its inevitable outcome, formed the theme and metaphor, if not explicit plot, of the literature and art depicting the Indian during this period. Indians, both noble and savage, had their destined place in the order of history according to the intellectuals of the time. Noble Indians could exist before the coming of White society or they could help the White settler and then die forecasting the wonders and virtues of the civilization that was to supersede the simplicity and naturalness of aboriginal life. Savage Indians could scalp helpless Whites or die under torture singing their defiant death songs according to the old ways of native life. Both kinds of Indians would be eliminated through disease, alcohol, bullets, or the passage of time to make way for the presumed superior White way of life. The noble Indian deserved White pity for his condition and his passing, but his way of life no less than that of the ignoble savage demanded censure according to the scale of progress and the passage of history. For this reason, American artists and authors could never espouse the thoroughgoing primitivism of their European counterparts.[51] What American authors preached in their novels, plays, and poems about the inevitability of civilization superseding savagery, regardless of nobility, American schoolchildren learned in their textbooks.[52]

These premises received marble embodiment in the few sculptures of Indians at the time. Horatio Greenough's "Rescue Group," commissioned for the Capitol in Washington, proclaimed one of the basic themes of the American imagination. As set in place in 1853, the statue resembling the Laocoön showed a brave White pioneer male restraining the tomahawk of a nearly naked Indian male from killing the settler's cowering, helpless wife and child (see Plate 7). Another sculptor appealed to the opposite image of Indian life in his "Indian and Panther," which portrayed a Noble Savage saving his small son from a fierce panther. The famed sculptor Hiram Powers depicted two other themes in his fleeing Indian maiden, called significantly "The Last of Her Tribe," and the wise but resigned Indian in his "Indian Chief Contemplating the Progress of Civilization," for Red like White men knew, according to the artistic and literary conventions of the time, that ultimately civilization must triumph over savagery, no matter how noble it might be.[53]

Even those American authors who depicted the nobility of the Indian agreed with most of their fellow countrymen on the fate both good and bad Indians deserved when measured against the destiny of the United States. The quest for American cultural identity, the role of the United States in history, faith in the future greatness of the nation, and the fate of the Indian and the frontier in general were all seen as connected by the White Americans of the period. What reconciled the ambivalent images of nature, the Indian, and the frontier was an ideology of social progress that postulated the inevitable evolution of the frontier from savagery to civilization. American nature was beautiful for its wildness, its great expanse, and its unspoiled picturesqueness, but it was equally or even more beautiful in the eyes of many Whites for what it promised to become—a land of farms and a treasure house of resources for exploitation. Regardless of whether the Indian was savage or noble, he would inevitably be replaced by White civilization and its benefits. The transition from wild, savage nature to a cultivated, domesticated garden in the American West was believed to be as certain as the westward movement of progress had been in European history.

Therefore the frontier must change from the abode of the Indian to the farms and cities of the White. Hence the fate of the aborigine was sealed even though savage warfare might postpone briefly that inevitable destiny. In this ideological geography of the American West, the earliest wave of White frontiersmen, or "foresters" as they were called then, that led the march of civilization westward were as doomed to disappear as the savages they replaced, because they too must make way for the pioneer farmers and cities that followed just as surely as they had followed the Indian in the march of progress. The future of American civilization was assured through the richness of her frontier, but that glory had to come over the dead bodies of noble and ignoble Indians and White foresters alike. Operating within these assumptions, authors of the period could never really depict

Native Americans for themselves but only in counterpoint to White values, as metaphors in the struggle between savagery and civilization.[54] (See Plate 8.)

More than any other American author, James Fenimore Cooper established the Indian as a significant literary type in world literature. Eleven of Cooper's many novels featured Indians, of which the best known now and the best sellers then were the five depicting the adventures of Leatherstocking or Natty Bumppo, known as Hawkeye or Deerslayer to the Indians in the stories. Like so many authors of his time, Cooper knew little or nothing of Native Americans directly, and so his works reveal the typical confusion of one tribe with another in customs, names, and languages.[55] He showed Indians as both good and bad according to the traditional favorable and unfavorable images, for their character and personality excited romantic emotions, as he admitted:

> Few men exhibit greater diversity, or, if we may so express it, greater antithesis of character, than the native warrior of North America. In war, he is daring, boastful, cunning, ruthless, self-denying, and self-devoted; in peace, just, generous, hospitable, revengeful, superstitious, modest, and commonly chaste. These are qualities, it is true, which do not distinguish all alike; but they are so far the predominating traits of these remarkable people as to be characteristic.[56]

Following the judgments of his chief source, the Moravian missionary John Heckewelder, Cooper's good Indians resemble Christian Delawares and his bad Indians behave like Heckewelder's descriptions of their enemies, the Iroquois.[57] Moreover, his good Indians, although not necessarily Christianized, act like Christian gentlemen and natural aristocrats, live apart from their tribe and/or are often the last members of their tribe, and play their roles in locales historically situated between savagery and civilization. These noblemen of the forest appear as if they stepped out of the paintings of the period. Thus did Cooper, for example, describe Uncas, the last of the Mohicans:

> The travelers anxiously regarded the upright, flexible figure of the young Mohican, graceful and unrestrained in the attitudes and movements of nature . . . there was no concealment to his dark, glancing, fearless eye, alike terrible and calm; the bold outline of his high, haughty features, pure in their native red; or to the dignified

elevation of his receding forehead, together with all the finest proportions of a noble head, bared to the generous scalping tuft. . . . The ingenuous Alice gazed at his free air and proud carriage, as she would have looked upon some precious relic of the Grecian chisel . . . while Heyward . . . openly expressed his admiration of such an unblemished specimen of the noblest proportions of man.[58]

Not only did Cooper subscribe to the contemporary tension between progress and simple nature, savagery and civilization, he also obeyed the romantic conventions of the novel of the time in not allowing an Indian, no matter how noble, to marry a White, and therefore no Indian could be a true hero in his novels if it meant wedding the heroine. Even Leatherstocking himself was too Indianized and too lower class to breach these conventions of the traditional romantic novel. Although Cooper's bad Indians far outnumbered his few noble ones, Lewis Cass, Governor of Michigan Territory and later Secretary of War under Andrew Jackson, and later Francis Parkman, the Boston Brahmin historian, among others, criticized his superficial and romantic portrayal of Indian thought and emotions.[59]

No one criticized his image of the frontier White, however, for all subscribed to the same larger pageant of White progress into the interior of the continent. The White on the frontier was as ill adapted for the full coming of that civilization of which he was the vanguard as the last of the Indians trying to accommodate themselves to the new order. Both possessed too little "Whiteness" and too much savagery to survive beyond a certain point in the history of the United States. Cooper's noble White foresters like his good Indians were anachronistic, as both Leatherstocking and the Last of the Mohicans revealed in speech after speech. Therefore Cooper's setting in his Indian novels is that area between savagery and civilization at that historic moment just before the full White advance, the same place literarily as the still largely unsettled West to which Catlin and other artists rushed in their battle with time.

At their best Cooper's good frontiersman represented the ideal blend of the two cultures in a somewhat primitivistic version. All authors, however, recognized that this balance of good qualities from the two societies could be lost and the White turn into a savage. So brutal did some White pioneers become in their defense of home and civilization that they adopted the savage ways of the Indians they hunted and scalped. These "Indianized" Whites became either renegades from civilization or the archetypal Indian haters. In a novel as popular in its day as the *Leatherstocking Tales*, Robert Montgomery Bird created in 1837 such a character in *Nick of the Woods, or the Jibbenainosay*, who was a peaceful Quaker transformed into a blood-thirsty killer of Indians by the savage slaughter of his family. From James Hall's story of Colonel John Moredock, Herman Melville fashioned the quintessential Indian hater in *The Confidence Man: His Masquerade* (1857). There he condemned "The Metaphysics of Indian-hating," as the chapter is titled, as a perversion of American and civilized values to justify extraordinary violence.[60]

By the 1850s the Indian in general and the Noble Savage in particular began to bore the sophisticated reading public and to reveal their literary limitations to the men of letters. Although Longfellow's *Hiawatha* achieved great success during this decade, it was quickly ridiculed in one satirical imitation after another. Other satires mimicked the standard Indian subjects of earlier plays and poems. John Brougham, for example, first burlesqued in 1847 the popular portrait of King Philip in his *Metamora; Or the Last of the Pollywogs* and then in 1855 mocked *Pocahontas; the Gentle Savage*.[61] The use of the Indian as a subject for an *American* literature in the quest for cultural identity and nationalism had run its course. The Indian now became mainly a literary staple of popular culture while serious men of letters searched elsewhere for inspiration and themes.

The great romantic historians of the period, George Bancroft and Francis Parkman, never really espoused the Noble Savage image. To them progress ruled history and the Indian deserved his fate. They employed the romantic conventions of scenery and character delineation to depict the deceitfulness of Indian diplomacy and the cruel horrors of savage warfare.[62] Parkman turned to the past to escape the crass commercialism and vulgar democracy of his day, but in doing so he did not glorify the Indian. After several weeks of living among the Oglala Sioux, he quickly abandoned his Cooper-like image of the noble Red man. For he concluded after his stay:

> For the most part, a civilized white man can discover very few points of sympathy between his own nature and that of an Indian. With every disposition to do justice to their good qualities, he must be conscious that an impassable gulf lies between him and his red brethren. Nay, so alien to himself do they appear, that having breathed for a few months the magic air of this region, he begins to look upon them as a troublesome and dangerous species of wild beast, and if expedient, he could shoot them with as little compunction as

they themselves would experience after performing the same office
upon him.[63]

From his *Oregon Trail*, published in 1847, onward through his
many histories, Parkman never wavered from the belief in the superiority of White civilization over Indian savagery. His histories of the
great conflict between France and England for the domination of
North America, beginning with the *History of the Conspiracy of
Pontiac* in 1851, celebrated the demise of the Indian race in the face
of White advance as well as the triumph of English enlightened institutions over French superstition and backwardness. Parkman has been
accused of being a racist of the polygenetic variety for these views,
and his writing certainly appears part of the fusion of scientific racism
with literature in the post–Civil War period.[64]

The Western and the
Indian in Popular Culture

AFTER THE CIVIL WAR, the Indian became more and more part of a
sectional tradition in American art and literature. As White settlement proceeded across the Missouri River and the Indian wars receded ever more westward, the Indian lost his place as an important
subject in what we might call elite or formal art and literature. The
Indian, however, did play a significant, if subordinate, role in the
popular arts. Both the elite and the popular arts differ from the folk
arts in their self-consciousness and their lack of anonymity. The elite
and popular artists create self-consciously for their audiences, but their
ends and their audiences are presumed different. If the elite artist
appeals to the few, the popular artist entertains the many. The elite
artist presumes a rather exclusive audience with high critical standards
searching for new ways of interpreting experience, while the popular
artist seeks as large an audience as possible, using the predictable,
familiar ways of looking at things. If the elite artist is expected to
create new visions and aesthetics, the popular artist generally reverts
to formulas that have been successful before. For the Indian in popular literature and art, that formula was the "Western," and the Indian

of the Western was usually the generic tribesman of the Plains—the new quintessential image of the Native American in White eyes.[65]

What had been the result of creative tension in Cooper's works had already become production by formula in the dime novel of the 1860s, for by that date the Western was fully developed. Although the medium for its presentation has varied greatly since that time, the basic ingredients of the Western have remained fundamentally the same for well over a century. What distinguishes a Western from other types of adventure literature is the setting and the costumes. Originally set in the forest like Cooper's conception, the Western quickly moved to the plains, deserts, and mountains of the trans-Missouri United States. More significant than its actual locale is its timing in the history of westward expansion of White society. It must be set at the moment when social order and anarchy meet, when civilization encounters savagery, on the frontier of White expansion, in order to give rise to the conflict that is the heart of the genre. In the Western formula, lawlessness and savagery must recede before the vanguard of White society, of which the town and particularly the educated White woman are the prime symbols, but they are still strong enough at that time to offer a local challenge to the advance agents of civilization. Although that moment was probably short in the actual history of any given locale, it becomes the "timeless epic" of all Western plots. The Western stresses strong individuals locked in combat with the enemy without customary social institutions or civilized law and order at their disposal, although the latter are not far behind in space or time. The actual settings used for the scene of the action enhance this sense of temporary isolation from the main part of White civilization by placing the story in a town, fort, or ranch removed from the rest of society on the frontier, with only a thin, easily broken link in the form of a trail, telegraph line, or railroad connecting the advance agents with the great body of White population that is to follow them.[66]

Into this setting are injected three main types of characters: (1) the agents of civilization, such as townspeople, settlers, especially the schoolmarm, (2) the outlaws or the Indians, and (3) the hero, who frequently represents some blend of both sides. In fact, his main task is to resolve the conflict between the two sides, usually according to the standard formula of physical combat. Originally the hero was a forester or scout in Cooper's Christian gentleman tradition, but the trapper and mountain man soon entered the action, and by the mid-1880s the cowboy eclipsed all others in popularity as hero, especially since the horse gave him complete mobility and his six-gun gave him a direct means of self-assertion. Given the conventions of rugged individualism, physical conflict, and the absence of civilized institutions, in the Western the hero regardless of nominal occupation was always athletic and masculine, even Calamity Jane! The simplest villains were outright opponents of law and order or White civilization in general. Hence the villains had to be either White renegades from their own society's justice or Indians. Since the role of the villain could be filled by White as well as Red savages, the Indian could be presented under either of his two guises. In the negative image the Indian was the usual bloodthirsty savage, often crazed, seeking vengeance or just malicious fun at the expense of innocent Whites, especially women. On the other hand, the good Indian was the typical Noble Savage acting as a friend to the Whites fighting the bad White or Red outlaws. Regardless of which guise the Western presented the Indian in, he was master of the wilderness and possessor of physical prowess and/or crafty wisdom. In short, the Western perpetuated the traditional White images of the Indian.

No matter how important the Indian might be to the Western plot and genre, he usually served in the end as the backdrop rather than the center of attention, for to do otherwise would have discarded simplicity for complexity and violated the premises of popular culture production. If the Indian was to be taken seriously, his motives and his culture would have to be presented as alternative values and lifestyles to White civilization, thereby introducing ambiguity into the genre. At the least, such introduction of Indian culture would imply the questioning of White values if not the criticism of White actions in history, and the popular artist would risk the possibility of alienating his audience. Thus, the Indian either posed an immediate threat to the hero who then wiped him out or he vanished shortly before the advance of civilization when it finally came in all its fullness to the West. In this way, the use of the Indian raised no real criticism of American values and presented no ambiguity in book or movie to puzzle the audience. Not until the arrival of the "adult Western" and the use of the Western formula for "countercultural" purposes was this basic rule violated and a supposedly Indian way of life presented as a serious alternative to general American values.

Although the Western figured prominently as a staple product in one medium after another in the popular arts, the evolution of the Western formula in itself did not really depend upon the history of any particular medium to any great extent. As soon as cheap periodicals began to exploit the new literacy of the Jacksonian era through the inexpensive production offered by the steam-powered rotary press, adventure stories of the Western type with Indians appeared in their pages. In regard to Indians, these stories depended as much upon the captivity narrative tradition as upon the growing legends of Daniel Boone and Davy Crockett and the popularity of Cooper's *Leatherstocking Tales.*[67] Distribution improved and the potential market enlarged with the expansion of the railroad network in the 1850s, and soon after the dime novel appeared. Although the publishing house of Beadle and Adams did not invent that genre of subliterature, it standardized the length, uniformly packaged the product, innovated in advertising it, and issued regularly for ten cents what had cost ten to fifteen times as much in hard covers. Their first number in mid-1860 reprinted from *The Ladies' Companion* a love story by the well-known author of the day, Mrs. Ann Sophia Winterbotham Stephens: *Malaeska; the Indian Wife of the White Hunter.* The protagonist promised her dying husband to raise their son in White rather than Indian ways, but Whites took him away from her, and she, upon return to her tribe, was condemned to death. Her old Indian suitor allows her, a princess, of course, to escape, but in the end she and her son both die as the son is about to marry a White woman. Thus the convention against miscegenation was doubly observed and combined with a sentimental romance taking place in the Hudson River Valley in the eighteenth century to produce a best seller for the time. Another best seller of that era published in the same year was written hastily by a nineteen-year-old schoolteacher, Edward S. Ellis. *Seth Jones; or, The Captive of the Frontier*, number eight in the same series as *Malaeska*, featured a Revolutionary War scout right after that conflict trying to help a White frontier family under attack by the Mohawks. The author has the hero captured by the Indians, tortured in vivid detail, chased melodramatically, and revealed finally as a person of sufficiently high status to marry a good White woman. In line with the morality of the dime novel, Seth calls the savage Indians "imps" or "varmints" but never "devils," which smacks of profanity. Ellis's paperback hit upon the right formula, and he went on to write many more of the genre. Beadle and Adams and their competitors sold hundreds of thousands of these little volumes during the Civil War and the decades after. In these series, frontier adventure provided more titles than any other subject, and the last battles with the Plains Indians after the Civil War did not harm sales or improve the image of the Indian in dime novels.[68]

The declining cost of paper, faster presses, still better distribution systems, and a larger literate population all conduced to increase competition among producers of cheap literature in the late 1870s. Their response was to lower prices to five cents for their fiction and to increase the violence and sensationalism of the genre. By the mid-1880s, the cowboy came to predominate over the former Western heroes: the Boones and Crocketts, the copies of Leatherstocking, and the mountain men and trappers of the far West. Whether based upon the supposed exploits of real men like Buffalo Bill Cody, Wild Bill Hickok, and others of the Plains West or upon the imagined adventures of the fictional heroes with the alliterative names of the Deadwood Dick variety, the new Westerns told of ever greater feats of gunmanship, riding, and escape from ever bloodthirstier savages and outlaws. With the increase in violence and sensationalism came heroes and heroines less pure in deed and past. Thus the savagery of the hero at times came to resemble that of the villain, as the following paragraph about Wild Bill Hickok illustrates:

> There was a wild, fierce yell, such as only Sioux throats could utter, as they leaped to their feet and made a dash toward him. Quick as was their movement, Bill had gained his feet ere the red devils gained the thicket. There was no time to use his Winchester, but the two six-shooters leaped from his belt, and the scout was soon surrounded by a flame as his deadly revolvers vomited leaden hail into the scarlet foe. The fight was short, sharp, and decisive, and was soon at an end, with seven scarlet bodies weltering in their blood under the midnight sky.[69]

Perhaps the increased action and gore signified that the dime novel and the nickel-library Western had become juvenile literature because the formula offered little new to the adult reader.[70] The "pulp literature" of the first four decades of this century and the paperbacks since then purveyed the Western and the Indian in the tradition of their cheap-literature ancestors as did the so-called comic books and comic strips in newspapers.

The Western formula and cheap literature had their impact upon the stage at home and abroad and on foreign literature as well. The Wild West shows and circuses were dime novels come alive, and they thrilled audiences in Europe as well as in the United States. Fittingly, the first prototype show in 1884 was named after and featured a hero made famous by the cheap literature of the period: *Buffalo Bill's Wild West Show and Congress of Rough Riders*. Among the standard performers in the show were, of course, "wild" Indians acting their savage images, and one year Sitting Bull even toured with the show.[71]

Europeans had already been exposed to the Wild West through their own authors as well as through Cooper and other American writers.[72] Perhaps the most prolific and certainly the best known today was Karl May of Germany. Inspired by Cooper and a vivid imagination, he created in the last decades of the nineteenth century one of the best known of German heroes, Old Shatterhand, modeled after Leatherstocking with a large dose of German romanticism, and his Red friend, the noble Apache chief, Winnetou. Without visiting the United States until late in his life, May produced scenery, dialogue, costumes, and plots revolving about his Teutonic hero, transported to the American West. In May's imaginative ethnography, the Apache were the most peaceful tribe in the trans-Mississippi West, suffering vicious attacks from the most warlike tribe, the Sioux, their dreaded enemies. Although written according to the Western formula and placed upon the American frontier, May's books nevertheless stressed German nationalism and shaped the outlook of many a German youth, including one devoted reader named Adolf Hitler.[73]

The images of the Indian according to the Western formula were impressed upon the American imagination by the popular artists of the day. Besides the vivid illustrations drawn to capture the cheap-literature reader's attention and money, Currier and Ives produced many chromo-lithographs depicting the various standard Indian themes.[74] Perhaps the most famous artist of the Old West in the late nineteenth century was Frederic Remington, another Eastern aristocrat gone cowboy like Theodore Roosevelt. His sculptures, engravings, and paintings, like his stories, portrayed a hostile Indian race. No matter how complete his knowledge of different individuals and their tribes or how authentic the detail in his Indian pictures, he, like all Western Americans who held what he termed a "cowboy philosophy," regarded Native Americans as an inferior race deserving of extinction. His archetypical Indian scowled and skulked as he passed off the stage of history.[75]

The transition of Native Americans from "wild" to reservation Indians after the Civil War was captured in a new medium by frontier photographers. Like painters earlier, many lensmen sought to portray the passing race before it was too late, and so their pictures frequently depicted the subjects before their cameras according to traditional themes. Their pictures recorded in minute detail the poses and costumes of brave and famous warriors, the vanishing native life-styles, and the degraded reservation Indian (see Plate 9). Perhaps no man dedicated himself to this task more than Edward S. Curtis, who reconstructed the past when he could no longer find the disappearing Indian ways of life. He received over a million and a half dollars from his backers. The task took thirty years of his life and resulted in forty volumes of photographs (see Plate 10).[76]

Visual representation of White Indian imagery immeasurably in-creased in the twentieth century through the motion-picture and tele-vision industries. The motion picture preserved old clichés and devel-oped new ones in the Western formula. The early nickelodeons and the penny arcades showed cowboys and Indians on their brief reels, and one of the first, if not the first, motion picture in the modern sense of sustaining a single narrative line depicted *The Great Train Robbery* in 1903 according to Western conventions. The elements of chase, action, violence, speed, suspense, and dramatic scenery natural to the Western lent themselves well to film presentation and became a staple of the developing motion-picture industry in the first decades of the twentieth century. These early Westerns got plots, themes, and heroes from elite and cheap literature in addition to the director's creativity. By World War One the feature film had been invented, films divided between class A and B pictures, and the basic subjects explored that were to dominate pictures thereafter. Among those sub-jects was the Western, of course, and its formulaic elements made it particularly suitable for the low-cost, hastily shot films designed for the B classification.[77]

The addition of sound in the 1920s and color in the 1930s did not change the basic Western formula or the popularity of the movies. Radio posed no threat to the motion-picture industry. One of the few Westerns on the radio was the famous Lone Ranger with his steady but stereotyped Indian companion, Tonto, which means *fool* in Spanish. The rapid acceptance of commercial television by the American public in the early 1950s, however, challenged the movie empire. As motion-picture theaters in the United States closed during that decade, the grade B Western merely switched after some diffi-culty to the new format of television. Now Americans could see Western heroes and Indians right in their own living rooms, as televi-sion executives bought old B movies for showing on the tube or paid to have new Western series ground out quickly as part of the tre-mendous amount of material consumed by the weekly entertainment schedule of television programming. Once again the Western formula rode to the rescue of a mass entertainment medium.[78]

No matter how new the media were, the old White stereotypes of the Indian generally prevailed in their presentations. Vicious and noble savages peopled the movie and television screens just as they had the cheap and elite literature of the past, from which scriptwriters had continued to borrow stories. The same old themes of Indians for and against settlers or miners or ranchers or soldiers or pony express riders or helpless White women were trotted out many more times on the new media. Indian princesses, squaw men, and friendly Red chiefs were joined by Indian football heroes after Jim Thorpe and soldiers after Native Americans served in the United States armies during the World Wars. In spite of these new heroes, the Indian was generally depicted as a person of little culture and less language. Speaking how! and ugh! dialogue and wearing combination, if not phony, tribal dress, Indians were usually portrayed with little concern for tribal differences in language, customs, or beliefs. Whites and Asians frequently acted the leading Indian parts, and those Native Americans hired for background action had to play any tribe because all Indians looked alike to movie and television directors. Because of the ignorance of writers, directors, and actors, the Indian was usually as stereotyped in a film supposedly sympathetic to the Native American cause as in one openly hostile to his plight.

Even those films of the 1960s and 1970s hailed as realistic and sympathetic to Indians by the White critics of American society still contained stereotypes typical of the motion-picture industry in the past, for all they usually did was to reverse the traditional imagery by making the Indian good and the White bad. In the more extreme countercultural films of the 1970s, the Indian hero becomes a mere substitute for the oppressed Black or hippie White youth alienated from modern mainstream American society. Although the action and locale purport to be laid in the past, the dialogue and thrust of the plot speak more to the recent conflict in Vietnam than to the battle over the American plains and mountains. As before, the latest countercultural use of the Indian reflects some Whites' disquietude with their own society and indicates that even today's sympathetic artists chiefly understand Native Americans according to their own artistic needs and moral values rather than in terms of the outlook and desires of the people they profess to know and depict.[79]

Only when the countercultural use of the Indian comes to dominate the mass media and modern literature in all its forms can we say that the classic Western has finally ended as one of the chief expressions of the basic American experience in the White imagination. Until then, the whole history of White settlement of the continent may be portrayed as one gigantic Western with the Indians "biting the dust" through the advance of civilization over savagery, both noble and ignoble. The modern novel or movie, like the Puritan history and captivity narrative, merely captures this larger story in microcosm.

Since the basic premises of the Western in regard to the Indian can be traced so directly from captivity narrative through Cooper's novels and pulp papers to modern literature and mass media, the persistence of the form as well as its premises points to a greater significance for the genre than entertainment value alone. What the captivity narrative started the Western novel and movie continued to finish long past the actual events of conquest—as if the American conscience still needed to be reassured about the rightness of past actions and the resulting present times. That the basic conflict over land and lifestyles should be so indelibly engraved upon the White mind so long after the actual events took place would seem to suggest the destruction of Native American cultures and the expropriation of Native American lands still demand justification in White American eyes.[80]

From Racial Stereotype to "Realism" in the Literary Indian

COMMENTATORS DISAGREE UPON when Native Americans first began receiving realistic portrayals by Whites in literature and the mass media. For the century after 1860, the Indian was stereotyped as part of the Western formula in most elite as well as popular literature.[81] Some analysts argue that any sympathetic portrayal of Native Americans and their plight in a White world is a realistic picture,[82] but others contend that the Noble Savage image is as much a stereotype as the ignoble one.[83] Neither nostalgia nor sympathy per se is a substitute for knowledge, in their opinion; only an accurate understanding of cultural diversity and ethnographic detail combined with firsthand experience constitutes a true basis for the realistic depiction of Indian life. From this viewpoint, the countercultural use of the Indian does not equal a realistic portrayal but merely a reversal of judgment upon the standard stereotype. For this reason, the modern anthropological image is important for the judgment of what is a realistic ethnographic approach to Native Americans as well as for its assumptions of cultural holism and moral relativism. Whether Native Americans themselves consider any White images realistic is quite another question.

What is called realism in literature did not necessarily produce realistic Indian imagery. Indian life was part of the regional or local-color school of that literary movement in the latter decades of the nineteenth century. Those authors like Mark Twain and Bret Harte who wrote of the Far West with its picturesque scenery and romantic styles of life included Indians in their detailed portrayal of locale, language, and customs on the frontier. If these authors often glorified the White outcast of society in the West, they also seemed to adopt those Whites' prejudices against the Indian. The vitriolic racism of literary realism found no more bitter expression than in Mark Twain's description of the Gosiute in his *Roughing It*. This deprived Great Basin tribe that lived in an extremely harsh environment disabused Twain of any noble Indian idea, for he considered the people among the most depraved and degenerate on earth:

> Such of the Goshoots as we saw, along the road and hanging about the stations, were small, lean, scrawny creatures; in complexion a dull black like the ordinary American negro; their faces and hands bearing dirt which they had been hoarding and accumulating for months, years, and even generations, according to the age of the proprietor; a silent, sneaking, treacherous-looking race; taking note of everything, covertly, like all the other "Noble Red Men" that we (do not) read about, and betraying no sign in their countenances; indolent, everlastingly patient and tireless, like all other Indians; prideless beggars—for if the beggar instinct were left out of the Indian he would not "go," any more than a clock without pendulum; hungry, always hungry, and yet never refusing anything that a hog would decline; hunters, but having no higher ambition than to kill and eat jackass rabbits, crickets, and grasshoppers, and embezzle carrion from the buzzards and coyotes; savages who, when asked if they have the common Indian belief in a Great Spirit, show a something which almost amounts to emotion, thinking whiskey is referred to; a thin scattering race of almost naked black children, these Goshoots are, who produce nothing at all, and have no villages, and no gatherings together into strictly defined tribal communities—a people whose only shelter is a rag cast on a bush to keep off a por-

tion of the snow, and yet who inhabit one of the most rocky, win-
try, repulsive wastes that our country or any other can exhibit.

He thought these "treacherous, filthy and repulsive" tribespeople deserving of pity, but he admitted that he could only feel such compassion when he was far removed from their actual presence.[84]

On the other hand, some lesser writers of the school romanticized the Indian. Joaquin Miller combined fancy with truth in his
autobiographical *Life Among the Modocs*, published in 1873, and
produced the usual Noble Savage clichés in his poetry, as can be seen
in his description of an Indian brave in his tritely titled "The Last
Taschastas":

> *His breast was like a gate of brass,*
> *His brow was like a gather'd storm;*
> *There is no chiseled stone that has*
> *So stately and complete a form.*
> *In sinew, arm and every part,*
> *In all the galleries of art.*[85]

Romantic fiction writer Helen Hunt Jackson, famous today for her
indictment of White Indian policy, *A Century of Dishonor* (1881),
tried to do for the Indian cause with *Ramona* in 1884 what *Uncle
Tom's Cabin* had done for the antislavery crusade before the Civil
War. Purporting to deal with the California Mission Indians, the
novel actually details little about Native American ways of life, for
her half-breed heroine of the novel's name and her supposedly pure
Indian hero reflect Spanish-American more than Native American
culture.[86]

If realism in the Indian novel means the treatment of Native
Americans as individuals rather than as Indians, as human beings and
not assemblages of tribal traits, then the Indian novel proper can
hardly be said to have begun before the 1920s. Realistic writing in
Indian novels demands sympathy for anti-White as well as pro-White
Native Americans, for medicine men as well as Christian converts, for
ordinary Indians as well as "princesses," for interracial love as well as
intraracial marriages. Neither White nor Red culture need be judged
superior, and the motives and behavior of the Indians should seem
natural to the modern reader in the situations described. Humanness
not race should be the essential criterion, and only stories depicting
the Native American in a full and rounded way can be called true
Indian novels, according to one school of critics.

Sympathetic treatment of Indian life combined with knowledge of a tribal culture began in the 1890s with Adolph Bandelier and other anthropologically inclined writers. To achieve this sympathy, however, Bandelier's *The Delight Makers*, published in 1890, and the other prose and poetry of those familiar in that period with Southwestern tribes placed their subjects far into the past before White contact, thereby avoiding the knottiest problems of the Indian genre of literature.[87] With the publication of Oliver La Farge's *Laughing Boy* in 1929, the genre of the Indian novel reached full maturity. Of an established New England family, La Farge received anthropological training at Harvard and fieldwork experience in the Southwest and Central America before he wrote his Pulitzer Prize–winning novel of love between a young Navajo man and woman confronted by the conflict between native and White American cultures. Possessing the same dignity and fallibility as other human beings, the two young lovers try several lifestyles in their efforts to cope with the commercialism and instability of the White world and the poverty, pride, and stability of the Navajo world.[88] In the wake of *Laughing Boy*'s popularity came the books of the first generation of White-educated Native American novelists: *Flaming Arrow's People* by James Paytiamo (an Acoma) in 1932; *Sundown* by John Joseph Mathews (son of an Osage mother and half-blood father) in 1934; *Brothers Three* by John Oskinson (Cherokee) in 1935; and the best novel of the group, *The Surrounded*, by D'Arcy McNickle (Flathead) in 1936.[89] White literary recognition of a Native American writing an Indian novel finally arrived with N. Scott Momaday (Kiowa) winning the Pulitzer Prize in 1969 for his *House Made of Dawn.*

The growing acceptance by White Americans of the Indian novel, with its themes of alienation from industrial society, praise for Indian ways, and quest for identity in the modern world, speak to countercultural trends in White society itself. As White American intellectuals first questioned the drive to Americanize immigrants and other minority groups in the early twentieth century, then the materialism and vulgarity of business civilization in the 1920s, the survival of capitalism itself in the 1930s, and the basic values of American society after World War Two, American authors increasingly looked to the experiences of other peoples to criticize their own society.[90] Beginning in the 1940s, writers began to use the Western novel for probing the human condition and employed the Indian as a symbol for a more humane way of life.[91] The Indian again entered the mainstream of formal literature with his brief appearance in the works of William Faulkner and Ernest Hemingway to represent a sentient, spiritually rich life compared to the desiccated, intellectualized life of White men in Western civilization.[92]

In the novels and plays as in the motion pictures of the 1960s, writers and directors increasingly employed the Indian as the hero and the White man as the villain in their efforts to raise questions about the direction of American society. The Indian assumed a central role for this purpose in such major works as *The Sot-Weed Factor* (1960) by John Barth, *One Flew Over the Cuckoo's Nest* (1962) by Ken Kesey, *Little Big Man* (1964) by Thomas Berger, and *Indians* (first performed in 1968) by Arthur Kopit. Thus the Vanishing American returned to significant literary use as the alien, often witty, critic of the industrial and mass society that White intellectuals find so hard to live in. Modern writers employed the countercultural Indian in a way equivalent to the eighteenth-century *philosophes'* use of the Noble Savage.

In this trend from racism to attempted realism in the understanding of the Native American, historians of the United States have followed other intellectuals during the century after the 1860s. Both popular and academic historians in the last decades of the nineteenth century accepted the premises of Indian inferiority and the necessity for the disappearance of Native Americans before the westward movement of White civilization. At first the Indian was treated as part of the colonial past or of the history of the Western section of the United States. Francis Parkman continued his magisterial history of the conflict between France and England for dominion over North America, in which he portrayed the Indian as both inferior and savage. Hubert Howe Bancroft also subscribed to the old ideas about savagism and civilization in *The Native Races of the Pacific States of North America*, published in 1874. Although he felt constrained to devote five 800-page volumes in his multi-volumed project to the aboriginal peoples of the area, he nevertheless pictured their lives as mere prelude to the more interesting White civilizations that were to come.[93] Similarly, Edward S. Ellis, author of dime novels, and Edward Eggleston, leader of the Hoosier school of local color, promulgated the same basic views in their popular histories written during the 1880s and 1890s and the first decade of the twentieth century.[94]

This view received full academic respectability when it became the dominant interpretation of United States history as a result of

Frederick Jackson Turner's so-called Frontier Thesis. In one of the most important papers ever delivered before the American Historical Association, Turner argued in 1893 that American character and history had been shaped primarily by the frontier experience of westward migration and settlement. As initially presented, the thesis rested upon premises of social progress and evolution fashionable in the later nineteenth century, and so, naturally, the Indian was pictured as an obstacle to White settlement and the coming of civilization. Even though Turner dropped the social Darwinian trappings of his argument as he continued to elaborate his ideas, the Indian remained the stage of society before the evolution of White American civilization from frontier settlement to agricultural development to full-fledged urban society. So persuasive was this view of the United States past in its correlation of geographical movement with historical time to reflect White American images of their own social progress and evolution that basic American history textbooks in schools and colleges across the nation purveyed this interpretation for at least the first half of the twentieth century.[95] (See Plate 8.)

Although scholars questioned details of Turner's thesis as early as the 1920s, its basic premises and interpretation of the Indian were not really challenged until after World War Two. Henry Nash Smith in *Virgin Land: The American West as Symbol and Myth* (1950) demonstrated that much of what Turner and other historians had accepted as the facts of White expansion westward constituted, as his subtitle suggested, nineteenth-century American mythology about the frontier, not empirical reality. In other words, Smith pointed out that the history of the American frontier was as much a mirror of American prejudices and ideology as it was a story of actual past events. Applying this idea specifically to Native Americans, Roy Harvey Pearce in his *Savages of America: A Study of the Indian and the Idea of Civilization* (1953) suggested how White Americans from 1750 to 1850 had created the image of the Indian out of the opposition of civilization and savagism in order to justify their policies of extinction and assimilation. In more recent years, some commentators have elaborated Pearce's argument about the psychological basis of racism as the foundation of White Indian imagery and the imagery in turn as a rationale for genocide.[96] To correct the views disseminated by White historians of the Native American past, Native Americans and others founded the American Indian Historical Society in the mid-1960s.[97]

By that time, the United States was undergoing what young

radicals and their older supporters and teachers were calling a cultural revolution. Haunted by the extremes of great affluence side by side with crippling poverty at home and a supposedly invincible war machine floundering in the guerrilla warfare of Vietnam, these vocal intellectuals and leaders of the late 1960s called for a complete over-hauling of American institutions to eliminate racism and imperialism at home and abroad. Inspired by the revolutions of the third world, they called for revolution at home in order to redirect America's priorities and to achieve a more humane way of life for all peoples. In this atmosphere the Indian appeared among all the other countercul-tural arguments of the day. If racism was a problem, then historians found it a basic strand during the centuries of United States Indian policy just as social scientists found it in modern American society's treatment of Native Americans. If alternative ways of life were pro-posed as the solution to America's problems, then the communal and spiritual foundations of Indian life offered a superior example. If affluent White lifestyles raped the earth and polluted its atmosphere, then the traditional Indian land ethic and economy demonstrated na-tive ecological sense valuable to the very survival of the nation and the world (see Plate 11). If countercultural dreams and profound truth emanated from drugged states of consciousness, then here too the Indian provided precept and practice as well as peyote.

Appreciation of Indian arts, crafts, poetry, and oratory boomed as it always does during such periods of White fancy, but the latest phase in the countercultural use of the Indian is seen best in the lessons preached by three writers whose works achieved instant rec-ognition in the brave new world of a greening America. Vine Deloria, Jr., a Standing Rock Sioux, moved from a critique of White Indian policy (*Custer Died for Your Sins: An Indian Manifesto*, 1969) to the proposal that Indian tribalism offered a more rational lifestyle for all Americans in face of the impending disaster Whites had brought the nation to through industrialism (*We Talk, You Listen: New Tribes, New Turf*, 1970).

More radical in his use of the Indian as countercultural lesson was the literary critic Leslie Fiedler in *The Return of the Vanishing American* (1968). Following the suggestion of D. H. Lawrence that Americans had always tried to exorcise the Indian demon in their midst only to fall prey to the demon of the continent, Fiedler sur-veyed the White imagination as embodied in the history of literature to capture the sense of the alien other than the Indian represented. Always one to combine and extend the fashionable insights of his day,

Fiedler perceived in the Indian the effort of the White to escape the rationalist, imperialistic life he led in favor of the madness of true sanity in a sick world. Indians, therefore, were the alien other selves the Whites had destroyed in their own capitalistic, Christian life, and only drug-induced states of altered consciousness might allow the self-alienated White to regain his wholeness.

What the literary critic suggested was made the principal theme of the anthropologist Carlos Castaneda in his books about Don Juan, the Yaqui sorcerer. Under the teaching of Don Juan, Castaneda had advanced (in his own opinion) from the imperceptive orientation of the social sciences to an expanded alternative consciousness that allowed a far fuller appreciation of the universe than the scientific narrowness of Western civilization and its cognitive tradition.[98] Thus the spectrum of countercultural uses ranged from an appreciation of Indian lifestyles as more rational and humane than the general American way of life to a repudiation of the whole epistemology and ontology of Western philosophy for the mystical strain in the universal human psyche.

Whether any of these countercultural uses of the Indian prove any more "realistic" than previous stereotypes will, of course, depend upon the future of White scientific opinion and politics. About the only conclusion a historian can safely derive from the history of the Indian in the White imagination is that, even if new meaning is given the idea of the Indian, historians of the future will probably chronicle it as part of the recurrent effort of Whites to understand themselves, for the very attraction of the Indian to the White imagination rests upon the contrast that lies at the core of the idea. Thus the debate over "realism" will always be framed in terms of White values and needs, White ideologies and creative uses.

~~~~~~~~~

PART FOUR

Imagery and White Policy: The Indian as Justification and Rationale

THE IDEA OF THE INDIAN has lasted as long in White policy making as it has in White imagination, ideology, and social science. Whether one looks to the history of the relationships between White claims and native lands, between White political sovereignty and Indian governments, between White commerce and native economies, or between White philanthropy and Red welfare, one finds the same fundamental imagery serving both as moral and intellectual justification for White policies and as explanation for their failure or success. The primary premise of that imagery is the deficiency of the Indian as compared to the White. At bottom, to Europeans and Americans this means Native Americans must be *reformed* according to White criteria and their labor, lands, and souls put to "higher uses" in line with White goals. The similarity of these goals over the centuries attests to the continuity of basic White values as well as the endurance of native cultures.

As remarkable as the persistence of the idea of the deficient Indian in policy making has been the variety of Whites who resorted to the standard imagery for their own purposes. Although the specific goals of missionaries and military officers, of philanthropists and politicians often conflicted, these diverse White officials and policy makers agreed upon the basic nature of the Indian, and therefore their policies, if not their aims, were usually compatible in the larger sense. In fact, what historians distinguish as high ideals and crass interests frequently combined in the past to justify specific policies, for ideals like interests derived from a larger intellectual and social context shared by the policy makers of a period or place. Moreover, what historians label good and bad motives or policies all too often produced like results for Native Americans. As the humane goals of past eras become ethnocide in present perspective, all historic White activities are judged racist in motivation and outcome.[1]

Reduced to its fundamental principle, policy is a matter of what policy makers want versus what they think they can get. What White Indian policy makers wanted derived from the major values and political objectives prevailing in European and American societies. What they thought they could get hinged upon their image of the Indian. What they actually got in the end depended upon the differing natures of Native American societies. In this view of policy making, the idea of the Indian performs the role of intermediary between the desired and the actual outcomes of policy. White desires and ends in regard to Native Americans and the image of the Indian mutually interacted—a dialectic, if you will—and both were products of the larger trends in White societies. In practice what was presumed desirable for Whites was also supposed by Whites to be desirable for Indians and conversely what was good for Indians was seen as beneficial for White societies as well. In this best of all policy worlds from the White viewpoint, the idea of the Indian served to explain both what had to be done and what could be done for the sake of both the Native Americans and the Whites who came to their lands. The larger trends of a period in a White society not only determined White perceptions of the Indians and what was wanted of or from the Indians but also how the policy results were to be assessed. The results, however, depended upon the nature of social hierarchy and the degree of political authority and centralization in the various native societies.

The Colonial Foundations
of White Indian Policy: Theory

THE FOUNDATIONS OF WHITE POLICY were laid during the initial century or so of contact by each of the major European nations.
Whether one looks at the social, economic, religious, political, or legal
side of that story, one traces the basic approach long pursued by
White policy makers back to those early years, for, at that time,
Native Americans as "Indians" became colonial subjects in their own
lands as Whites advanced toward their goals as imperial powers in the
New World. Future generations of Native Americans, whether
descended from peoples conquered then or subsequently, inherited
that subordinated status.

Because this early period was so formative in the history of
White-Indian relations, historians have long cast their story of that
time in terms of heroes and villains among the policy makers,
allotting praise and blame among the colonizing powers, as if that
accounted for the supposedly different national histories of Indian
relations. Francis Parkman over a century ago summarized the conventional wisdom on this matter in his oft-quoted apothegm: "Spanish civilization crushed the Indian; English civilization scorned and
neglected him; French civilization embraced and cherished him."[2]
Parkman subscribed to one myth already hoary by his time and
helped through his own writings to establish others. He perpetuated
the so-called Black Legend of Spanish cruelty and genocide that
French and English propagandists derived initially from Las Casas
and exploited for their own nationalistic purposes.[3] Parkman's own
epic story of French and English exploration and conquest portrayed
the English as disdainful of intermarriage with "savages" and far less
zealous in the extension of Protestantism than of agriculture and commerce. He showed the French, however, enamored of Red mates and
as successful in the spread of Catholicism as they were of the beaver
trade. Some writers have countered the Black Legend with a White
Legend of Spanish accomplishment in giving the Indians Christianity
in place of human sacrifice and cannibalism and in providing beasts of

burden and plows to ameliorate or replace the heavy manual labor exacted in aboriginal times. Still other commentators have noted the large numbers of English people who became "White Indians"[4] and the sincerity if not accomplishments of English missionaries.

Such a comparison appears to me to emphasize the seeming differences in aims at the expense of their similarities, and it implies the outcomes depended more upon these aims and motives than upon the natural resources and the level of tribal socio-political organization available for exploitation by the three nations' policy makers and settlers in any given area. Where aims or, more important, consequences appear to differ among the colonial powers, one should look more to dissimilar physical environments and differing tribal governments and social organization than to fundamental contrasts in national idealism or racial sentiment. I do not mean to suggest that policies did not differ at all or that race prejudice and missionary zeal did not vary among the three nations. Rather I maintain that these latter are minor matters compared to the larger similarities of aims among the three nations' policy makers and settlers.[5]

In colonial charter and royal edict, in propaganda pamphlet and theoretical treatise, in missionary leaflet and public law, the Spanish, French, and English spokesmen espoused the same basic goals to justify the exploration and settlement of the New World: the spread of Christianity through the conversion of the heathen, the augmentation of private and public wealth through trade, and the enhancement of national and personal prestige and glory through colonization. If some scholars see the transition from one set of aims to another over time in the course of settlement,[6] and others say the Spanish theorized in post-hoc rationalization of their conquest as opposed to the French and English, who theorized to justify exploration and settlement to get what the Spanish had already obtained, they all agree that cross and crown, gold and glory constituted the legitimating symbols in European eyes for the invasion and takeover of the Americas. Although historians also disagree over whether public avowals of goals equaled the true motives of missionary and settler, of monarch and merchant, of conqueror and government official, they all concur in listing the same set of basic aims and motives in aggregate for the various groups of population within the nations. To Spanish crown and missionaries, the propagation of the faith seemed enjoined by the papal bulls on the settlement of newly discovered lands, which also happened to restrict most of the settlement of the Western Hemisphere to that nation. If the French and English denied the Spanish monopoly of American soil based upon papal grant, they nevertheless felt directed by God's command to spread the true faith as much as the Spanish. Colonies to supply gold and silver from precious mines or trade and raw materials through commerce were thought desirable for the increase of private wealth and public weal according to the mercantilistic tenets of the day. Whether colonies belonged technically to the crown or to the country as a whole, writers felt they enhanced the prestige of the monarch and the nation-state as it emerged in the new era of international relations and constant warfare.[7]

Ideals and interests of settlers and missionaries, of policy makers and private profit seekers were touted as compatible, even intertwined, in official statement and public propaganda—if not in practice, as all were to discover in actual settlement. Religion subdued the natives for economic advantage and paved the way for national expansion through peaceful conquest at the same time that it saved souls from eternal damnation. Trade and agriculture were presumed to extend national power and glory while they also converted the heathen to Christianity and European civilization through the social interaction of the commercial nexus. Thus propagandists for the missionary enterprise presented arguments for the increase of trade, while proponents of the commercial advantages of colonies mentioned the desirability of spreading Christianity. No people more than the English fused this diversity of aim into one rationale. George Peckham summarized succinctly in 1583 this fusion of ends in his statement of thesis for a book justifying the voyage of Sir Humphrey Gilbert: "to proove that this voyage, late enterprised, for trade, traficke, and planting, in America, is an action tending to the lawfull enlargement of her Majesties dominions, commodious to the whole Realme in generall. Profitable to the adventurers in perticuler, beneficial to the Savages, and a matter to be attained without any great daunger or difficultie."[8] Or as the buccaneer John Hawkins put it in a poem:

> *If zeale to God, or countries care, with private gaines accesse,*
> *Might serve for spurs unto th' attempt this pamflet doth expresse.*
> *One coast, one course, one toile might serve, at ful to make declard*
> *A zeale to God, with countries good, and private gaines regarde.*[9]

Many writers justified, as Peckham and Hawkins did, the invasion and settlement of native lands as beneficial to the Indians as well as to the Whites, for the Indians received the blessings of Christianity and civilization in exchange for their labor and/or lands. Sepúlveda, opponent of Las Casas in the great Spanish debate over the nature of the Indian, advanced such an argument that in effect idealized the activities of his countrymen in the New World. He favored dividing the Indians "among honourable, just and prudent Spaniards, especially among those who helped to bring the Indians under Spanish rule, so that these may train their Indians in virtuous and humane customs, and teach them the Christian religion; which may not be preached by force of arms but by precept and example. In return for this, the Spaniards may employ the labour of the Indians in performing those tasks necessary for civilized life."[10] The Virginia Company in 1610 issued a statement equally blunt in terms of the quid pro quo offered the Indians by the English, for the latter "by way of merchandizing and trade, doe buy of them the pearles of the earth, and sell to them the pearles of heaven."[11] Thus European policy makers and their propagandists not only presumed that the various ends and desires of Whites were or ought to be compatible but they also assumed that what was good for the Europeans must be equally good for the Indians.

White hopes for the exploitation of Indians and their lands certainly shaped their perceptions of Native Americans from the very beginning of contact. Conceptions of what the natives had to be so they could satisfy the demands Europeans would make of them influenced, if not fostered, the descriptions explorers, missionaries, and settlers provided financial backers and policy makers. Images of the good Indian suggested the ease of exploitation as well as the ability of natives to be exploited, for peaceful behavior, a quick wit, and willingness to listen all made the accomplishment of European settlement, religious conversion, and labor exploitation seem as easy as it was presumed profitable to White and Red alike. Therefore, the explorers' use of the primitivistic version of the good or Noble Savage must be suspected of catering to motives other than mere objective description. Thus Columbus concluded from his very first meeting with the Indians: "They should be good servants and of quick intelligence, since I see that they very soon say all that is said to them, and I believe that they would easily be made Christians, for it appeared to me that they had no creed."[12] Surely Barlowe's idyllic descriptions of the genteel Indians living along the Carolina coast as in the Golden Age were meant to cater to the hopes of his sponsor, Sir Walter Raleigh, as much as to record his impressions of native hospitality.[13]

If the primitivistic version of Indian goodness promised easy fulfillment of European desires, the image of the bad Indian proved the
absolute necessity, if difficulty, of forcing the Native Americans from
"savage" to European ways through the exploitation of their physical
bodies, spiritual souls, or tribal lands. That the Caribs were cannibals
justified, in Columbus's view, his selling them into slavery, and the
human sacrifice practiced by the Aztec required, in the opinion of
Sepúlveda and other Spaniards, the forced labor of all Indians. In fact,
the whole debate among the Spanish over the nature of the Indian can
be viewed as a dispute among colonists, clergy, and crown officials
about the proper method of exploiting the native, for the consequences of the arguments benefited some groups at the expense of
others.[14]

Not only did the image of the savage Indian rationalize European conquest but it also spurred missionaries to greater zeal and their
patrons to larger contributions. Although Samuel Purchas thought
the Virginia Indians little better than animals after the massacre of
1622, he nevertheless considered them "fit objects of zeale and pitie"
for their very badness and savagery.[15] Images of the good and bad
Indian proved as useful, therefore, to policy makers and others who
wished to exploit Native American minds, bodies, or resources as they
did to intellectuals and artists fighting the ideological controversies of
European high culture at the time. Beneath both the good and bad
images used by explorer, settler, missionary, and policy maker alike
lay the idea of Indian deficiency that assumed—even demanded—that
Whites do something to or for Indians to raise them to European
standards, whether for crass or idealistic motives.

In line with these general impressions of the basic nature and
ultimate purposes of the Indian, European monarchs and their coun-
selors developed policies that gave their fellow countrymen access in
the end to Native American labor, souls, and resources. In fulfilling
what they considered the basic obligation to Indian and White, European policy makers took not only a possessive view of the Indian but
also a possessory view of him and his lands as the means proper to the
"higher" ends all Whites agreed upon. In theory and in practice, each
colonizing power, except Sweden, asserted the same basic legal power
over the persons and territory of Native Americans. If the precise
legal theories whereby monarchs and policy makers justified such
intervention and invasion of native lives remain obscure or compli-
cated by the emergence of new conceptions of political sovereignty,
international law, and mercantilist doctrine, the basic claims and

their implications for Native Americans are clear enough. The exact kind of political jurisdiction and land tenure asserted by a monarch differed according to whether the claims were made under feudal customs or modern state law, and so in turn what grants and powers individuals received from the monarchs for the discovery and settlement of the Americas varied, but they all asserted legal jurisdiction over native persons and title over native lands.

In examining European claims to Indian lands, one must distinguish between what the colonial powers asserted against each other's claims as opposed to what they asserted against the native title. Among themselves, they argued whether visual discovery alone sufficed to establish a valid claim to areas of the Americas or whether occupation and settlement were also necessary to secure permanent title for one nation against other European powers. The assertion of title against native claims was of quite another order: it rested upon the image of the Indian as deficient. Charters and grants to explorers and settlement agencies usually stipulated that they possess lands uninhabited by a Christian prince. *Terra nullius* was an ambiguous term, however, for it could mean lands totally vacant of people or merely not inhabited by peoples possessing those religions and customs that Europeans recognized as equal to their own under the international law arising in this era.

If the land was vacant of any human occupancy, then a nation could claim both land title and political jurisdiction on the grounds of *vacuum domicilium*. Discovery and certainly occupation of such land by a European nation conferred both land title and political jurisdiction upon that nation's monarch, who in turn could pass on such title and jurisdiction to settlement agents as was customary in that country. Such title and rights in the land and in political power offered no problem in White opinion, but the degree of vacancy was often a matter of differences in European and native land usage. What to White eyes appeared empty or underutilized according to European practices was seen as owned and fully utilized according to tribal custom and economy.

Since large areas of America were occupied by tribes who moved their housing often by European criteria or who pursued hunting as well as horticulture, the Whites quickly leaped to the conclusion that such land awaited their immediate settlement because it was vacant. Europeans also believed that sparsely settled and underutilized lands could be shared by the Indians with the "higher" uses of the Europeans without harm to native economy and lifestyles, and perhaps to their improvement. The English particularly conceived of Indian occupancy in this manner. As John Winthrop before he left England answered in his own mind the objections to planting in New England, he concluded: "As for the Natives in New England, they inclose noe Land, neither have any setled habytation, nor any tame Cattle to improve the Land by, and soe have noe other but a Naturall Right to those Countries. Soe as if we leave them sufficient for their use, we may lawfully take the rest, there being more then enough for them and us."[16] If Native Americans challenged such a White view of their ownership and economies, White laws, customs, and courts existed to prove them wrong and to decide the matter of emptiness and title in favor of the invaders.[17]

Contrary to modern assumption, most title and jurisdiction over native lands were not claimed upon the basis of *vacuum domicilium*, for the presence of Native Americans, hostile at times, indicated that they indeed claimed an area even if they had not settled it densely enough in European eyes. While the English and the French might pretend otherwise some of the time, the size of the native population encountered by the Spanish on the mainland demanded some other rationale than "empty" land for laying claim to American territory. No European government, in fact, asserted that the Indians had no claim at all to any of their lands. Rather they questioned just what sort of title and political jurisdiction native rulers and their peoples possessed under national and natural law, since they lived without the Christian religion and without the customs deemed necessary for equality in international relations at the time. Did savagery and even barbarism remove the restraints imposed upon Christian princes and their subjects in claiming these regions, or did the natives of America have natural rights to their lands and their persons? What temporal relationships must be established with these peoples in fulfilling spiritual obligations to spread the Christian faith? Did native peoples have legitimate rulers, and, if so, what was the rulers' relationship to European monarchs? What legal and political rights remained to native peoples after conquest and White settlement? What rights in their lands did they forfeit and retain after conquest? Did they come under the civil and ecclesiastical courts common to European nations at the time? In response to these questions, European theorists and legal philosophers as well as policy makers developed a body of law and custom to deal with the spiritual and temporal relationships Native Americans bore to the colonial powers. Without examining the specific answers to all these questions, let us look at the major theory put forth at the time as the resolution to these many perplexing problems.[18]

To overcome the ambiguities of the situations posited in these questions, the European colonial powers evolved a doctrine of conquest applicable to American peoples that established White rights and jurisdiction by extinguishing or augmenting previous Indian title and rights—in White eyes, of course. Conquest in its broadest sense at the time meant seizure resulting not only from war but also from peaceful means according to Christian ideas of *occupatio bellica*. Such peaceful seizure required gaining the tacit, if not actual, agreement of the natives to the surrender of their lands and persons to European crowns.

Pacific methods whereby the European powers gained such conquest were various. Explorers of the several nations performed symbolic acts of possession. Columbus, for example, erected crosses upon each island he visited "as a sign that your Highnesses held this land as your own, and especially as an emblem of Jesus Christ Our Lord, and to the honor of Christendom," as he explains in his journal.[19] Later, Spanish as well as French and English explorers performed public ceremonies of erecting crosses or plaques with the royal arms upon them, claiming the soil and jurisdiction for the crown, and creating a public record of the action. Those few natives who sometimes witnessed the charade were presumed to acquiesce in the claim. The even fewer natives who protested such ceremonies were duped or cajoled into seeming agreement.[20] Under the theory of *occupatio bellica*, colonial charters represented a declaration of title against natives as well as against other European powers. At times, explorers or early settlers obtained explicit recognition of European suzerainty from native rulers. Perhaps the most famous example aside from Montezuma was the crowning of Powhatan.[21] Colonization and settlement by Whites constituted de facto and therefore de jure evidence of conquest, no matter how peacefully done. All methods presumed tacit agreement to European claims by the native peoples. Whether conquest resulted from peaceful or military means, therefore, the native lands and inhabitants came under the legal authority of the Europeans in White theory, if not always in actual control.

Conquest, whether pacific or violent, had to be for just cause according to Christian or "civilized" criteria. Since the Spanish coped with this problem first owing to priority of settlement, that nation's theologians developed the doctrines that justified the Spaniards' rapid conquest. Originally, they expropriated the land they needed for forts and habitations and enforced the labor service they demanded of the natives in mines and on farms without official rationale or legal basis. To rationalize the brutal warfare and oppression of those natives who resisted such exploitation of their bodies and lands, the Spanish policy makers extended to the Americas the doctrine of just war against the infidel used for centuries in Europe, but with modifications adapted to the new circumstances and based upon the theory of international law evolving at the time. To legalize this view of forceful conquest and prove its righteousness, Spanish policy required that a document, probably composed around 1512 by Palacios Rubios, an authority on just-war doctrine, be read to native populations about to be colonized. Although ship captains had the *Requerimiento*, as it was called, read from ship deck as they approached an island or brave commanders had it delivered in safe but empty places far from the Indian enemies to be attacked, the natives were to understand that they possessed a choice of peace or war as a result of the history of God's creation of the world and patronage of the Catholic Church. After learning of the Petrine theory of the papacy and the right of the Pope to donate the territories of the New World to the monarch of Spain, the Indians, who were invited to inspect the documents of this donation if they wished, were offered a choice based upon this knowledge:

> . . . Wherefore, as best we can, we ask and require that you consider what we have said to you, and that you take the time that shall be necessary to understand and deliberate upon it, and that you acknowledge the Church as the ruler and superior of the whole world, and the high priest called Pope, and in his name the king and queen Doña Juana our lords, in his place, as superiors and lords and kings of these islands and this mainland by virtue of the said donation, and that you consent and permit that these religious fathers declare and preach to you the aforesaid.
>
> If you do so you will do well, and that which you are obliged to do to their highnesses, and we in their name shall receive you in all love and charity, and shall leave you your wives and your children and your lands free without servitude, that you may do with them and with yourselves freely what you like and think best, and they shall not compel you to turn Christians unless you yourselves, when informed of the truth, should wish to be converted to our holy Catholic faith, as almost all the inhabitants of the rest of the islands have done. And besides this, their highnesses award you many privileges and exemptions and will grant you many benefits.
>
> But if you do not do this or if you maliciously delay in doing it, I certify to you that with the help of God we shall forcefully enter into your country and shall make war against you in all ways and

manners that we can, and shall subject you to the yoke and obedience of the Church and of their highnesses; we shall take you and your wives and your children and shall make slaves of them, and as such shall sell and dispose of them as their highnesses may command, and we shall take away your goods and shall do to you all the harm and damage that we can, as to vassals who do not obey and refuse to receive their lord and resist and contradict him; and we protest that the deaths and losses which shall accrue from this are your fault, and not that of their highnesses, or ours, or of these soldiers who come with us.[22]

Whether the Indians chose peace or war, they were to exchange their resources, labor, and religions for the Spanish version of Christianity and civilization as the document made clear.

Although some scholars have written extensively about the religious opponents within Spain and her colonies to the forceful conquest and enslavement of the Native Americans by their fellow countrymen, what these charitable religious people and the legal philosophers argued did not challenge the essential points of the doctrine of conquest in its broader outlines. Though these people denounced the enslavement of the natives upon the grounds of their natural inferiority, they did not question the ultimate political and legal jurisdiction of the Spanish over the native peoples and their lands. Though they opposed the forced conversion of the Indians to Catholicism, they did not doubt that missionaries had a right to preach the gospel in native lands and be protected, even unto warfare, in that holy mission. Though they argued against the natives' losing their legal rights and lands just because they were heathen and barbarian, they still upheld the desirability, even the necessity, of conversion to Christianity and civilization in the end. Though they protested the brutality of the *encomienda* and *repartimiento*, the two chief methods of compulsory labor, they did not wish to undo the whole of Spanish intervention in the New World. In the end, they too agreed with their opponents that resistance to the spread of Christianity demanded force and lazy native work habits (as the Spanish saw it) necessitated some form of control. The point of contention therefore was the means, not the ultimate ends. In denying the brutal oppression of the conquest, the reformers substituted Christian charity, as they understood it, for naked exploitation as the grounds for the Spanish invasion of the Americas, without challenging or changing very much the basic outcome for native political power and land title.[23]

In line with the prodding of those religious people opposing the naked exploitation of native labor through *repartimiento* and *en-*

comienda, first the king and then the Council of the Indies promulgated laws recognizing the freedom of the Indians, but such "freedom" changed little in theory and less in fact the actual lives of the natives under Spanish rule. As a result of the ascendance of the charitable religious rationale over the more blatant justifications for conquest and empire, the *Requerimiento* was abolished in 1556 and Spanish colonization declared a missionary enterprise. In 1573, Philip II ordered the subsequent extension of empire in America be termed "pacifications" instead of "conquests," and the Junta of 1582 defined the crown's relationship to the Americas as a "universal overlordship" giving the Spanish monarch a special guardianship in trust designed to further the spread of the Catholic faith. By the time the *Requerimiento* was abolished, however, the Spanish had conquered most of the major population groups worth exploiting according to their customary methods. Though the kings of Spain espoused a new theory of empire, they never reduced their territorial or jurisdictional claims over the New World or its inhabitants.

What the Spanish theorists propounded about the justification for the peaceful and forceful conquest of Native Americans and the resultant title and control over Indians and their lands was adopted in practice and, so far as scholars can tell, in theory by other European nations (except Sweden). Whether based upon feudal law or modern political sovereignty, England and France treated natives and their lands as ultimately under the control of the crown. Symbolic acts of possession, settlement practices, and formal rationales followed the doctrine of peaceful or violent conquest for just causes. If English theorists of empire added the right of commerce among the "savages" to the right to preach the gospel among the heathen, their addition may reflect not only the proverbial shopkeeper mentality said to be so prevalent in that nation but also the growing legitimacy of secular reasons as supplement to, if not replacement for, theological ones in international law as Europe moved from the Middle Ages into modern times. George Peckham argued in his treatise justifying English colonization of the New World "that it is lawfull and necessarye to trade and traficke with the Savages. And to plant in their countries," because, he argued,

> . . . that the Christians may lawfully travaile into those Countries and abide there whom the Savages may not justly impugne and forbidde, in respect of the mutuall society and fellowship betweene man and man prescribed by the Lawe of Nations.

For from the first beginning of the creation of the world and from the renuing of the same after Noes floode, all men have agreed, that no violence shoulde be offered Ambassadours. That the Sea with his Havens shoulde bee common. . . . And that Straungers sholde not be dryven away from the place of Countrey whereunto they doo come.

If it were so then, I demaunde in what age, and by what Lawe is the same forbidden or denied since? For who doubteth but that it is lawfull for Christians to use trade and traficke with Infidels or Savages, carrying thether such commodities as they want, and bringing from thence some parte of theyr plentie.[24]

What Peckham argues so incompletely here is amplified in the writing of the Dutch jurist Hugo Grotius, one of the founders of modern international law and the resident of another seafaring nation.[25] Secular rationale therefore supplemented those claims already asserted against Native Americans by the European powers.

The Colonial Foundations
of White Indian Policy: Practice

SUCH GRAND THEORIES of justification for the transfer of native title and jurisdiction to European crowns and their subjects did not solve the difficulties of gaining actual political control and possession of the land and its inhabitants. Monarchs usually granted the initial explorers title and jurisdiction over what lands and peoples they could peacefully or otherwise conquer and control. Under such speculative grants of power and title, the early explorers appropriated what lands they could and controlled the native inhabitants as best they could in relation to their ends. Under each of the three major colonial powers, subsequent policy and results developed according to the resources found in a region and the level of the native sociopolitical organization in the area. Of the three leading colonial powers in North America, the Spanish encountered the widest spectrum of native societies. From the viewpoint of the other colonizers, the Spanish also obtained the best of all possible colonial worlds in the Aztec empire.[26]

In addition to the rich mines and farmlands, the Aztec empire was especially exploitable by colonial standards, because Spanish feudal tenure and practices were so compatible with former native control of peoples and resources under the Aztec conquest state. Although the conquistadores and early colonists expropriated some Aztec lands upon their own or royal authority, they were more interested in receiving tribute and labor to work the land and its resources. Under the *encomienda* system, the conquerors in essence substituted their demand for labor and tribute for that of the former native rulers. Thus they essentially imposed their own level of lordship and tenure according to Spanish feudal practice upon native authority and title, and the Spanish crown's efforts to break this revival of feudalism in the New World accounted as much for the freeing of the natives from the control of the *encomendero* as the urging of clergy and conscience in the great debate over the nature of the Indian. In releasing the natives from the *encomenderos*, however, the crown placed them under its own system of tribute and compulsory labor service as part of the *corregimiento*. Under either system, *encomendero* and *corregidor* demanded local native leaders supply from the people they ruled the required quota of labor or tribute. Increasingly during the sixteenth century, Aztec communities came under the jurisdiction of the crown and its representatives through the local nexus of *corregidor* and Indian *gobernador* and other native village officials, and Indian town government in turn became increasingly Hispanized. Working through the same local native leadership, the clergy sought to bring the Indian masses into the Church. Thus Spanish secular and spiritual policy allowed the continuance of local native rule and jurisdiction insofar as it served Spanish ends. In this manner, the Aztec empire became part of the Spanish empire.[27]

Although the French and English approached exploration and settlement with visions of Spanish achievement shimmering before their eyes, the natural resources and, more important, the native societies they encountered in the areas they settled precluded a duplication of Spanish success. As soon as extensive exploration by both nations began, their policy makers and settlers alike quickly discovered the lack of mineral resources in their respective areas of colonization. Moreover, the French found little land suitable for farming in the St. Lawrence Valley, and so they turned to the fur trade as the only valuable resource other than the fishing banks off the coast of Canada. In the fur trade, the French and Native Americans formed a sym-land or to exercise obvious political control. In the valley of the St. biotic relationship that did not require the French to occupy much

Lawrence, where the French made the only extensive settlement in mainland Canada, the land had been mostly abandoned by native tribes on the eve of White settlement in the seventeenth century. Furthermore, the peculiarities of topography and the lack of French *habitants* confined White occupation to thin lines along the sides of the river.[28] Some pressure for conversion was exerted by priests in the field or on the few reserves founded by *religieux* along the St. Lawrence.[29]

The policy of *Francization,* or converting the Indians to French civilization as well as religion, so much the aim of secular authorities and religious leaders alike in the beginning of the colony, proved a failure without containment upon a reserve, and even here many questioned the results.[30] Even after the abandonment of the policy of *Francization,* some efforts were made to bring the Indians into full-fledged legal and social equality in New France, but the achievement of such an aim still depended as much as ever upon the ability of the French priests and politicians to control the life of a tribe or its members individually. De facto sovereignty unlike de jure sovereignty depended upon actual control rather than theoretical jurisdiction, and so the high ideals of integrating the inhabitants of the Franco-American colony into one people hinged as much upon concrete power as upon good intentions. Integration still presumed acculturation and French dominance, and discrimination underlay Franco-Indian relations as actually practiced.[31]

In the end, the success often attributed to French Indian policy must be ascribed to the failure of Canada as a colony when judged by Spanish and English achievement. French settlement seemed compatible with Indian occupancy because the French settled and farmed so little of mainland Canada and that principally where the natives had vacated. The fur trade required minuscule portions of land and rested primarily upon a reciprocal economic relationship beneficial to both sides in contact. Even though the fur trade can be described as the least destructive of the White methods of exploiting native resources, still it promoted profound changes in Native American societies. These transformations, however, came as much in response to the desires of native peoples as at the behest of Whites.[32] Under these circumstances, the pressures for assimilation to White ways remained as minimal as the French desire for extensive native lands. Wherever the French attempted the type of agricultural settlement pursued by the English, however, they encountered similar native resistance and engaged in the same kind of warfare.[33]

If in general the French during the seventeenth century did not need native labor as the Spanish employed it, the English needed but could not use native labor, given the nature of tribal social and political organization they encountered in the areas of mainland North America they settled. Although both nations' settlers came upon the same type of stateless bands and tribes, the French fur trade needed no higher level of social organization for its exploitation, but English agriculture, especially in the southern colonies, could have used a captive labor force of the kind employed by the Spanish in central Mexico. Like the French, the English also turned to fish and furs at first, but their permanent settlements soon came to depend upon agriculture and the trade associated with it as the main support of their economy. The English fur trade appeared as compatible with native lifestyles as that conducted by the French.[34] English political jurisdiction and land claims as represented by the fur trade impinged as lightly upon native title and ways as those carried into the forest by voyageur and priest. English farming, however, whether of the southern or northern variety, depended upon the extensive and exclusive use of the land and so demanded, at the same time that it promoted, the rapid expansion of White settlement upon native territory. Virginia alone had a larger population in 1650 than all of New France in 1700, and Massachusetts counted almost as large a population at mid-century as Canada did fifty years later.[35]

Moreover, English agricultural practices presumed exclusive White usage of the land, thereby precluding any sharing of resources with Red neighbors, and English tenure and legal jurisdiction recognized this approach to territorial control. White uses of the land destroyed Indian subsistence from hunting as well as native horticulture and forced each tribe to contest White destruction of its economy, or to convert to White ways and methods, or to remove further into the frontier and encroach upon another tribe's territory. As a result of this conflict between native and English economies as well as cultures, the history of the mainland English colonies in the seventeenth century (and later) consists primarily of the expansion of White settlement onto native lands and the peaceful or forceful transfer of ownership of those lands from Red to White hands.

After the initial years of English settlement, this transfer of title took place through two main means of cession. Although the early English explorers claimed vast territory in the name of the monarch, who in turn granted portions to the various agents or agencies empowered to settle America, the colonists acquired actual possession and completed title to the land by slower but more certain means. The English in Virginia gained a foothold through a combination of methods: permission from some chiefs who lived there, the claim of sovereignty symbolized in Powhatan's coronation ceremony, and out- right seizure.[36] Certainly of all the native societies encountered by the English on the east coast of what was to become the United States, the so-called Powhatan Confederacy possessed the greatest potential for exploitation along Spanish lines. Since Powhatan was apparently establishing a nascent conquest state through which he received tribute, the English could have asserted a feudal overlordship consistent with the Spanish practice of receiving tribute and labor service. Such a possibility never came to pass, however, as the initial gentlemen adventurers gave way to tobacco-raising settlers.[37] Pil- grims and Puritans located their first settlements upon lands tempo- rarily depopulated by what the pious considered providential plagues and therefore they claimed title by virtue of *vacuum domicilium*.

Subsequent land possession and title were obtained north and south through native cession by purchase or warfare. Apparently colonial leaders thought the practice of buying tracts of land from the natives as a means of quieting Indian title claims cheaper than forceful seizure in warfare and equally effective in theory—even though cajolery and coercion often entered into the actual negotiations. Scholars debate just when cessions through formal and recorded pur- chase started in New England, but the practice became general throughout the colonies after the 1630s.[38] As the seventeenth cen- tury progressed, colony after colony adopted legislation restricting the right of purchase from Indians to the official agents of the gov- ernment. By thus placing the right of preemption in the hands of official colonial representatives, the legislatures hoped to avoid the conflict between individual Whites and Indians over the legitimacy of various cessions and purchases. The other source of cession resulted from White victories over native tribes in warfare. Under the impres- sion that Indians should recompense the colonists for conquering them, White leaders demanded substantial land cessions from hostile tribes as the price of renewed peace—if any tribespeople survived warfare.[39]

Whether obtained in war or through purchase, whether re- corded in deed and treaty or by informal arrangement, the English demanded and received title and possession of tract after tract from the tribes they encountered in their expansion westward. By this gradual process of cession, the colonists brought their actual control of native resources and populations into line with the exorbitant territorial claims made by the early explorers for the English crown. The justification of the process and the means was expounded as early as 1636 by Peter Heylyn in his geographical survey of the world, *Microcosmus:*

> He that travelleth in any Part of America not inhabited by the Europeans shall find a world very like to that we lived in, in or near the time of Abraham the Patriarch about three hundred years after the flood. The lands lie in common to all Natives and all Comers, though some few parcels are sown, yet the Tiller claims no right in them when he has reaped his crop once. Their Petty Kings do indeed frequently sell their kingdoms, but that in effect is only taking Money for withdrawing and going further up the Country, for he is sure never to want land for his subjects because the Country is vastly bigger than the Inhabitants, who are very few in proportion to its greatness and fertility. . . . Sometimes whole Nations change their Seats, and go at once to very distant places, Hunting as they go for a Subsistance, and they that have come after the first discoverers have found these places desolate which the other found full of inhabitants. This will show that we have done them no Injury by settling amongst them; we rather than they being the prime occupants, and they only Sojourners in the land: we have bought however of them the most part of the lands we have, and have purchased little with our Swords, but when they have made war upon us.[40]

In this brief statement he combines the image of the deficient Indian with the doctrine of just war and the new method of land purchase to justify the English title to American lands.

Just as the colonists had to acquire the land through cession to substantiate England's claim to title, so they had to gain control over the tribes to extend English law and jurisdiction over the natives. Although law and political control extended in theory over the natives as part of the territorial claim, in practice de facto sovereignty was limited to those tribes that willingly surrendered or were subjugated to the colonists' authority. In other words, the power of the respective sides determined the legal system to which individual natives were responsible. The status of Indians in colonial law can be divided into three categories according to de facto sovereignty. First, those individuals separated from their tribes, whether as slaves, servants, or as free persons, came under the colonial laws applicable to their respective categories without any question.[41] Second, members of independent tribes were treated as nominal foreigners under their own customs, although colonial authorities insisted that Indians of those tribes under treaty arrangement breaking English laws be tried in White courts according to English justice. Whether these Indians were tried according to English justice for the offenses of murder, trespass, or theft depended upon the wishes of their own chiefs and peers, since the power of the colonists over their lives was nominal at best.

The third jurisdictional category was an anomalous but significant one for the future of Native Americans. Some tribes existed for a period neither independent nor socially assimilated. Either through conquest or for other reasons, these tribespeople rendered homage to the monarch, held their lands from the crown, acknowledged themselves to be English subjects, and existed as communities and tribes under colonial protection. Often rendering tribute to colonial governments, the members of these tribes came under English law and colonial courts, although special laws and practices were often promulgated for their governance. Such tribes, whether settled on colonial frontiers or in enclaves within colonial societies, possessed an anomalous status that foreshadowed the reservation system to come. Indians of all three categories were to be given justice under law equal in theory and practice to that rendered Whites, but, even under the best of circumstances, that justice and law were to be according to the English model and interpreted by White officials and judges, not native chiefs and peers according to tribal customs.[42]

As in New France and the borderlands of New Spain, English policy makers delegated the task of converting the Indians to White civilization mainly to the missionaries. Like their Catholic counterparts in the other areas of North America, the Protestant missionaries of the English colonies expected to propagate English customs and values along with the doctrines of Anglicanism and Congregationalism. English missionaries of these persuasions recognized the close connection between White secular and religious values and practices. The most famous of the seventeenth-century New England missionaries, John Eliot, counseled his charges using the deficiency image:

They began to enquire after baptism and church ordinances, and the way of worshipping God as the Churches here do, but I showing how incapable they be to be trusted therewith, while they live so unfixed, confused, and ungoverned a life, unsubdued to labor and order; they began now to enquire after such things. And to that end

I have propounded to them that a fit place be found out for cohabitation wherewith they may subsist by labor, and settle themselves in such a way: And then they may have a Church, and all the Ordinances of Christ amongst them.[43]

In this fusion of secular and religious ends, the work of the English missionaries, like that of the *religieux* engaged in the *Francization* program and of the Spanish friars proselytizing on the frontiers of New Spain, can be viewed not only as bringing the Indians more fully under White law and jurisdiction but also making them more amenable to White economic exploitation. The praying towns of New England, like the reserves along the St. Lawrence and the mission villages on the Spanish borderlands, rendered the Indians docile in demeanor, trained in lowly White economic skills, and ready for incorporation into the European economic system. Although the English missionaries may have thought their motives and goals quite different, the effect of their efforts—to the extent that they succeeded in accomplishing their program at all—was to bring the Indians into some sort of economic as well as spiritual and cultural relationship with the colonists of their lands. In the end, the English missionary program, whether measured by these secular purposes or by its professed spiritual goals, must be judged a failure.[44]

Scholars have assigned many reasons for the failure of the English missions as compared to Spanish and French achievements: Protestant apathy versus Catholic zeal; Catholic, especially Jesuit, flexibility versus Protestant rigidity in the field; the ceremonialism of Catholicism versus the dull services of the Protestants; and even Latin racial sentiment versus Anglo-Saxon prejudices.[45] Without minimizing the importance of these and other factors in explaining the differences in the missionary results achieved by the various colonizing powers, one must still place these factors into the larger context of each European nation's overall relationships with Native Americans for the perspective necessary in understanding the diverse outcomes. The English missionaries, like their French colleagues, found no hierarchical and centralized native political administrations that they could use as the Spanish missionaries had in the Aztec empire to gain nominal mass conversion. In fact, the Spanish friars ran into the same kind of problems as the English and French missionaries when they entered tribes with the same type of stateless and "democratic" organization faced by their northern peers. Neither could the English missionaries operate under the permissive contact conditions associated with the fur trade because of the rapid expansion of agriculture by their fellow colonists and the resultant hostilities. All English religious work among the Virginia Indians aborted in Opechancanough's two uprisings in 1622 and 1644. Only four of the fourteen praying towns established by Eliot survived King Philip's War, and even these disintegrated by the end of the seventeenth century.

Thus the propagation of the faith, like the other White uses of the Indian, ultimately depended upon the compatibility of White aims and methods of exploitation with native social organization and natural resources. If Spanish and French missionary success is measured by complete conversion to the Roman Catholic religion rather than nominal allegiance to form and syncretic practice, then perhaps the discrepancy between English and Latin achievements diminishes considerably. In the end, the religious toilers of all three nations faced tribespeople, no matter how little or much organized politically and socially, who preferred their own beliefs and practices to those of the foreign invaders.[46]

If the European powers did not get all they wanted from the Indians, they accomplished their basic goals of transforming many natives into colonial subjects in their own homelands, transferred title in theory and often in fact from native inhabitants to crown and settlers, and exploited native resources in ways consonant with European economies and tribal organization. Toward these ends, policy makers used the image of the Indian to justify the necessity as well as to prove the desirability of their policies. They also used the image of the Indian as the base line for measuring how far they had succeeded in their efforts to convert Native Americans to White civilization and religion.

Early United States Policy: Expansion with Honor

How and what one nation built upon these colonial foundations may be seen in the history of United States Indian policy. Comparison of the larger aims and results of two hundred years of White American policy making with those of the preceding period reveals a remarkable similarity. From the founding of the nation until recent times, and some would include today as well, United States policy makers placed two considerations above all others in the nation's relation with Native Americans as Indians: the extinction of native title in favor of White exploitation of native lands and resources and the transformation of native lifestyles into copies of approved White models. Whether White Americans pursued their crassest interests or their highest ideals throughout most of the two centuries, the results for Native Americans resembled those achieved earlier by the European powers, particularly England: dispossession of native lands and frequently displacement from native locales, disruption if not destruction of native cultures, and demographic decimation from White diseases and warfare. Given the larger similarities in goals and effects of the two periods of policy, the basic question then becomes not the morality or hypocrisy of United States Indian relations as such or in comparison to other nations' dealings, important as this may be in another context,[47] but why did the old policies (and consequences) persist so long in the new nation, even as its social, political, and economic organization changed so dramatically? The answer lies once again in the long-term competition for the same natural resources by peoples with different cultures and levels of social organization.

What was new in United States Indian policy was not, therefore, the continuing conflict over lands and resources or the persistence of old goals and results, but the ideology of "Americanism" that played such a crucial role in formulating and evaluating that policy over time. Although competition for the same natural resources by peoples of different social organization and economic institutions goes far to explain the general similarity of outcomes between the colonial and later periods, the cluster of ideas and images leading White Americans had of what their nation was and should be as a society accounts for the specific ways in which United States Indian policy was formulated and implemented to produce those similar outcomes—and even to judge them subsequently. To claim that this cluster of ideas and images, so conceptually integrated and consciously articulated by leading Americans as to constitute an ideology,[48] demanded the idea of the Indian to rationalize and justify the continuing conflict oversimplifies the role of ideology in human affairs. The idea of the Indian, however, probably served more often to reconcile national interests with national ideals in regard to Native Americans than basic American values were held to condemn the policies formulated for the Indian. In any case, the Native American as Indian posed a moral as well as a practical problem in national life, since such a large component of Americanism stressed the normative side of American institutional arrangements.[49]

To be an "American" therefore was as much an image in the minds of the leading citizens of the United States as it was to be an "Indian," and for most, if not all, of the two centuries of United States existence the two images were antithetic. The Native American understood as an Indian represented an affront to the cherished values of the vast majority of White Americans, whether those values were crass or idealistic according to their own standards. Therefore principles of morality as well as expediency dictated, nay demanded, the "Americanization" of the Indian and his lands, either through transforming the Native American into an approved White American model or by placing White Americans upon former Indian lands. Either method substituted an "American"[50] for an "Indian," and eliminated the latter in favor of the former, on the territory claimed by the United States under international law.

The creation of the United States at the end of the eighteenth century gave new meaning to the words "America" and "American." Just as the New World carried a larger symbolic meaning as a result of European intellectual currents during the age of discoveries, so the new nation seemed to represent the fulfillment of enlightened liberal ideals in the eyes of European social theorists as well as of its own citizens. What had only been philosophized about in Europe appeared to be actual practice in the newly independent United States. To the social equality that seemed to prevail there were added the blessings of political and religious liberty. In their revolt against monarchy the states singly and collectively instituted republican governments founded upon popular sovereignty and dedicated to the natural rights of men. To secure political freedom and liberty for the individual, these governments operated under written constitutions that embodied the principle of checks and balances and specified the civil liberties of citizens. To foster religious liberty, most of these constitutions subscribed to freedom of conscience. In this religious equivalent of laissez-faire, the founding fathers assumed that the religious and moral foundations of the republic would remain untouched, because they presumed a republic far more dependent upon the virtue of its citizenry than a monarchy with its alternative source of power. Could, in fact, a republic, especially one large in extent and population, long endure based upon such novel principles? The new United States thus became an experiment in the history of the rights of man, which its own leaders watched as anxiously as those overseas.[51]

Americans sensed their place in history and sought innovations in line with that larger destiny as they conceived the future greatness of the nation. Their leaders revised law codes, sought a new foreign policy, and created land and colonial systems all in accordance with what they thought were the most liberal ideals of the age. As Jefferson, one of the most self-conscious of these leaders, exclaimed to a friend in 1784, "This is surely an age of innovation, and America the focus of it."[52] Both the ideas of progress and religious millennialism hinted at the coming role of the United States in history.[53] No wonder the Continental Congress adopted in 1783 as mottoes on the Great Seal of the United States both *annuit coeptis*, "He [God] has smiled on our undertakings," and *novus ordo seclorum*, "a new order of the ages."[54]

Given the perspective of the time, land played an important role in the preservation as well as the fulfillment of what had been achieved in America. To leading Americans of the Revolutionary generation, agriculture was the preferred (as well as the predominant) means of existence for the vast majority of the population, because it provided the best economic foundation for the political and social arrangements considered ideal in the new nation. If a citizen was economically independent, he would be politically autonomous in their opinion. Under republican ideals of the period, property was connected with life and liberty because its ownership was the surest guarantee of those other inalienable rights. To perpetuate the social hierarchy leading Americans deemed desirable to preserve public virtue as well as to provide the stake in society thought necessary for responsible decision making, republican constitutions restricted the franchise to property holders.

Widespread ownership of property was also believed to afford the basis for the social equality believed so prevalent at the time. Americans as well as Europeans thought the vast majority of (White) inhabitants of the United States belonged to the middle ranks of society, neither rich nor poor but a "happy mediocrity" as they said, due to the extensive property ownership in the new nation. This combination of substantial land ownership and new political system made for the historical uniqueness of America in the eyes of Ezra Stiles, president of Yale. In his sermon of 1783, "The United States Elevated to Glory and Honor," he observed, "But a Democratical polity for millions, standing upon a broad basis of the people at large, amply charged with property, has not hitherto been exhibited."[55] From our vantage point, only the existence of cheap, readily available land for the general populace allowed the reconciliation of the general equality of condition with equality of opportunity. Without cheap lands and access to them, the paradox, or even conflict, of these two sides of American political and economic liberalism would have become apparent. If republican institutions and social structure constituted the ideal America in the opinion of the era's leaders and its people, then the future of that America depended upon the continued availability of cheap lands as the population increased.[56]

Thus geography took on a moral as well as an economic dimension under the ideology of Americanism that had direct implications for Native American occupancy. First, to preserve the American political and social system, certain ways of using the land were preferred to others, and the idea of the Indian and his way opposed these modes. According to the imagery, Indians were hunters and Americans were farmers or at least industrious in other ways in transforming nature into property. As John Quincy Adams queried in 1802 in words that were to haunt him decades later during the removal debate: "What is the right of a huntsman to the forest of a thousand miles over which he has accidentally ranged in quest of prey? . . . Shall the fields and vallies, which a beneficent God has formed to teem with the life of innumerable multitudes, be condemned to everlasting barrenness?"[57] The deficient Indian, as usual in this doctrine of uses, possessed more land than he could utilize in approved fashion. Second, American ways of life were fated to expand within the boundaries of the United States and even beyond in accord with the ideas of progress and destiny.

If national destiny at this time was not as manifest as it would become when premised upon assumptions of evolutionism and racism in the second third of the nineteenth century, its course and implications were evident enough to Jedidiah Morse in his *American Geography* of 1789. He discussed whether American citizens venturing beyond the Mississippi River, which was the western boundary of the United States under the peace treaty of 1783, would be lost to the nation's commerce and to Americanism as they came under Spanish rule. After some practical arguments upon the matter, he ended with a peroration premised upon an ideal of America that expressed clearly what United States expansion meant in terms of who would use the land and how they would use it:

> Besides, it is well known that empire has been travelling from east to west. Probably her last and broadest seat will be America. Here the sciences and the arts of civilized life are to receive their

1. THE LANDING OF CHRISTOPHER COLUMBUS. *Woodcut from title page of a rhymed edition of Columbus's first letter describing his discovery, published in Florence, 1493.*

While purporting to represent the natives of the newly discovered Indies, this woodcut is probably a reprint of an earlier one depicting another discovery of the period. In any case, the only feature that distinguishes the "Indians" from the Europeans or other peoples is their nakedness. It was nearly impossible, given the techniques of the time, to show racial differences among people depicted in printed illustrations.

2. THE PEOPLE AND ISLAND WHICH HAVE BEEN DISCOVERED . . . *Woodcut, German, probably Augsburg or Nuremberg, ca. 1505.*

This woodcut is usually claimed to be the first picture showing Native Americans in some ethnographic detail. Since the artist depicts Indian life according to the widely circulated description of Vespucci, he emphasizes cannibalism, open love-making, and their scanty feather dress. Not having seen his subjects, he erroneously gives them beards.

3. A WEROAN OR GREAT LORDE OF VIRGINIA. *From Theodor de Bry's edition of Thomas Hariot,* A Briefe and True Report of the New Found Land of Virginia, *published in Frankfurt, 1590.*

Although copying the on-the-spot drawings of John White, de Bry's engravers gave a classical stance and Europeanized physical features to the Carolina natives. Such pictures as this one of a "prince" established the muscular handsomeness and athletic virility of the Noble American Savage in European minds. The lack of clothing and the careful distribution of artifacts upon and about the prince's body only enhanced the image.

4. THE DISCOVERY OF AMERICA. *Jan van der Straet (Stradanus),
pen and bistre, ca. 1575.*

In this drawing showing the supposed discovery of the New
World by Vespucci in 1497, the artist develops the symbolism of
Europe confronting America. Vespucci appears with the symbols
of European scientific knowledge and dominion: astrolabe, ships,
crosses, flag, and armor. The Indian maid representing America lies
supine in a New World hammock, barely clothed in feathers, with
club, instead of bow and arrow, nearby. In the background are
cannibals and the exotic fauna and flora sixteenth-century
Europeans associated with the New World. This image of America
as an Indian maiden was retained in iconography for another two
centuries.

5. LES FUNERAILLES D'ATALA (THE ENTOMBMENT OF ATALA).
Anne-Louis Girodet-Triosin, oil on canvas, 1808.

In what is probably the most famous of all the works inspired by
Chateaubriand's novel, the painter uses romantic conventions to
evoke the passion the ill-fated lovers felt and the purity they
lived. The specific scene combines two scenes from the novel: the
all-night vigil of Chactas and Père Aubrey over the dead Atala and
the burial next morning under a bridge of rock. The Indianness of
Chactas and Atala is barely seen in the physical features and dress
of the two lovers, while the Christian symbolism of the monk and
the crosses in the hands and on the hill all emphasize the essence of
Chateaubriand's religious fervor. By playing down the Indianness
of the lovers, the painter stresses the universal aspects of romantic
melancholy common to the arts at the time.

6. WI-JÚN-JON, THE PIGEON'S EGG HEAD (THE LIGHT), GOING TO
AND RETURNING FROM WASHINGTON. *George Catlin, oil on canvas,
1832.*

In the "before" picture, Catlin depicted the Assiniboin chief in
all his romantic glory and noble bearing, untainted in clothing or
psyche by White civilization. This was the image Catlin hurried to
the Plains to capture before the race passed into oblivion. It was also
the image that became the classic Indian in the nineteenth century,
replacing finally the noble American of the de Bry engravings of
the 1590s. The colonel's uniform, the umbrella, the fan, the cigarette,
and the clownish, foppish strut in the "after" picture all reveal in
Catlin's opinion how civilization corrupted the natural nobility and
manners of the Indian.

2

3

4

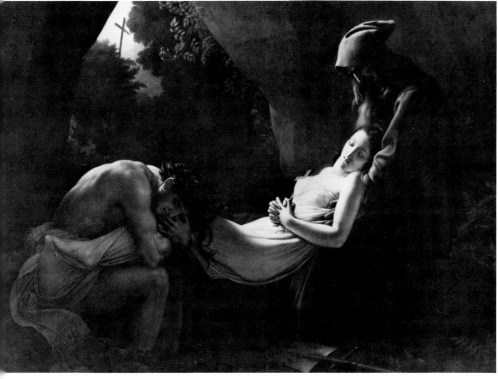

5

7

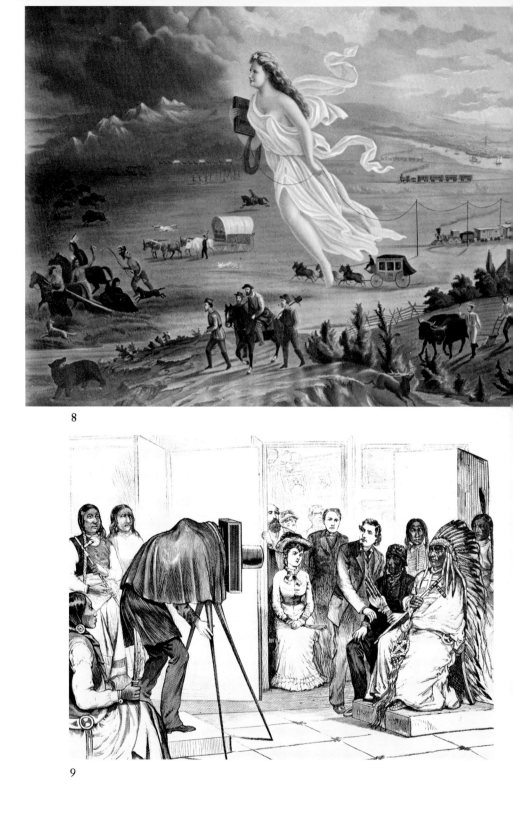

8

9

Pollution: it's a crying shame

People start pollution.
People can stop it.

Keep America Beautiful

Advertising contributed for the public good

11

7. RESCUE GROUP. *Horatio Greenough, commissioned 1837, placed in the East Portico of the Capitol, Washington, D.C., 1853.*

Greenough chose a classic image of the bad Indian for display in the national capitol. The savage, still depicted as muscular and handsome, menaces White society, represented by a helpless woman and child. Only the superior strength of the brave pioneer man, garbed in contemporary clothing and ancient helmet, prevents the intended blow from the upraised tomahawk. The physical superiority in size and strength of the White pioneer man over the savage Indian symbolizes the moral and racial superiority of civilization over savagery, and presumably indicates the destiny of the two races.

8. AMERICAN PROGRESS. *Chromolithograph, after a John Gast painting, 1872, issued by George Crofutt's* Western World, *1873.*

The artist, according to the description on the back of the picture, illustrates "at a glance the grand drama of Progress in the civilization, settlement and history of our own happy land." In showing the progress of civilization according to nineteenth-century evolutionary assumptions, the artist has the Indians, along with bears, wild horses, and buffalo, fleeing before the Spirit of Progress, who wears the star of empire on her forehead, carries a book representing common school education, and trails a telegraph wire behind her. Following her are the various stages of transportation and the different occupations to trace the growth of civilization and the westward movement of White American society. What the artist portrays so graphically becomes the foundation premise of the frontier interpretation of American history advanced by Frederick Jackson Turner in 1893.

9. PHOTOGRAPHING AN INDIAN DELEGATION, IN BELL'S STUDIO, FOR THE GOVERNMENT. *After a sketch by A. B. Shults, published in* Frank Leslie's Illustrated Newspaper, *Vol. LIII (Sept. 10, 1881), p. 24.*

This sketch shows vividly the gap between the social context of a photograph and its contents. The Secretary of Interior, pleased by a land cession made by a visiting delegation of Omaha, Winnebago, Sioux, and Ponca, had each of the chiefs photographed by C. M. Bell in his Washington, D.C., studio at government expense. It was customary for Indians visiting the national capital to be photographed for the Smithsonian Institution or for other purposes.

10. THE VANISHING RACE—NAVAHO. *Photograph by Edward S.*
Curtis in The North American Indian, *supplementary plates, vol. 1,*
plate 1, 1907.

Curtis chose this photograph as the first one in his supplementary
series, because, as he explained, "The thought which this picture is
meant to convey is that the Indians as a race, already shorn of their
tribal strength and stripped of their primitive dress, are passing into
the darkness of an unknown future." In line with this impression,
he often posed Indians in costumes they no longer wore and
re-created environments in which they no longer lived. To ensure
the authenticity of his photographs, he carried with him a box of
wigs to lend to his subjects so they would have the proper long hair.

11. POLLUTION: IT'S A CRYING SHAME. *Poster for Keep America*
Beautiful, Inc., by Marsteller, Inc., through the Advertising
Council, Inc., 1972.

This close-up of the Cherokee actor Iron Eyes Cody, who sheds
a tear in sorrow for the land the Indians kept clean but Whites
littered and polluted, has appeared in television and other
advertisements during the 1970s as part of an educational campaign
conducted by Keep America Beautiful, Inc. This nonprofit, public-
service organization seeks to persuade individuals of their personal
stake in maintaining a clean and healthy environment. The
effectiveness of the advertisement depends upon the use of two
standard images of the Indian: the image of the stoic Indian (who
never weeps) and the image of the Indian who respects nature and
possesses an ingrained sense of ecology. That such a brave, taciturn
Indian could be brought to tears over the White rape of the
environment is an effective countercultural use of a reverse image to
make a point about ecological concerns stick in the mind of the
onlooker.

highest improvement. Here civil and religious liberty are to flourish, unchecked by the cruel hand of civil or ecclesiastical tyranny. Here Genius, aided by all the improvements of former ages, is to be exerted in humanizing mankind—in expanding and inriching their minds with religious and philosophical knowledge, and in planning and executing a form of government, which shall involve all the excellencies of former governments, with as few of their defects as is consistent with the imperfection of human affairs, and which shall be calculated to protect and unite, in a manner consistent with the natural rights of mankind, the largest empire that ever existed. Elevated with these prospects, which are not merely the visions of fancy, we cannot but anticipate the period, as not far distant, when the AMERICAN EMPIRE will comprehend millions of souls, west of the Mississippi. Judging upon probable grounds, the Mississippi was never designed as the western boundary of the American empire. The God of nature never intended that some of the best part of this earth should be inhabited by the subjects of a monarch, 4000 miles from them. And may we not venture to predict, that, when the rights of mankind shall be more fully known, and the knowledge of them is fast increasing both in Europe and America, the power of European potentates will be confined to Europe, and their present American dominions, become, like the United States, free, sovereign and independent empires.[58]

In not discussing the effects this "empire for liberty," to use Jefferson's phrase, would have for Native American occupancy, Morse presumed that the natural increase of the White American population, the intentions of Providence, and the spirit of progress all would overwhelm the Indian like the Spaniard. For him, as for so many other leading intellectuals and politicians in the new United States, American nationality, defined as allegiance to American ideals and institutions, excluded the "foreigner" and the Indian as aliens. As a result many wished to deny asylum to immigrants presumed still loyal to foreign, i.e. un-American, values and institutions, and they thought the Indian should and would inevitably be replaced by proper Americans upon the lands Native Americans inhabited as the United States fulfilled its destiny.[59]

Under these impressions of the future of the American empire, what would and could United States policy makers do for the Indian in accord with both the ideals of the new nation and the necessities of the situation? Indians constituted but one part of the problem of the West the Continental Congress inherited from England. In a diplomatic coup, the United States negotiators obtained an area, ranging from the Appalachian settlements of the Americans to the shores of the Mississippi River, that the new national government could not control so long as the English retained forts and soldiers within its boundaries and the Native Americans who dwelt there opposed occupation. So the West and the Indians posed both a military and diplomatic problem for the American leaders. Since many of the original states claimed lands within this trans-Appalachian region according to their colonial charter boundaries, their leaders challenged the right of the Continental Congress to set policy for the region and therefore made Indian policy another matter of conflict between the states and the central government.

Even if these states ceded their claims in this region to the central government, Congress faced the additional problems of, first, how to settle this area while raising desperately needed revenue for the empty Confederation treasury and, secondly, how to govern this huge area so far removed from the original states. Would a strong military force be necessary in the West to preserve law and order among the settlers and to keep peace between them and the Indians? Such a solution, however, violated republican prejudices against a standing army inherited from the conflict with England's troops of occupation before the Revolution. All these problems appeared connected in the minds of the new nation's policy makers, and so Indian policy influenced the solutions to the others and vice versa.[60]

In efforts to resolve some of these problems, the Continental Congress bequeathed to posterity a new kind of colonial and land system in line with both the ideals of the era and the necessities of the moment. Congress laid the foundations for the American public land system in the Ordinance of 1785. After survey according to the now familiar rectangular coordinates, the national public domain was to be sold to individuals in fee simple, the most liberal land tenure of the time, without any further quitrents as had been collected by the crown and proprietors in the colonial period. This method of land disposal sought to settle the huge Western regions in an orderly fashion with industrious republican farmers at the same time that the sales raised revenue for the depleted central treasury.[61]

The Continental Congress created a new kind of colonial system with the Northwest Ordinance of 1787, which set up territorial government for those who settled the West. What had once been proposed as colonies under the crown now were to become new states under the ordinance after spending some period as territories under control of Congress. To allow for the independent spirit of the set-

tlers fostered by the distant trans-Appalachian environment, this system provided for the addition of new states equal to the old in the
Confederation. Since the frontier produced lawlessness and civic irre-
sponsibility as well in the eyes of good republicans, the period spent
as a territory would teach lessons in public virtue under the tutelage
of Congress. After recapitulating in brief the history of the original
states, these territories were to become their coequals in the Confederation. And so the American empire was to expand according to a
novel colonial system, which came to be called "territorial" to distinguish it from the old imperial type.[62] Both of these important
ordinances presumed the solution of the Indian and other problems of
the West, because they provided for the settlement and governance
of Americans on lands still under native occupancy at the time.

What Indian policy was depended upon who managed it. As
part of the centralization of imperial administration before the Revolution, English officials had sought to remove the control of Indian
trade and policy and the purchase of native lands from the hands
of colonial legislatures. In a series of proclamations and instructions to colonial governors and through treaty negotiations by their
agents, English home officials had defined and bounded for the first
time an Indian country in which colonial settlement was prohibited
and the sole right of land purchase reserved to the crown. With the
appointment of officials responsible to London to grease the wheels of
Indian diplomacy, the English officials also had hoped to restrict the
trade malpractices that irked the Indians as much as the advances of
White settlers upon their lands. The colonists had objected to these
efforts to restrict their expansion and their profits from speculation
and trade. Once the colonists had declared their independence, they
watched warily any attempt to re-create such central authority over
their affairs. States with claims to trans-Appalachian lands opposed
giving too much power over Indian affairs to the Continental Congress in the Articles of Confederation. After the war, New York challenged the authority of Congress to negotiate a peace treaty with the
Iroquois, over whom it claimed jurisdiction, and the Southern states
opposed congressional authority over Indian tribes within or near
their borders.

Perhaps because of such controversial implications, the federal
Constitution barely mentions the Indian. Although the founding
fathers meant to strengthen the central government at the expense of
the states, the only power expressly granted Congress under the Constitution to control Indian policy is the brief mention in the commerce clause: "to regulate Commerce with Foreign Nations, and

among the several States, and with Indian Tribes." Whether the authority to manage Indian affairs in general derived from that specific clause or the power to make treaties or to promote the general welfare, the new federal government acted as if it possessed such authority in full. State leaders questioned the federal government's right to set policy at times as it applied to tribes in which they asserted particular interest. Differ as the two sides might over the ultimate authority over Indian affairs, both state and federal officials assumed that the United States as a nation possessed full sovereignty according to international law over its territory, regardless of whether they actually had military control over the region between actual White settlement and the boundaries of the nation upon the Mississippi.[63]

Both of the men who laid down the principles of the new nation's Indian policy, George Washington as the first President under the federal Constitution and his Secretary of War, Henry Knox, looked beyond the immediate hostilities inherited from the Confederacy with the trans-Appalachian tribes to a permanent solution to Indian affairs. In summarizing the lessons of the Confederation experience for long-range policy, Knox ruled out destruction of the Indians in favor of conciliation. To defeat let alone wipe out the Indians with the small military forces at the command of the United States had proved impossible and, besides, would cost the poverty-stricken republic too much money. Moreover, Knox reasoned such a policy was as unnecessary as it was inconsistent with the new nation's honor in light of the natives' future. The importance of the image of the Indian in coming to these conclusions can be seen from his actual argument:

> When it shall be considered that the Indians derive their subsistence chiefly by hunting, and that, according to fixed principles, their population is in proportion to the facility with which they procure their food, it would most probably be found that the expulsion or destruction of the Indian tribes have nearly the same effect: for if they are removed from the usual hunting grounds, they must necessarily encroach on the hunting grounds of another tribe, who will not suffer the encroachment with impunity—hence they destroy each other.[64]

In formulating the principles proper for an enlightened federal policy, Knox assumed that White advance upon native lands was as unpreventable as it was inevitable, but it should be restrained and regulated in the interests of keeping peace with the Indians. Given the republican image of frontier inhabitants and the lessons of previous experience, illegal White intrusion upon native territory had to be curbed in the short run in order to achieve relatively peaceful, and therefore cheap, expansion in the long run.

To conciliate and attach the Indians to the United States as opposed to England or Spain required the recognition of native occupancy rights and their transfer through purchase, for the attempt by the Continental Congress to gain cessions through mere expropriation in the treaties after the Revolution had failed in practice. In arguing this point, Knox suggested why Indian affairs ought to be considered the province of the new federal government rather than of the states. Careful reading of his actual words indicates that his argument for Indian sovereignty aimed to restrict state authority in favor of federal control, not to declare that tribal governments possessed sovereignty vis-à-vis the United States as such:

> It would reflect honor on the new Government, and be attended with happy effects, were a declarative law to be passed, that the Indian tribes possess the right of the soil of all lands within their limits, respectively, and that they are not to be divested thereof, but in consequence of fair and bona fide purchases, made under the authority, or with the express approbation, of the United States.
>
> As the great source of all Indian wars are disputes about their boundaries, and as the United States are, from the nature of the government, liable to be involved in every war that shall happen on this or any other account, it is highly proper that their authority and consent should be considered as essentially necessary to all measures for the consequences of which they are responsible.
>
> No individual State could, with propriety, complain of invasion of its territorial rights. The independent nations and tribes of Indians ought to be considered as foreign nations, not as the subjects of any particular State. Each individual State, indeed, will retain the right of pre-emption of all lands within its limits, which will not be abridged; but the general sovereignty must possess the right of making all treaties, on the execution or violation of which depend peace or war.[65]

So the ascendancy of the federal government over the states through the treaty power of the Constitution as well as the honor of the nation prompted an enlightened policy based upon principles consistent with the ideals of the new republic.

Expansion could be achieved with honor if the United States offered American civilization in return for native lands. This policy would redound to the future reputation of the nation at the same time that it contributed to the acquisition of native lands according to Knox's image of the Indian, for the advance of White civilization brought the inevitable demise of the Indian. Federal policy could only hope to mitigate this decline, as his argument stated:

> As population shall increase, and approach the Indian boundaries, game will be diminished, and new purchases may be made for small considerations. This has been, and probably will be, the inevitable consequence of cultivation.
>
> It is, however, painful to consider, that all the Indian tribes, once existing in those States now the best cultivated and most populous, have become extinct. If the same causes continue, the same effects will happen; and, in a short period, the idea of an Indian on this side of the Mississippi will only be found in the page of the historian.
>
> How different would be the sensation of a philosophic mind to reflect, that, instead of exterminating a part of the human race by our modes of population, we had persevered, through all difficulties, and at last had imparted our knowledge of cultivation and the arts to the aboriginals of the country, by which the source of future life and happiness had been preserved and extended. But it has been conceived to be impracticable to civilize the Indians of North America. This opinion is probably more convenient than just.
>
> That the civilization of the Indians would be an operation of complicated difficulty; that it would require the highest knowledge of the human character, and a steady perseverance in a wise system for a series of years, cannot be doubted. But to deny that, under a course of favorable circumstances, it could not be accomplished, is to suppose the human character under the influence of such stubborn habits as to be incapable of melioration or change—a supposition entirely contradicted by the progress of society, from the barbarous ages to its present degree of perfection.
>
> While it is contended that the object is practicable, under a proper system, it is admitted, in the fullest force, to be impracticable, according to the ordinary course of things, and that it could not be effected in a short period.[66]

If assumptions of progress and environmentalism offered hope of "civilizing" the Indian, the image of the "dying Indian" and progress made such a hope a close contest with native disappearance through laws seemingly as inevitable in their operation as those that pushed the frontier people westward. Regardless of the outcome of the program, Knox recognized that the certain demise of the Indian in a relatively short time would make the price of their lands a bargain while the effort to do them some good according to White definition made the policy honorable in the view of posterity. Thus were national interests reconciled with national ideals in a federal Indian policy that can be called, for short, expansion with honor.[67]

Expansion with Honor:
Problems in Practice

IN LINE WITH THESE LARGER policy considerations, Congress enacted a series of laws "to regulate trade and intercourse with Indian tribes, and to preserve peace on the frontiers," as the first summary codification of 1802 phrased the intent. Designed at first to supplement and to uphold the treaty obligations of the United States with various Indian tribes, these laws came more and more to embody the legal framework of federal Indian policy. Thus, from the initial laws licensing traders, prohibiting private purchase of Indian lands, and punishing murder and other crimes committed by Whites on native lands, Congress increasingly tried to control both sides of Indian-White relations. It went on to regulate, and even conduct from 1796 to 1822, trade with Indians. It at first restricted, then prohibited liquor in the Indian country in 1832 and provided more generally for the punishment of crimes in Indian country and native crimes committed outside that area. After 1819 Congress began to finance the education and "civilization" of Indians. By defining and bounding an "Indian country," regulating trade, and reserving to the federal government the preemption, or exclusive right, to purchase land, Congress adopted the program England had attempted before the Revolution. By continuing the negotiation of treaties for the establishment of peace and for the purchase of lands, Congress continued colonial and Confederation policy. In any case, peace and expansion with honor depended upon the federal government's ability to implement these laws and treaties as much as on the correctness of Knox's and other White leaders' assumptions about the nature of Indian life.[68]

The implementation of these laws rested with the executive branch of the federal government. In the 1789 legislation establishing the first executive departments—Treasury, State, and War—Congress placed the management of Indian affairs under the branch handling military matters, which indicates as much about Congress's conception of native sovereignty as its fear of native warfare. In the early years, the officials and clerks designated to handle Indian matters became known as the "Indian Department." Congress created the Superintendent of Indian Trade in 1806 and Indian affairs came under his direction. After the dissolution of the factory system of trade, Secretary of War John C. Calhoun established in 1824 without congressional authorization a Bureau of Indian Affairs, which was called by its head, Thomas L. McKenney, the Office of Indian Affairs. This bureau was not regularized by congressional enactment until the creation of the Commissioner of Indian Affairs in 1832.[69]

The field apparatus of the Confederation period evolved into the superintendencies, agencies, and subagencies of the new federal service. In territories, the governor served, invariably from the first appointee by the Continental Congress until the 1850s and often thereafter until the 1870s, as Indian superintendent both over the Indian country and the ceded land in his jurisdiction. Not until 1834 was the post of Indian agent given permanent legal status, but the agents before that time, temporary as was their tenure under the law, were expected to accomplish a great deal with their charges. As the instructions of 1802 to the agents worded these aims:

> The motives of the Government for sending Agents to reside with the Indian Nations, are the cultivation of peace and harmony between the U. States, and the Indian Nations generally; the detection of any improper conduct in the Indians or the Citizens of the U. States, or others relating to the Indians, or their lands, and the introduction of the Arts of husbandry, and domestic manufactures, as means of producing, and diffusing the blessings attached to a well regulated civil society.[70]

In actuality, the agents and even the superintendents and the central Indian office lacked both the power and the money to accomplish such high-sounding goals.[71]

Enforcement of the trade and intercourse acts as well as the maintenance of peace in the Indian country depended upon the power of the army. Indian superintendents and agents had to call upon the military establishments in their area to remove Whites who intruded upon native lands or to apprehend Whites who murdered or stole from Indians on those lands. But Congress denied the army the right of summary punishment so many officers thought desirable in favor of civilian courts. Although both the Indian office and the army were branches of the same executive department, the military commandants resented orders from civilians, whether they came from Washington, the territorial governor, or the agents. In many cases, the officers thought that another Indian policy should have been pursued rather than the official one from Washington, and these men believed, moreover, that Indian policy on the frontier should be under military control. Civil-military conflict over Indian policy and its control lasted throughout the nineteenth century.

If maintenance of peaceful Indian relations hinged upon the power of the army, then Congress frustrated this end in the pursuit of other goals. As a result of their pre-Revolutionary experience, Americans distrusted a standing army in times of peace as dangerous to their civil liberties and freedom. This attitude plus the tendency of Congress to economize on the appropriations for the military kept the army small in size and inadequate to frontier needs. In fact, Congress only supported an army in "peace time"—a phrase that discounted battles with Native Americans as mere police actions and not full-fledged wars with foreign powers—as a result of Indian hostilities. Congress, at the same time, funded too few troops to be effective in preventing White depredations against Native Americans or in maintaining peaceful relations with and among tribes. A cordon of forts followed the frontier westward in the nineteenth century, but neither Red nor White peoples could count upon the army to preserve peace and expansion with honor.[72]

For the apprehension and prosecution of White and Indian crimes committed outside the Indian country, the agents had to rely upon the local law-enforcement agencies and judicial systems. Besides being inadequate to the task, local agencies and courts refused frequently to find White criminals guilty when committing crimes against Indians. Superintendents and agents in the field reported numerous times that White murderers and thieves went scot-free after the clearest evidence of their guilt, to the great disgust of Native Americans. On the other hand, the local militia rushed out all too often to punish Indians presumed to be murderers and thieves and, in their trigger-happy haste, killed innocent as well as guilty Indians. As the actions of the local militia and the decisions of local juries suggest, frontier state and territorial citizens often opposed federal policy. These people saw little reason not to violate Indian country or to kill Native Americans at will, justifying their actions by summoning up the image of the Indian as horrible savage. In this way they were as bloodthirsty and as lawless as the image republican leaders held of the frontier inhabitant. On the other hand, frontier Americans justified their actions ultimately upon the same grounds as the federal policy: the laws of nature and nations and the principle of higher uses. As the governor of frontier Tennessee argued in 1798: "By the law of nations, it is agreed that no people shall be entitled to more land than they can cultivate. Of course no people will sit and starve for want of land to work, when a neighbouring nation has much more than they can make use of."[73]

The territorial system, in fact, by continually creating new territories that would eventually become states in the union, only added new voices in Congress for native land cessions and war. It thereby counteracted the whole policy of peaceful relations with Indians at low cost and expansion with honor. Thus the oft-quoted third article of the Northwest Ordinance, which was readopted by the first federal Congress, expresses an ideal made less attainable by the very territorial system the law created:

> The utmost good faith shall always be observed towards the Indians; their lands and property shall never be taken from them without their consent; and in their property, rights and liberty, they never shall be invaded or disturbed, unless in just and lawful wars authorized by Congress; but laws founded in justice and humanity shall from time to time be made, for preventing wrongs being done to them, and for preserving peace and friendship with them.

Given the sensitivity of Congress to special interests, nineteenth-century committees on Indian Affairs in the two houses soon contained members and even chairmen from frontier states and, in the House of Representatives, delegates from territories. The constant addition of new states to the Union and their representatives in Congress meant that, as the older frontier became the East and new areas became the West, the traditional East-West conflict over Indian policy continued throughout the nineteenth century. That conflict concerned not so much the ultimate ends of Indian policy as the speed and method of its execution. Citizens of both the older and newer areas of the country agreed on the desirability of White expansion upon native lands, for both held the same basic image of the Indian, and on the desirability and, indeed, inevitability of progressive American individuals and institutions replacing the Indian tribes and their ways upon native lands. What separated Eastern and Western leaders in Washington and in home capitals were the issues of how fast and by what means such supersession should take place. Both sides envisaged national interests in the long run in the same way but differed over their accomplishment in the short run. They also differed about the desirability as well as possibility of achieving expansion with honor if this end had to wait for the "civilization" of the Indians. Frontier people doubted whether Indians were capable of such a drastic transformation. The ambivalence of legislative policy produced by this dual vision found its counterpart in the dilemma of the territorial governor who, according to his instructions, must civilize and protect the Indians from White intrusion but also must gain new cessions as quickly as possible to extend White settlements.[74]

To transform the Indian into a White-approved model citizen was an integral part of the expansion-with-honor program from the beginning, but the means to its accomplishment barely existed until after the War of 1812. Most of the monies appropriated for Indian affairs by Congress in the first three decades paid agents in the field and bought presents for chiefs. The agents and factory traders supposedly exemplified civilized life for Indian imitation, and some chiefs' gifts and annuity monies went for White agricultural implements. Some treaties in this early period provided blacksmiths for certain tribes, and the Indian office funded a few persons to teach farming to native men and spinning and weaving to native women. Before the War of 1812, few missionaries served among the Indians. Only after that war did national missionary societies arise with sufficient treasuries to support extensive establishments and numerous missionaries among the tribes.[75]

Congress, beginning in 1819, appropriated ten thousand dollars annually "for the purpose of providing against the further decline and final extinction of the Indian tribes adjoining the frontier settlements of the United States, and for introducing among them the habits and arts of civilization," but only after arguing about the possibility of ever achieving such an unlikely goal. Thomas McKenney, who headed Indian Affairs in the War Department at that time, used the money to subsidize missionary societies in the establishment of schools and the instruction of Indians in agriculture and domestic arts. Soon afterward, newly negotiated treaties contained articles appropriating tribal annuities to the same agencies for the same purposes.

The close relationship between state and church in this endeavor was mutually advantageous to both parties: the missionary societies received some money to support the secular side of their stations and the federal government obtained civilization agents at low cost. Given the lack of occupational specialization, government policy makers had to support missionaries in these tasks until after the Civil War if the Indians were to be acculturated at all by anyone. Such an arrangement saved the government money, moreover, through sharing costs. In this deal so dependent upon the realities of American society and economy at the time, the missionaries received some federal money and moral support, the Indians supposedly obtained "civilization," and the government leaders salved the American conscience while they hoped soon to acquire native lands no longer needed by their transformed inhabitants.[76]

As the federal support of mission activities indicates, the separation of church and state in the United States was never meant by its proponents to eliminate the moral and spiritual foundations of American society. Government officials joined missionaries and their patrons in subscribing to the same basic version of Christian civilization to be promulgated among the Indians. Americanism rested upon a firm religious and moral groundwork in the opinion of all policy makers, and so naturally religion, preferably Protestantism,[77] was presumed to be an inextricable part of the acculturation process for Indians. Whether missionaries favored civilizing or Christianizing their charges first, erecting small stations and day schools or building large manual labor boarding schools,[78] they sought to re-form the Indian into a model American husband or wife, who farmed his private property, attended church faithfully, could read and write and keep accounts, and participated in government as an American citizen. Regardless of denomination, missionaries in the early period, placing their faith in millennial hopes and perhaps environmental theory, expected the rapid conversion of Indian tribes to White civilization and Christianity. Since the superiority of the American Way of Life appeared self-evident to them, they thought that Indians too would see it in their immediate self-interest to adopt the habits and beliefs of the (good) White American after a brief demonstration.[79]

With enough money and prayers, the soon-expected millennium would bring Christian civilization to the Indians throughout the American empire, as the board of directors of one missionary society envisaged Manifest Destiny in 1823 according to a standard view of the Indian and Americanism:

Let then, missionary Institutions, established to convey to them the benefits of civilization and the blessings of Christianity, be efficiently supported; and with cheering hope, you may look forward to the period when the savage shall be converted into the citizen; when the hunter shall be transformed into the mechanic; when the farm, the workshop, the School-House, and the Church shall adorn every Indian village; when the fruits of Industry, good order, and sound morals, shall bless every Indian dwelling; and when throughout the vast range of country from the Mississippi to the Pacific, the red man and the white man shall everywhere be found, mingling in the same benevolent and friendly feelings, fellow-heirs to a glorious inheritance in the kingdom of Immanuel.[80]

Even as the immediate future revealed the gulf between these hopes and the actual accomplishment of missionaries, their societies and the government affirmed the possibility of Indian transformation and eventual acculturation and assimilation through the increasing support and staff thrown into the process.[81] As Enlightenment belief in the rationality of all people and the environmental theory of human behavior and diversity gave way to romantic racism and democracy, missionary societies and governmental officials continued to urge civilizational transformation of the Indian as the last best hope of peaceful expansion with honor and the preservation of an otherwise doomed race. As one missionary to the Eastern Sioux exclaimed in 1846: "*As tribes and nations the Indians must perish and live only as men!* With this impression of the tendency of God's purposes as they are being developed year after year, I would labor to prepare them to fall in with *Christian Civilization* that is destined to cover the earth."[82] Missionaries more than other persons tended to believe Christianity and civilization were in direct conflict with Indianness, but all White policy makers subscribed to this fusion of religion and lifestyle. For the missionaries the goal of Christian civilization justified their increasingly larger budgets and numbers. For government officials, Christian civilization increasingly became the only pacific method of dealing with the Indian problem in the nineteenth century. So an old policy inherited from colonial times continued to be espoused in the midst of changing intellectual currents and new social and economic institutions, in a United States whose territory as well as population were expanding. Only now larger sums of money, better organization, and more missionaries carried out the old aims with much the same results as before.[83]

From even this brief survey of the formative period of United

States Indian policy, the contradictions built into the system emerge clearly. Who should formulate and execute Indian policy? What should be its specific methods and who should carry them out? At what rate should land cession and White settlement proceed? Whose view of the Indian should prevail? These questions point to some of the consistent inconsistencies of United States Indian policy that prevailed throughout the nineteenth century and made honorable, peaceful, and inexpensive expansion difficult or impossible.

Less apparent but equally important were the contradictions at the very heart of the policy of expansion with honor. The preemption doctrine presumed that Indian tribes would be ready to sell whenever Whites were ready to buy. By making American expansion contingent upon Indian consent, government policy makers predicated a delicate balance of conditions and a certain set of assumptions about the Native American as Indian. First, the policy implied that Indians possessed more land than they could or would use and that the Indians would readily surrender those lands to Whites for relatively small amounts of money and gifts. The Indians would cede the lands wanted by Whites because they (1) could withdraw westward easily and resume their migratory ways, or (2) would die of disease or other natural causes as White society approached, or (3) would become "civilized" and thus disappear as Indians. Since all Indians were presumed alike, policy makers thought that a tribe could easily roam westward before the White advance and continue their hunting without difficulty upon the large amounts of land underutilized in the same manner by other tribes. When Congress, for example, first bounded the Indian country in 1796, only an eastern line of separation was stipulated, apparently under this assumption. If most members of a tribe died off as usually happened when White civilization approached, then surely the remainder needed less territory than the whole tribe originally claimed. If the Indians switched from hunting to farming, the policy makers supposed they would use the soil more intensively than previously and thus be able to surrender the large amount of surplus land. For this reason, White policy makers viewed civilizational transformation useful to expansion as well as good for the Indian per se. All in all, the basic policy of expansion with honor rested upon the assumption that Indians would not cede more lands than their changing status encouraged or required them to, and that Whites would not ask for more land than the orderly advance of the frontier necessitated or stimulated them to require. The policy, moreover, optimistically presumed that cessions could be obtained from the various tribes before White expansion overwhelmed them, and that presupposed in turn a relatively slow speed of White settlement advance westward.

Under such a policy, whatever was good for the White American was assumed good for the Native American also, even if the Indians had to be manipulated against their own inclinations for the larger good as the Whites saw it. How much cajolery, disingenuousness, bribery, or even coercion this justified remained a matter of practice, of the means available, and of White morality. The last persons presumed to know their own larger interests were the Indians, and policy makers therefore assumed a stewardship over native interests in the American scheme of things. Whether ethnocentrism, racism, high idealism, or sheer self-interest prompted such stewardship made little difference to Native Americans as they felt its effects.

On the other hand, what was good for the Indian under the expansion-with-honor policy was not necessarily good for White society, given the paradoxical assumptions of Americanism. How would and should Indians be accepted into American society as a whole? Would and should they be assimilated as individuals or as whole tribes? Would and should White Americans welcome them as full-fledged citizens? Would they allow their children to marry Indians? To raise these problems of social incorporation, cultural assimilation, and marital amalgamation points beyond the inconsistencies of Indian policy to the great consistencies among nineteenth-century American values and institutional arrangements.

Democracy, American Liberalism, and Indian Policy in the Nineteenth Century

THE CHANGING INTELLECTUAL CURRENTS of the nineteenth century made the Indian and the American more antithetic than ever in theory if not in actual practice. As the ideal of democracy replaced republicanism, old words took on new meaning and new words came into use to characterize newer concepts basic to Americanism. Foremost among these semantic shifts was the word *democracy* itself, which was lifted out of its narrow and often disparaging political context in the days of the early nation and broadened to embrace that peculiar fusion of social equality and political freedom that Americans believed they lived. Whether grounded on the romantic absolutes of the decades before the Civil War or the naturalism of the late nineteenth century, American democracy designated a belief in the goodness of majority rule, a minimal government supposedly beneficial to all alike, and free enterprise—in short, the classic liberalism of the age.

America became the symbol to Europeans as well as to its own citizens of what the future of liberal democracy would be in the world, as Alexis de Tocqueville expounded it in his famous analysis of the United States in the 1830s. To describe the effects of American liberalism on the inhabitants of the United States, Tocqueville employed the word *individualism*, and the word was introduced into the English language through the translation of his *Democracy in America*.[84] Americans had long prided themselves upon their individualism without having a word for it, but in the decades before the Civil War romantic connotations of dynamism and potentiality infused new meaning into the concept of the free individual, different from what the republican founding fathers understood or meant. Now individuals needed more than uncoerced options to have freedom; they also had to have the opportunity to develop their natural talents to the fullest in order to realize their inner potential. Only a liberal government beneficial to all in theory and an untrammeled economy offered equal opportunity to every American, and conversely all good Americans ought to take advantage of their opportunities because they supposedly could. With the artificial barriers of class privilege presumably removed under the new regime, the self-made person became the ideal American. Therefore, if every American did not become a success it was his own fault. If Black slavery violated more than ever an individual's freedom under these democratic and romantic assumptions of human potentiality, so too White failure to achieve material success indicated a defect in personality or ambition. Liberal institutions supposedly offered the chance and individualism afforded the motive under this theory. Freedom of opportunity under liberalism had as its goal the freedom to become unequal in wealth and position, all in the name of equal rights.[85]

Democracy, liberalism, and individualism possessed important implications for understanding frontiersmen and Indians. The frontier acquired greater symbolic importance than ever as the place offering upward social mobility through the acquisition of property and the exploitation of resources at low cost.[86] Moreover, the White frontier population gained new respectability under the assumptions of democracy and racism. From the lawless image of republican days, they personified increasingly as the century passed the self-help and self-reliance considered so desirable in a good American.[87] By the end of the century they represented, to historian Frederick Jackson Turner, the people who had made American history American.

With the rise of racism, whether based upon romantic principles or upon "scientific" research, Americans became ever more aware of the biological basis of their ideal society. Measured by their ideal of individualism and the liberalism of American institutions, they found other nationalities deficient in or opposed to American values and customs. Apprehensive about the impact of foreign immigration upon American society, leading politicians and intellectuals more and more linked Americanism to Anglo-Saxonism, especially in images of Manifest Destiny. The laws of progress and the biology of racism combined with the self-image of Americanism to justify continental expansion of the truly American populace against Indians within the enlarging boundaries of the United States and against Mexicans and others to enlarge those boundaries. When congressmen debated whether or not to annex all of Mexico after American victory in the war against that nation in the 1840s, many opposed the wholesale absorption of a population said to be biologically Indian on the grounds of the danger these people posed to American institutions.[88] For Native Americans, then, these new intellectual trends exacerbated the racial exclusion traditional to British and American policy. Thus, in spite of the policy makers' stress on the civilizational transformation of the Indian and incorporation of the Red man into American society, very few of them ever advocated marital amalgamation as an important means to those ends.[89]

The emphasis on individualism and liberal institutions, moreover, placed Indian tribalism in direct opposition to Americanism even more under democracy than under republicanism. Indians must join American society as individuals in the liberal state and economy rather than as tribes. Cultural assimilation, likewise, must proceed according to the values of individualism and not those of tribalism. What the proper White individual should be and therefore what the proper Indian individual must be represented an absolute antithesis to how Americans assumed Indians lived as tribal members. By definition, the tribal Indian lacked the industry, the self-reliance, and the material desires and success appropriate to the good American. Throughout the nineteenth century, missionaries and philanthropists, government officials in Washington and on the frontier, military officers and Western settlers measured the tribal Indian by their standard of Americanism and found him wanting, according to the traditional deficiency image.

While American thought changed during the nineteenth century, so too did American social, political, and economic organization. Of these latter changes, three major developments affected the formulation and execution of Indian policy as much as, or more than, the altered intellectual climate. In the economy, the improved means of transportation not only speeded up settlement of the West but also integrated those who settled there into a national economic system at a faster pace. Better roads, the building of canals, and, most important of all, the expansion of railroads brought to the West at increasing rates Eastern and European farmers, merchants, speculators, and others seeking their fortune, and once there, these people could find ever bigger markets through the same transportation modes in the evolving industrial economy.[90] In the political system, the development of permanent party organization made Indian policy a partisan issue like any other question before the politicians. Party voting, once thought disreputable in the republican era of the new nation, now became one of the foundation stones of a democracy based on majority rule. Partisan affiliation and individual conscience made strange alliances under the auspices of party brokerage in Congress and the executive.[91] Accompanying the changing economy and politics was the third major development: the proliferation of voluntary associations devoted to philanthropy, religion, education, and reform. Not only did some leaders of these many organizations participate directly in either formulating or executing Indian policy, but they also through the mobilization of public opinion as represented by their members brought pressure to bear on the political process in that formulation. In turn, reform leaders' opinions and positions became just another aspect of partisanship under the political party system.

The interaction of all these trends with the idea of the Indian and the formulation of Indian policy can be followed in the three chief policy determinations of the nineteenth century: removal under Andrew Jackson, the so-called Peace Policy under President Ulysses Grant, and the General Allotment Act associated with the name of Senator Henry Dawes. In not one of these instances was the basic policy new at the time. Removal in a larger sense, conflict between civilian and military administration of policy, the role of missionaries in policy execution, and the allotment of lands in severalty (the division of tribal properties into individual holdings) all had long histories before they assumed center stage in the history of United States Indian policy. But the decisions and debates of the time in each case bring into sharp focus the persistence of Indian imagery and the continuity of policy toward Native Americans during the nineteenth century.

Democracy and Removal: Defining the Status of the Indian

ALTHOUGH THOMAS JEFFERSON in 1803 originated the idea of exchanging lands west of the Mississippi River for Indian lands in the East, the policy of removal only developed as a "permanent" solution to the Indian problem in the 1820s during the administration of James Monroe. For Jefferson, removing the Indians into the newly acquired Louisiana Purchase was, like his plan for colonizing emancipated Blacks in Africa,[92] a way of expelling from within the nation those influences he believed deleterious to the American spirit and the continued vitality of American institutions. For his fellow Virginian James Monroe, the Tennessean Andrew Jackson, and others in the period after the War of 1812, however, removal offered a solution to pressing practical problems, in addition to being the only method calculated in their opinion to preserve the Indian from total extinction. Citizens of states and territories with rapidly growing populations demanded further cession of native lands and preferably the expulsion of all Indians from within their borders. States and territories to the west of these states not only demanded the same policy but in addition did not want to be the homeland for Indian emigrants displaced from areas to the east.

Under these circumstances, only allotment in severalty and native assimilation in the places where Indians lived or removal to an area not desired by White settlers in the immediate future offered any hope for solving the twin problems of further land cessions for the frontier Whites and the preservation of the Indian from intrusion and decimation. Some of the treaties negotiated by Jackson and other United States commissioners after the War of 1812 contained provisions for the exchange of lands and financial aid to Indians in the move beyond the Mississippi. A few treaties with Southern tribes provided in addition for allotments of 640 acres in trust to those Indians who wished to remain in their native lands and become citizens.

Not until the end of his administration, however, did Monroe recommend to Congress the enactment of a law providing for the general removal of tribes east of the Mississippi. Although impelled by the urgent demand of Georgia for the United States government to fulfill its part of the compact of 1802 (in which the state surrendered its claim to western territory beyond its boundaries in return for the federal government's extinguishing the title to Indian lands within its borders), Monroe laid down principles upon which he thought the new policy could be achieved with honor to the United States and still promote the "welfare and happiness" of the Indians. Fearing their "degradation and extermination" if they remained in the East, Monroe proposed that removal might be made honorable to the United States and attractive to the Indians if Congress guaranteed the emigrant Indians a permanent title to their Western lands, organized some kind of government among the removed tribes to protect their territory from intrusion, preserved peace among the tribes native to the West and the emigrant tribes, and continued funding of civilization agents among them to prevent further "degeneracy."

Monroe thought such a program not only made removal practical but offered a positive boon to the Indians while it served the ideals and basic interests of the American people:

> The digest of such a government, with the consent of the Indians, which should be endowed with sufficient power to meet all the objects contemplated—to connect the several tribes together in a bond of amity and preserve order in each; to prevent intrusions on their property; to teach them by regular instruction the arts of civilized life and make them a civilized people—is an object of very high importance. It is the powerful consideration which we have to offer to these tribes as an inducement to relinquish the lands on which they now reside and to remove to those which are designated. It is not doubted that this arrangement will present considerations of sufficient force to surmount all their prejudices in favor of the soil of their nativity, however strong they may be. Their elders have sufficient intelligence to discern the certain progress of events in the present train, and sufficient virtue, by yielding to momentary sacri-

fices, to protect their families and posterity from inevitable destruction. They will also perceive that they may thus attain an elevation to which as communities they could not otherwise aspire. . . .

It may fairly be presumed that, through the agency of such a government, the condition of all the tribes inhabiting that vast region may be essentially improved; that permanent peace may be preserved with them, and our commerce be much extended.[93]

So once again Indians were offered civilization for land as a boon supposedly to both parties, but now assimilation was to be achieved through segregation. Both the rationale and the basic principles of guaranteed land title, preservation of peace, organization of government, and the funding of civilization agents were embodied in the program proposed by Andrew Jackson after he entered the presidency.[94]

By that time removal had become thoroughly entwined with the debates over Indian title and sovereignty, over the success of the Indian civilization program, and, most important, over states' rights versus federal powers, as a result of the conflict between Georgia and the Cherokee Nation. According to Georgia politicians, the civilizational transformation of the Cherokee had been all too successful because their leaders refused to cede any more lands within that state and because they had adopted in July 1827 a constitution establishing a national government modeled upon American principles. In response to what many members of the Georgia legislature considered an affront to and violation of their own state's sovereignty, they asserted Georgia's sovereign rights in a set of resolutions that ended with a succinct summary of how they viewed Cherokee title and what they proposed to do about this insult to their state by the "savages":

> *Resolved*, That all the lands appropriated and unappropriated within the conventional limits of Georgia, belong to her absolutely; that the title is in her; that the Indians are tenants at her will; that she may at any time she pleases determine their tenancy, by taking possession of the premises; and that Georgia has the right to extend her authority and laws over the whole territory, and to coerce obedience to them from all descriptions of people, be they white, red, or black, within her limits.[95]

In line with the resolution's intent, the legislature at the end of 1828 added Cherokee lands to existing counties and the next year extended state laws over all inhabitants of those lands.

When the Cherokees sought protection from Congress and the new President for this infringement of their traditional right to self-government and customary title, presumably guaranteed by treaty and the intercourse acts, Jackson and his Secretary of War advised the tribal representatives that the executive of the United States would not interfere with Georgia's rightful prerogatives. Instead they advised the best interests of the tribe lay in emigrating across the Mississippi.

Old Hickory had long opposed treating tribes as independent entities and favored removal, and he now combined these views with states' rights in regard to federal-versus-state jurisdiction over the so-called Civilized Tribes of the South. In that portion of his first annual message to Congress on December 28, 1830, discussing "the condition and ulterior destiny of the Indian tribes within the limits of some of our states," he denied the "pretences" of the Cherokees to an independent government in favor of Georgia's sovereignty and requested that Congress pass a law setting apart lands west of the Mississippi outside the limits of any state or territory "to be guaranteed to the Indian tribes as long as they shall occupy it," where the "benevolent may endeavor to teach them the arts of civilization, and by promoting union and harmony among them, to raise up an interesting common-wealth, destined to perpetuate the race and to attest to the humanity and justice of this government." Through the use of the wild and dying Indian images, Jackson justified the removal of the acculturated Cherokees as well as other tribes from the lands they farmed to "wild" lands in the West—all in the name of eventually civilizing them. No matter how inapplicable in this case, traditional Indian imagery rationalized the needs of the United States in the continued push of Native Americans from lands desired by Whites.[96]

With these events as prelude, the debate over removal produced lengthy analyses of the very fundamentals of United States Indian policy: the nature of Indian title and the right to self-government, federal and local authority over Indians, and the legal standing of treaties with tribes. In alignments foreshadowing the national political parties to come, politicians in Washington and the state capitals in the South, public figures in and out of government, and missionary society officers and members all disputed whether Jackson's approach to Indian affairs was a new and dangerous departure from past practice toward Native Americans. Jackson's opponents felt the federal government was obligated through treaty, legislation, and custom to recognize tribal title to native lands and the right of Indians to self-government as tribes. So long as a tribe had not surrendered its title to certain lands, then those lands remained guaranteed to the tribe by treaty and continued occupancy. To the opponents of Jackson's policy, treaties, including those with Indians, were the supreme law of the land, in which the citizens of the United States had pledged their word and honor. Even the new Cherokee government in the view of these partisans was but the latest development in a long-standing tradition of the Indians' being a "distinct and separate community governed by their own peculiar laws and customs," to use the words of Senator Theodore Frelinghuysen, who was dubbed the "Christian statesman" for his support of the Cherokee cause and who in 1844 appeared as the vice-presidential candidate on the Whig ticket.[97]

On the other side, the supporters of Jackson and the Georgians considered treaties nothing more than convenient, humanitarian devices to obtain Indian lands already under the sovereignty of the United States. As Governor George Gilmer of Georgia phrased it in the usual-uses argument: "Treaties were expedients by which ignorant, intractable, and savage people were induced without bloodshed to yield up what civilized people had the right to possess by virtue of that command of the Creator delivered to man upon his formation— be fruitful, multiply, and replenish the earth, and subdue it."[98] In this view, Indian occupancy amounted to mere tenancy at the will of the people of the United States, who had granted the Cherokees some land for their use when that tribe acknowledged by treaty the sovereignty of the Continental Congress after the Revolution. Moreover, according to this side, the Cherokee government had erected an *imperium in imperio*, to use their favorite phrase, which went beyond the customary authority and governance of Indians over themselves to become a threat to the official government of the state and by implication the nation.

Since the Georgia leaders questioned federal authority over their relations with the Cherokees and other tribes within the state's borders (although arguing that the United States government must carry out the compact of 1802), the conflict over sovereignty was actually a three-way division among the federal government, the Georgia government, and the new Cherokee national government, which for its protection in turn looked to the federal branches of government for redress against the actions of Georgia. Jackson and the executive branch favored the claims of Georgia over those of the Cherokees and their congressional and missionary backers. Jackson's opponents saw the conflict in terms of Christian humanitarianism, national honor and union, and opposition to the executive's usurping new prerogatives and destroying the balance of powers under the Constitution. The supporters of Old Hickory believed their opponents to be a "Christian party" seeking partisan advantage from the convenient issue of the Cherokees and removal.[99]

Because the Cherokees became the focus of the removal debate, the whole question of the possibility as well as desirability of civilizing Indians was argued with this tribe as reference. Was removal compatible with or destructive of the efforts to civilize Indians? To their supporters the Cherokees exhibited in their habits and government the success of the philanthropic efforts of the preceding decades, and they should therefore be left upon their own lands to develop even further along the path to American institutions. Removal would only hinder if not destroy these achievements.

While the opponents of removal emphasized the great transformation of the Cherokees, the proponents of emigration played down the amount of acculturation within the tribe. To the latter the vaunted civilization of the tribe was the product of those Cherokees with White blood in their veins, and the new government was the deliberate tyranny of this mixed-blood elite over the Cherokee masses in its own interests rather than for the welfare of the entire tribe. Since this government with the aid of the missionary "fanatics from New England" resisted removal in the interest of the mixed-bloods, this tyranny must be destroyed. The Georgians proposed to achieve this destruction through the extension of state law over the tribe. This solution forced the Cherokees as individuals to live by their wits in the White land speculator's world while denying to them the civil and legal rights of White citizens to protect their newly acquired private property.[100]

In the end, the Georgians wanted the Cherokee lands, and no amount of acculturation would be allowed to stand in the way of their greed. The Georgians and their supporters everywhere argued, therefore, that Indians through temperament and habit were incapable of becoming civilized—thus contradicting the grand rationale of removal but true to the idea of the timeless Indian. Neither side to the removal debate doubted the superiority of Americanism and the desirability of civilizing the Indian; rather they differed over how soon or whether it could be accomplished. All sides agreed upon the higher uses of native lands, but they disagreed upon just how well the Civilized Tribes of the South had achieved this desirable end.

With the passage of the removal bill at the end of May 1830 by close vote of the House of Representatives and with Jackson's signature enacting it into law, the Cherokees at the behest of their political allies looked to the Supreme Court for relief from both Georgia and the President. The decision in *The Cherokee Nation* v. *The State of Georgia* (1831), rendered for the majority by Chief Justice John Marshall, an avowed opponent of Jackson and an advocate of federal supremacy over the states, side-stepped the basic issue in an effort to avoid a confrontation between the judiciary and the executive. He argued that the Cherokee Nation could not seek redress before the Court because it was not a foreign nation under the Constitution. In attempting to explicate the long-time anomalous relationship existing between the United States government and Indian tribes, Marshall employed phrases that were to define that relationship for the future as well as summarize what presumably had been past theory and practice. What Henry Knox had hoped would be the relationship between the federal government and the tribes Marshall asserted had been the actual case:

> The condition of the Indians in relation to the United States is perhaps unlike that of any other two people in existence. In the general, nations not owing a common allegiance are foreign to each other. The term *foreign nation* is, with strict propriety, applicable by either to the other. But the relation of the Indians to the United States is marked by peculiar and cardinal distinctions which exist no where else.
>
> The Indian territory is admitted to compose a part of the United States. In all our maps, geographical treatises, histories, and laws, it is so considered. In all our intercourse with foreign nations, in our commercial regulations, in any attempt at intercourse between Indians and foreign nations, they are considered as within the jurisdictional limits of the United States, subject to many of those restraints which are imposed upon our own citizens. They acknowledge themselves in their treaties to be under the protection of the United States; they admit that the United States shall have the sole and exclusive right of regulating the trade with them and managing all their affairs as they think proper. . . .
>
> Though the Indians are acknowledged to have an unquestionable, and, heretofore, unquestioned right to the lands they occupy, until that right shall be extinguished by a voluntary cession to our government; yet it may well be doubted whether those tribes which reside within the acknowledged boundaries of the United States can, with strict accuracy, be denominated foreign nations. They occupy a territory to which we assert a title independent of their will,

which must take effect in point of possession when their right of possession ceases. Meanwhile they are in a state of pupilage. Their relation to the United States resembles that of a ward to his guardian.

They look to our government for protection, rely upon its kindness and its power; appeal to it for relief to their wants; and address the president as their great father. They and their country are considered by foreign nations, as well as by ourselves, as being so completely under the sovereignty and dominion of the United States, that any attempt to acquire their lands, or to form a political connexion with them, would be considered by all as an invasion of our territory, and an act of hostility.

These considerations go far to support the opinion, that the framers of our constitution had not the Indian tribes in view, when they opened the courts of the union to controversies between a state or the citizens thereof, and foreign states.[101]

In line with this reasoning, Marshall concluded that Indian tribes were at best "domestic dependent nations." These words describe as accurately as any succinct phrase could the theory of Indian sovereignty asserted from the beginning by United States policy makers.[102] The idea of wardship Marshall expounded came to define the nature of the relationship achieved after the Civil War.

As revealing of the general American conception of native dependency at the time as this decision was the effort to establish an Indian territory for the emigrant tribes. Some sort of Indian government to make good the promise of self-rule and a permanent home in the West was envisaged as part of removal from the mid-1820s. The American territorial system with its commitment to eventual statehood would have seemed the logical and ready-made solution to the problem—if Americans had truly believed in the eventual assimilation of the Indian into their society upon an equal basis. Throughout the 1830s the Jackson and Van Buren administrations urged the creation of an all-Indian territory, and congressmen regularly drafted bills to erect such a government. Not one of these many bills ever became law although passed by one or the other house at times. Often these bills failed to establish a true territory, and all interfered with actual Indian rule by imposing federal supervision over the tribes. For that reason, the Southern tribes resisted the creation of an all-Indian territory, or even a confederation, as did the enemies of Jackson, who opposed another fiefdom under administration control and patronage. More important from our standpoint were the fears of Northern and Southern, pro- and anti-removal people alike of the creation of an exclusively Indian territory and perhaps state. Both Northerners and Southerners feared the precedent of a racially based territory and state. Southerners, in particular, worried about the influence of such an example for slave emancipation. They also opposed the creation of a permanent Indian state as an obstacle to their further expansion westward. As consolidation and concentration of Indian tribes continued in succeeding decades, the idea of an Indian territory was broached sporadically but it never again received the support it mustered in the 1830s.[103]

By the end of that decade most Indian tribes had been removed from the Eastern half of the United States to beyond the Mississippi, but the enlargement of national boundaries and the increasing rate of White settlement transferred the problems once faced in the East to the trans-Mississippi West. The expansion of the United States under President James K. Polk brought the tribes of the Southwest, California, and the Northwest under American jurisdiction and policy. Moreover, this extension of boundaries to the Pacific placed the old Louisiana Purchase, once the edge of the United States, smack in the middle of the bustling nation. Lands just designated as permanent Indian country in the 1830s became desirable as settlers followed the trails to Santa Fe, Oregon, and California. They requested that the federal government remove and concentrate the Indians inhabiting the midsection of the newly expanded America. The treaties negotiated with the tribes inhabiting this area in the 1840s and 1850s started the second phase of removal.

To concentrate the Indian population and to bring intertribal peace to the Plains, the Commissioner of Indian Affairs in 1849 proposed that the Indians inhabiting this area be compelled to live upon limited reservations with definite boundaries beyond which the Indians were forbidden to travel and where they would undergo civilizational transformation. These policies produced the usual wars as the United States sought to establish de facto control of land and tribes claimed under the de jure sovereignty always asserted by the policy makers. As leading Whites displayed interest in building a transcontinental railroad in the early 1850s, the tribes once removed from the East to supposedly permanent homes in what is now Kansas and Nebraska were forced to remove once again to make way for the organization of a White, not an Indian, territorial government in that region. Like the emigration of the Northern tribes earlier, this second phase of removal did not draw the protests or even the attention elicited by the original removal of the Southern tribes. Perhaps reformers like politicians were so preoccupied with the abolition of slavery and the impending sectional crisis that they could not divert their attention to what they considered a minor cause. More likely, the lack of protest shows that removal per se was never the real issue in the earlier period. The sustained campaign in favor of treaty rights and acculturation among the more civilized Southern Indians would not have occurred without the larger political issues and partisan rivalry that stirred White leaders and philanthropists at the time. Not until after the Civil War did Indian policy regain the public spotlight it held during the time of Jackson.[104]

Reservations and Allotment: Acculturation and Detribalization

THE IMMEDIATE DECADES AFTER the Civil War marked a transition more in the circumstances than in the basic goals of United States Indian policy. Foremost was the collapse of armed resistance to that policy by Native Americans. The United States government essentially completed the conquest of the Indians by the end of the 1870s, although the actual last battle occurred in the massacre at Wounded Knee in 1890. With all Native Americans finally under the effective control of American sovereignty, the effort to acculturate and assimilate the entire native population became more efficient. The drive to greater bureaucratic organization in the government during these decades carried over to the Indian service and made these efforts at acculturation more disruptive than ever of tribal life. Aiding in this process of assimilation were the self-professed humanitarian organizations that arose specifically to reform the Indian. With the end of the Civil War and slavery, some reformers turned their attention to the Indian "problem." Like the government, they too brought new organizational resources to the task. Increasingly in the eyes of these reformers and government officials alike, the only hope of transforming the Indian lay in detribalizing him as prelude to acculturation and assimilation. By 1890, these circumstances had produced what reformers and government officials of the day thought was the final solution to the Indian problem—allotment of reservation lands combined with American citizenship.[105]

The impetus for a new policy after the Civil War came from the dramatic warfare with the Plains Indians, who by this time represented the timeless Indian in White eyes—nomadic, horse-mounted hunters of the buffalo, who fought and died bravely when portrayed as noble and massacred the innocent when pictured as ignoble. These tribes, caught between the eastward advance of the mining frontier and the westward movement of the ranching and farming frontiers, naturally turned to war to protect their homes from swift encroachment. Even as White frontier people intruded onto the lands of these tribes, they demanded army protection from and extermination of the "bloodthirsty savages" they had aroused.

To this end or merely to prevent further wars, Westerners, military officers, and others thought the army should be given complete control of the problem, and they therefore favored returning the Bureau of Indian Affairs to the Department of War from the Interior Department, to which it had been transferred upon the creation of the Interior Department in 1849. The proponents of such a transfer were certain that the army was both more capable of the vigorous policy necessary for the subjugation of the Indians and more efficient and less corrupt than the "Indian Ring" said to control the Indian Bureau. Although the House of Representatives passed several bills effecting this transfer, they all died in the Senate as a result of pressure from Eastern reformers and the expensiveness of Indian warfare. Not only was it considered more honorable but it was shown to be far cheaper to feed these nomadic buffalo hunters upon a reservation until they could learn to farm for their own subsistence than to finance costly wars against them. The expenditures of millions of dollars for each of the military campaigns needed to return some bands to their assigned reservations afforded ample proof for those who argued the cheaper alternatives of feeding the Indians.

Peace came to the Plains less from the victories (and defeats) of the army than from the destruction of the buffalo herds, death from disease, and the extension of the railroad. No matter what the effectiveness of the army in arranging peace, this phase of reservation formation was as forced as earlier removals had been. The end of the Indian wars terminated the transfer issue, and so the Indian Bureau remained under the Interior Department.[106]

Military force, common as it may have been in the two decades after the Civil War, was no more the official Indian policy per se than it had been in earlier periods. In fact, the official policy under President Ulysses S. Grant was known as the "Peace Policy." Although

Grant should probably receive less credit for originating the policy associated with his name than either General Sherman, Commissioner of Indian Affairs Ely S. Parker (a Seneca Indian), or even certain philanthropists of the period, it was under his administration that church nomination of Indian agents and philanthropic supervision of the Indian office combined with the use of the army on the Plains to produce the so-called Quaker or Peace Policy. The army coerced the tribes to live within the confines of the reservations assigned them. Any band of tribesmen caught outside its designated reservation was presumed to be at war and therefore liable to military reprisal. On the reservation the tribes were subject to the authority of the agent, who was nominated by a missionary society or church board. By replacing the corrupt agents affiliated with the notorious "Indian Ring" with devout men dedicated to God and not Mammon, philanthropists and the Grant administration hoped to achieve honest, and therefore cheaper, distribution of annuities and rations to Indians on reserves.[107] To further prevent the fraud of the Indian Ring as well as to encourage Christian civilization, Congress authorized Grant in 1869 to establish a Board of Indian Commissioners, independent of the Interior Department, to supervise Indian affairs. Composed of prominent religious persons serving without pay, the board soon learned it lacked effective authority to change the system as much as reformers had hoped. The old patronage system replaced the church nomination of agents by the early 1880s. Many vocal Westerners opposed the Peace Policy as just another example of sickly sentimentalism toward savage Indians, while Eastern humanitarians looked to new ways of converting the Indian to Christian civilization after the 1870s.[108]

At the heart of the Peace Policy lay the idea of the reservation. Although the idea of reservations for the Plains Indians can be traced back directly only to the 1850s, the placement of native peoples upon specially designated lands reserved from their cessions originated in the colonial period of Anglo-American policy. Short-lived as the Peace Policy was, its basic goals remained the old ones while its methods pointed to the future. The rationales for the policy were the usual need for cheapness and the traditional aim of acculturation, as can be seen in the summary of the plan by the Secretary of Interior in 1873:

> The so-called peace policy sought, first, to place the Indians upon reservations as rapidly as possible, where they could be pro-

vided for in such manner as the dictates of humanity and Christian civilization require. Being thus placed upon reservations, they will be removed from such contiguity to our frontier settlements as otherwise will lead, necessarily to frequent outrages, wrongs, and disturbances of the public peace. On these reservations they can be taught, as fast as possible, the arts of agriculture, and such pursuits as are incident to civilization, through the aid of the Christian organizations of the country now engaged in this work, cooperating with the Federal Government. Their intellectual, moral, and religious culture can be prosecuted, and thus it is hoped that humanity and kindness may take the place of barbarity and cruelty. . . . [It] is the further aim of the policy to establish schools, and through the instrumentality of the Christian organizations, acting in harmony with the Government, as fast as possible, to build churches and organize Sabbath schools, whereby these savages may be taught a better way of life than they have heretofore pursued, and be made to understand and appreciate the comforts and benefits of a Christian civilization, and thus be prepared ultimately to assume the duties and privileges of citizenship.[109]

So once again "wild" Indians according to the deficiency image were to be transformed into Americans by traditional means of acculturation and assimilation, this time through the supposedly new method of the reservation.

What policy makers and philanthropists saw as novel about the post–Civil War reservations was the furious pace at which assimilation of even these "wild" Indians was to take place as a result of the greater funds and larger bureaucratic apparatus brought to bear on the process. To achieve Christian civilization and eventual assimilation, the reservation policy gave the agent absolute authority over his charges and demanded, as a consequence, the total subordination of Native Americans within their assigned enclaves. While such a power structure ruled from Washington may not have been achieved in the 1870s, the goal of total control by the agent and the utter dependence of the Indians was the lasting legacy bequeathed from this decade to later ones.[110] Thus did the wardship postulated by John Marshall in his 1831 decision become actuality as Indians were denied self-government and particularly religious freedom in the very hope of giving them democracy and liberty according to the American model. With new means at the command of the Indian Bureau, many government officials, army officers, and Eastern humanitarians believed that the task of assimilating even these "wild" Indians would take no longer than twenty-five years or so.[111] The new evolutionary anthropologists of the time questioned not the desirability of achieving acculturation through such harsh methods but rather its possibility, given their scientific analysis of stages: could hunters advance to the farming stage without first passing through the prior herding phase? They, like other leading Whites of the era, never doubted the need to transform Indians into "good" Americans as the long-term solution to the Indian problem.[112]

Coinciding with the increasing subordination of Native Americans on reservations went a growing effort at detribalization in order to render the communalistic Indian an individualistic American in line with the changing economic and intellectual atmosphere in the last decades of the nineteenth century.[113] The end of treaty making in 1871 signaled one aspect of this transformation. Although the immediate occasion for the end of treaty making was the quarrel over the prerogatives of the Senate at the expense of the House of Representatives in controlling Indian policy, the more important trend was the growing feeling on all sides of the incongruity between the status of native tribes presumed under the etiquette of treaty negotiations and the actual state of White conquest and native subjugation. Grant's Commissioner of Indian Affairs, Ely S. Parker, expressed succinctly the new attitudes as well as the changed circumstances of Native Americans vis-à-vis federal authority in his report of 1869. Although a Seneca Indian himself, he resorted to old clichés in his arguments:

> The Indian tribes of the United States are not sovereign nations, capable of making treaties, as none of them have an organized government of such inherent strength as would secure a faithful obedience of its people in the observance of compacts of this character. They are held to be wards of the government, and the only title the law concedes to them to the lands they occupy or claim is a mere possessory one. But because treaties have been made with them, generally for the extinguishment of their supposed absolute title to land inhabited by them, or over which they roam, they have become falsely impressed with the notion of national independence. It is time that this idea should be dispelled, and the government cease the cruel farce of thus dealing with its helpless and ignorant wards. . . . As civilization advances and their possessions of land are required for settlement, such legislation should be granted to them as a wise, liberal, and just government ought to extend to subjects holding their dependent relation.[114]

What Andrew Jackson and others had argued decades earlier now became official policy as Congress proceeded to legislate directly for tribes. Thus, after some 370 treaties, most for land cessions, Native Americans moved officially and legally from being domestic dependent nations represented through their own governments to being wards of the state, to be acted upon by the agents of a bureaucracy in their midst.[115] On the reservations, the agents for their part attempted to side-step tribal authorities through the establishment of their own native police and courts, thereby administering the tribes under their control through people beholden and responsible to them rather than to the tribal government or traditional kinship ties. These native police and judges were to exemplify in their own lives, as well as to enforce, the individualistic foundations of American law and the protection of property deemed so basic to American liberalism.[116]

Developments in the funding and nature of White-sponsored native education pointed in the same direction of increased subordination and individualization of the Indian. The federal government assumed full responsibility for native education during the fiscal year 1871 for the first time by making a general appropriation. The efficacy of the reservation day school versus the off-reservation manual-labor boarding school was once again debated in spending this money. The most famous of the off-reservation manual-labor boarding schools was the Carlisle (Pennsylvania) Indian Industrial School, founded in 1879 by Captain Richard H. Pratt. In its distance from its pupils' homes, its close, prisonlike supervision of the students, and its outing system, in which students spent summer months or a year living in the home of a good Christian White family, Pratt hoped to destroy the "Indian" in the "race" in favor of the "man," as he was fond of saying. Although the school fielded a famous football team that played the Eastern colleges, its own curriculum resembled that taught in White elementary schools of the period. Pratt, in effect, treated his Indian students as utterly dependent wards in order to prepare them for American individualism.[117]

Administration of Indian education was centralized in the 1880s with the establishment of a bureaucracy devoted solely to the task within the Bureau of Indian Affairs. Codification of rigid rules, uniformity of texts and curriculum, compulsory attendance, and separation of church and state support of schools followed within the next decade as the federal government tightened its supervision over Indian education. By the end of the century nearly half of all native children attended school for some period of time.[118]

In addition to education as a means of detribalizing Native Americans, members of the new Indian rights and reform organizations arising in the 1880s looked to allotment of reservation lands in severalty, the extension of the American legal system over Indians on reservations, and the grant of full-fledged United States citizenship to Native Americans as absolutely necessary for the individualization of the Indian. As the Indian Affairs Bureau consolidated its power over Native Americans through the reservation system, more and more of the self-styled "friends of the Indian" concluded that the reservation system itself hindered the goal of total Indian assimilation into American society. The reservation provided the social and economic foundations for the very Indian values and customs these people so detested in Native American life. The reservation offered the land base and communal reinforcement of traditional economic and governmental patterns in the tribe which the "friends of the Indian" thought so "communistic," to use their word. If American Indians were ever to become individualistic Americans, then these traditional patterns of economic, social, religious, and political relations must be eliminated through the destruction of the reservation community that fostered them in spite of the best efforts of federal agents and dedicated missionaries.

Total detribalization demanded nothing less in their minds than bringing crimes among Indians under the penal statutes of the United States instead of the customs of a tribal government, granting Indians the responsibilities as well as the privileges of United States citizenship, and, most of all, allotting reserved lands in severalty so Indians would feel the powerful effects of private property through its sole and exclusive ownership. Through the destruction of the reservation and consequent detribalization, reformers and policy makers sought to end the wardship of the Indians embodied in the peculiar and anomalous relationship they bore to the federal government, unlike that of any other nationals living in the United States. The achievement of these goals would be measured by the disappearance of the Bureau of Indian Affairs, itself a bureaucratic monument to the peculiar relationship with its expensive services.[119]

Some reformers of the late nineteenth century had as much faith in the magical effects of property and laissez-faire in transforming the Indians as some missionaries of the early decades of that century had in the miraculous influence of the Bible and the institution of the Sabbath. As Merrill E. Gates, the president of both Amherst College and the famed Lake Mohonk Conference of the Friends of the Indian, extolled in glowing terms the moral implications of private property, he resorted to the old stereotypes of the Indian to make his point:

> We have, to begin with, the absolute need of awakening in the savage Indian broader desires and ampler wants. To bring him out of savagery into citizenship we must make the Indian more intelligently selfish before we can make him unselfishly intelligent. We need to *awaken in him wants.* In his dull savagery he must be touched by the wings of the divine angel of discontent. . . . Discontent with the teepee and the starving rations of the Indian camp in winter is needed to get the Indian out of the blanket and into trousers,—and trousers with a pocket in them, and with a *pocket that aches to be filled with dollars!* . . .
>
> There is an immense moral training that comes from the use of property. And the Indian has had all that to learn. Like a little child who learns the true delight of giving away only by first earning and possessing what it gives, the Indian must learn that he has no right to give until he has earned, and that he has no right to eat until he has worked for his bread. Our teachers upon the reservations know that frequently lessons in home-building, and providence for the future of the family which they are laboriously teaching, are effaced and counteracted by the old communal instincts and customs which bring half a tribe of kins-people to settle down at the door of the home when the grain is threshed or the beef is killed, and to live upon their enterprising kinsman so long as his property will suffice to feed the clan of his kins-people. We have found it necessary, as one of the first steps in developing a stronger personality in the Indian, *to make him responsible for property.* Even if he learns its value only by losing it, and going without it until he works for more, the educational process has begun. To cease from pauperizing the Indian by feeding him through years of laziness,—to instruct him to use property which is legally his, and by protecting his title, to help him through the dangerous transition period into citizenship,— this is the first great step in the education of the race.[120]

With such views of the Native American as deficient Indian, no wonder the reformers of the period treated all tribes as alike no matter what their degree of acculturation or the conditions upon their reservations. Nor did the reformers and policy makers consult Native Americans in proposing or carrying out their programs, for according to their image the Indian was as incapable of appreciating the benefits of these reforms as he was of understanding the motives of his supposed benefactors.

This phase of the Indian reform movement culminated in congressional passage of the General Allotment Act of 1887. Hailed at the time as the final, comprehensive solution to the Indian problem, the act linked citizenship to private land ownership. The principle of allotting lands to individuals and even the connection of citizenship to allotment had been tried before in various treaties dating from the 1830s onward—with a notable lack of success conspicuously disregarded in the new enthusiasm. The application of these two principles to all tribes in general, regardless of the degree of acculturation or the nature of their economic resources, was the new feature of the policy. So was the compulsory nature of the law. General allotment bills were first introduced into Congress in 1879, but the final passage of such an act awaited compromise between the interests of the reformers and of Westerners. Reformers at first opposed both the allotment of lands without adequate safeguards to their new native owners as well as the sale of reservation lands left over after severalty. Westerners, except for those already grazing cattle on Indian lands, at first resisted any kind of allotment as depriving them of potential land, and then wanted as much of the surplus lands as possible.

Eventually, Senator Henry L. Dawes of Massachusetts, a noted "friend of the Indian" at the reform conferences of the time, sponsored the compromise that allotted each native family head a quarter section of 160 acres, typical under the Homestead Act, and half that amount to orphans and single persons over eighteen years of age. The patent for the land was to be issued only after being held in trust for twenty-five years by the Secretary of Interior, during which time the land could not be sold or the title encumbered. For those Indians who failed or refused to select their allotment, the Secretary of Interior was empowered to make the choice. Once the patent was issued, the new native owner became subject to the laws of the state or territory in which the land was located. United States citizenship was conferred upon allottees or other Indians who resided "separate and apart from the tribe" and who had "adopted the habits of civilized life." Citizenship was granted, however, only to those natives born within the bounds of the United States. Reservation lands remaining after allotment to tribal members were to be purchased by the federal government with Indian consent, and the sale price held in trust for the "education and civilization" of the former tribal members. Through such temporary wardship, policy makers and philanthropists hoped to thrust upon the Indian the independent spirit and institutions of modern times. For this reason, the reformers celebrated the allotment act as a new order of things comparable in historical importance to the Magna Charta or the Declaration of Independence for Whites or the Emancipation Proclamation for Blacks.[121]

In practice the new order for the Indians worked out more like the old order by favoring Whites at the expense of Native Americans. With the Secretary of the Interior forcing allotment upon tribes faster than reformers expected or thought the Indians ready for—ironically the Five Civilized Tribes and some other acculturated tribes were exempted from the Dawes Act at first[122]—the lands of the Indians fell into the hands of Whites far more quickly than Native Americans adopted White ways of life. Congress enacted legislation in 1891 permitting the leasing of allotted lands in trust for agriculture, grazing, mining, and lumbering. Tribal lands and economic resources therefore passed as quickly into White control under the new policy as under the old ones, as individualistic Whites converted individual Indian lands into the usual "higher uses" according to their own ideals and pocketbooks.

The effectiveness of the allotment policy toward this profitable end can be measured roughly by the diminution of Indian lands between the passage of the Dawes Act in 1887 and its reversal under the so-called Indian New Deal in 1934. Of the original 138 million acres, over 60 percent was lost through sales of the lands declared surplus and another 20 percent through disposal of allotments. When the amount of allotted lands leased is added to this total, the consequences for Native Americans is as devastating as the previous preemption policy. Thus did reform and crass interests team up to perpetuate old results under a new guise. President Theodore Roosevelt's characterization of the General Allotment Act in his first annual message to Congress as "a mighty pulverizing engine to break up the tribal mass" described better the effects of allotment for land transfer to Whites than acculturative transformation of Reds, but then "good" Americans no more doubted the desirability of both ends at the beginning of the twentieth century than they had earlier.

A New Deal for Native Americans: Cultural Pluralism in Practice

GIVEN THE REMARKABLE CONTINUITY of basic objectives and results in United States Indian policy from the founding of the nation until well into the twentieth century, we may wonder whether any basic changes have occurred in recent times. The 1920s marked a fundamental shift in the scientific and scholarly understanding of the Indian through acceptance of the concept of culture and the ideal of cultural pluralism. Did these conceptions so basic to a changed view of the Indian also influence the formulation and execution of Indian policy in the same period? Did the alienation from industrial society and the new definition of political liberalism that arose in the United States during the 1930s also fundamentally modify the foundations of the national Indian policy? In other words, have the political, social, and economic trends that transformed the larger White society during modern times also reversed the historic tendencies of American Indian policy?

Congress did not grant United States citizenship to Native Americans born within the country but still living on unallotted reservations until the third decade of the twentieth century. By that time, two-thirds of all Native Americans had acquired federal citizenship through old treaty provisions, special statutes, or under allotment. Birth in the United States did not make the first Americans citizens of the country in which they lived, although after the end of treaty making and under the reservation system they were subjects of that nation and its government. In the flurry of activity after the Civil War enfranchising the newly emancipated Blacks and making the former slaves citizens of the United States, Indian reformers sought the same privileges and duties for Native Americans. The Civil Rights Act of 1866, however, specifically exempted from its provisions Indians who were not taxed. A special Senate committee reported in 1870 that the fourteenth amendment, which defined federal citizenship for the first time, did not apply to Indians because of their anomalous tribal status, and a court held the next year that Indians could not be citizens as long as they were subject to tribal and not state jurisdictions.

Indian rights associations demanded immediate citizenship for Native Americans, particularly as judges ruled that Congress could and must extend citizenship to Indians if they were to obtain it at all. Hence, the General Allotment Act combined citizenship with private property to provide traditional and individualistic American grounds for granting federal citizenship to Indians. Once allotments destroyed the tribal communalism in government and land and forced Indians to cope with life as individuals like all other Americans, then they were considered ready to receive the boon of citizenship.

Congress finally bestowed citizenship in 1924 upon all Indians born within the bounds of the United States. At last, the first Americans became citizens of the country their ancestors had inhabited and ceded. The passage of the law, often ascribed to congressional gratitude for Indian enlistments in the United States Army during World War One, was probably due to partisan politics and the traditional effort to curb the authority of the Interior Department and the BIA by getting them out of the Indian business. Enfranchisement of the Native American, of course, did not follow federal citizenship automatically, for in many Western states White prejudice against the Indian continued to discriminate in this area of civil rights as in others. Nor did citizenship remove the Indian from being a ward of the federal government. In fact, the definition of guardianship had expanded during the early twentieth century, and so the new Indian citizen was more than ever under the legal power of his federal controllers.[123]

In the same year as congressmen gave citizenship to the Indians, they also restricted foreign immigration into the United States. The influx of millions of Southern and Eastern Europeans appeared more dangerous in their eyes than a few hundred thousand pacified Indians. Paralleling the decades-long drive to restrict immigration was the movement to Americanize those foreigners already in the United States. Supporting both restriction and Americanization was the new scientific racism and its corollary doctrine of Anglo-Saxon superiority. Racial thinking justified the quotas set in immigration restriction and equated 100 percent Americanism with Anglo-Saxon blood and institutions. In the eyes of its proponents, Americanization strove to produce conformity to Anglo-American institutions in the United States through extinguishing diverse un-American heritages or even the cultural amalgam of the metaphorical melting pot. Eugenics, racial anthropology, and fear of the Bolshevik experiment in communism, like the movements to Americanize and to restrict immigrants, peaked in the years immediately after the First World War. At the same time, Woodrow Wilson's Commissioner of Indian Affairs speeded up the allotment process in order to hasten Native American detribalization and assimilation.[124]

By that time a minority of intellectuals and reformers had repudiated the stress upon racism and Anglo-Saxon institutions in favor of cultural pluralism. Rather than wanting to stamp out minority groups, with their different attitudes and separate heritages, these thinkers and social reformers favored instead their preservation as a vital part of a better American life for all. In immigrants, Blacks, and Indians, these intellectuals found the virtues and a humanity they thought lost in the White, Anglo-Saxon, Protestant world. To these persons, the living traditions embodied in minority communities offered a challenge and a counter-example to both the rugged individualism preached by 100 percent Americans and the atomization of the modern industrial world.[125]

Important for the future of Indian policy among this group of intellectuals and reformers was John Collier, who discovered among the Pueblos of the Southwest the sense of community and harmony of life he thought White American industrial society lacked. After losing hope of re-establishing neighborhood communities and grass-roots democracy among the immigrants and poor of New York City through the aptly named People's Institute, Collier joined a group of intellectuals who, alienated from the business civilization of the 1920s, had fled to Taos, New Mexico, instead of Paris. There, among the same Pueblo peoples that Ruth Benedict later took as her model for Apollonian society in *Patterns of Culture*, Collier found hope for the survival of civilization in his rediscovery of the integrated primary social group and community lived by the "magical" Indians. He saw the Indians as repudiating the materialism, the secularism, and the fragmentation of modern White life under industrialism for a simpler, more beautiful way of life that emphasized the relationship of humans with one another, with the supernatural, and with land and nature. The integrated life of the Pueblos stood as a reproach to atomized modern civilization; and their harmonious, democratic ways a vital lesson to all White Americans. To Collier, the survival of this "Red Atlantis" into the modern era offered a hope for the future of the world in spite of industrialism. He romanticized the heritage of these folk societies as part of his alienation from his own "sick" times, and the Pueblos became his own personal countercultural utopia.

With the clarity of hindsight, Collier expounded in his autobiography on the cosmic significance the Pueblos held for a social worker interested in local, democratic community organization:

> The discovery that came to me there, in that tiny group of a few hundred Indians, was of personality-forming institutions, even now unweakened, which had survived repeated and immense historical shocks, and which were going right on in the production of states of mind, attitudes of mind, earth-loyalties and human loyalties, amid a context of beauty which suffused all the life of the group. What I observed and experienced was power of art—of life-making art—greater in kind than anything I had known in my own world before. Not tiny, but huge, this little group and its personalities seemed. There were solitary vigils which carried the individual out into the cosmos, and there were communal rituals whose grave, tranquil yet earth-shaking intensity is not adequately suggested by anything outside the music of Bach.
>
> And the experience was not a fantasy, but has been borne out by many and cumulative experiences in the years since, among many tribes. I was conscious all the time, that the significance was not local to Indians, but was universal. Yet it might be that only Indians, among the peoples of this hemisphere at least, were still the possessors and users of the fundamental secret of human life—the secret of building great personality through the instrumentality of social institutions. And it might be, as well, that the Indian life would not survive.[126]

For the sake of White as well as Red peoples, then, the Indians' tribal life must be preserved, and this became his aim first as executive secretary of the American Indian Defense Association formed in the 1920s and then as Commissioner of Indian Affairs under Franklin Delano Roosevelt from 1933 to 1945.[127]

The American Indian Defense Association was but one part of the whole reform effort in Indian affairs during the 1920s that prepared the ground for the Indian New Deal under Roosevelt and Collier. In many ways, reformers applied the lessons learned under Progressivism earlier to the plight of Native Americans in the decades after the First World War. Prominent in focusing public attention upon reservation conditions of Indians during the 1920s were the muckraking exposés of fraud and mishandling of native oil and mineral resources by the same political leaders involved in the other scandals of the era. More important in the long run, however, were the series of reports prepared by professional specialists in public health, irrigation, and education. These reports reflected the newly acquired professional status of social work and the applied social sciences as much as they explored the problems of Native Americans through the specialized knowledge represented in the new academic departments of the modern university. The new professional analysts of society's ills searched for the causes of poverty and other social problems within the social and economic system rather than in the faults of individuals. They preferred the treatment of social pathology by rising new specialists rather than handling by the amateurs who had donated their services previously.[128]

The most famous of the reports dealing with Indian problems was commissioned by the Secretary of the Interior from the independent Institute of Government Research (later the Brookings Institute) and written by a team of experts headed by Dr. Lewis Meriam and including one Indian, Henry Roe, a Winnebago graduate of Yale. The Meriam Report, issued in 1928, employed the recently developed scientific survey to provide detailed information about the conditions among Native Americans before making its recommendations. Often hailed as the most complete study of the Bureau of Indian Affairs ever conducted, the eight-hundred-page report applied the standards advocated at the time by authorities in public health, progressive education, resource management, and family and community development to the condition of Indian tribes and the reform of federal Indian administration. Naturally the report advised the greater use of higher-paid professionals in education, conservation, vocational training, public health, and community organization to bring the administration of Indian affairs into line with contemporary practices in those areas of specialization. To measure the effectiveness of the proposed new staff as well as to explore further the dimensions of the problems, the report's experts called for more of the new social statistics to be collected, just as they had done in arriving at their own conclusions about the abject poverty, the poor schooling, and the wretched health of the demoralized Indians.

Among the recommendations that were to become important in shaping future Indian policy were the questioning of allotment, the use of corporations for the management of tribal resources, the strengthening of family and community life, and cooperation among various governmental agencies on the federal and state levels. Ultimately, the report's experts viewed the Indian problem as educational, for the goal of helping Indians to help themselves was "so that they may be absorbed into the prevailing civilization or be fitted to live in the presence of that civilization at least in accordance with a minimum standard of health and decency."[129]

Such a goal did not mean a complete denial of native cultures, but the Indians in the end were to be manipulated as usual for their own best interests—even under an inchoate ideal of cultural pluralism:

> In the execution of this program scrupulous care must be exercised to respect the rights of the Indian. This phrase "rights of the Indian" is often used solely to apply to his property rights. Here it is used in a much broader sense to cover his rights as a human being living in a free country. Indians are entitled to unfailing courtesy and consideration from all government employees. They should not be subjected to arbitrary action. Recognition of the educational nature of the whole task of dealing with them will result in taking the time to discuss with them in detail their own affairs and to lead rather than force them to sound conclusions. The effort to substitute educational leadership for the more dictatorial methods now used in some places will necessitate more understanding of and sympathy for the Indian point of view. Leadership will recognize the good in the economic and social life of the Indians in their religion and ethics, and will seek to develop it and build on it rather than to crush out all that is Indian. The Indians have much to contribute to the dominant civilization, and the effort should be made to secure this contribution, in part because of the good it will do the Indians in stimulating a proper race pride and self respect.[130]

Like previous reports, this one also looked to the end of the separate handling of Indian affairs through the wise administration of its recommendations. Once more, another group of reformers thought assimilation would be achieved within a generation:

> The belief is that it is a sound policy of national economy to make general expenditures in the next few decades with the object of winding up the national administration of Indian affairs. The people of the United States have the opportunity, if they will, to write the closing chapters of the history of the relationship of the national government and the Indians. The early chapters contain little of which the country may be proud. It would be something of a national atonement to the Indians if the closing chapters should disclose the national government supplying the Indians with an Indian Service which would be a model for all governments concerned with the development and advancement of a retarded race.[131]

If this report employed new phrases to express its goals and new social engineering to discuss the Indian problem, the ultimate ends resembled those traditionally espoused for Indians. Cultural pluralism seemed but the icing upon the cake of assimilation.

What the Meriam Report recommended and the Quaker heads of the Indian Bureau under President Herbert Hoover advanced tentatively became official policy and practice under Collier and the opportunity presented by the Great Depression and the New Deal.[132] The conjunction of Collier's philosophy, like-minded people in the Department of Interior, headed by his friend Harold Ickes, and the power and influence of Franklin Roosevelt during the initial years of his administration overcame the objections of the traditional advocates of Indian assimilation and dispossession to halt if not reverse the long-time policy of allotment and detribalization. Part of Collier's program to preserve the strengths of tribal culture and life could be achieved through executive order and administrative decisions: the abolition of the Board of Indian Commissioners initiated under President Grant, prevention of the interference with native religions that had become policy in the 1920s, the encouragement of native crafts and arts, the transfer of pupils from distant boarding schools to day schools located upon the reservation close to the people, the transformation of these schools into centers for community activities and adult education as well as the teaching of the children, and the decentralization of BIA activities and the promotion of decision making more responsive to the grass-roots level of tribal societies. In the end, however, fundamental policy change depended upon congressional approval and funding.

What Collier wanted from Congress was embodied in a long omnibus bill drafted by him and his allies in the Indian Bureau and on the Interior Department legal staff and introduced by the chairmen of the congressional Indian Affairs Committees, Senator Burton K. Wheeler of Montana and Representative Edgar Howard of Nebraska. In one fell swoop, Collier and his friends hoped to supersede previous congressional legislation they considered outmoded and to redirect United States policy to the rehabilitation of tribal economies, the promotion of self-determination of tribal affairs through home rule, and the extension of civic, religious, and cultural freedom to Indians, while transferring as many duties and services of the Indian Bureau to the hands of the Indians as possible. To foster native economic independence, the bill not only halted the diminution of tribal land bases through the ending of allotment and restored unsold sur-

plus lands to tribal ownership but it also pledged the federal government to buy lands for homeless Indians to create new reservations and
to consolidate allotted landholdings fragmented through inheritance
into viable economic units. To further protect tribal resources, the
bill empowered the Secretary of Interior to regulate herding, timber
cutting, and soil usage according to the latest conservation practices.
In an amendment, Collier proposed that Congress establish a five-
million-dollar revolving fund to finance Indians in attaining economic
independence through development of their resources.

The bill also encouraged the political independence of tribes
through permission to form tribal governments with the powers common to municipalities in the United States: the election of officials,
the adoption of legislative ordinances, the establishment of local
courts, the management of tribal property and resources, and the
handling of those Indian Bureau activities transferred to the tribes.
To effect such self-government, a tribe had to adopt by three-fifths
popular vote a charter specifying the powers of the tribal corpora-
tion. These governments could vote to have federal services performed by the Indian Bureau turned over to them, and the bill provided for the advice and at times the consent of tribal authorities to
federal expenditures for Indians. To adjudicate the conflicts and
claims arising under the new law as well as old policies, the bill
created a seven-member federal Court of Indian Affairs with original
jurisdiction over crimes committed upon reservations and in disputes
arising from the new governments and with appellate jurisdiction
over tribal court judgments. This federal court was empowered to
adopt its own procedures, which Collier hoped would be nontechni-
cal and compatible with the needs and customs of native litigants.

Lastly, the bill provided funds to educate Indians in ways consonant with the need to administer their own affairs. As a result, the
last section of the title on education stated:

> It is hereby declared to be the purpose and policy of Congress to
> promote the study of Indian civilization and preserve and develop the
> special cultural contributions and achievements of such civilization,
> including Indian arts, crafts, skills, and traditions. The Commis-
> sioner [of Indian Affairs] is directed to prepare curricula for In-
> dian schools adapted to the needs and capacities of Indian students,
> including courses in Indian history, Indian arts and crafts, the social
> and economic problems of Indians, and the history and problems of
> Indian administration.

In no uncertain terms the bill looked to "curb the administrative absolutism" of the Indian Bureau in Native American affairs and to foster home rule and economic rehabilitation through reorganized and revitalized tribal governments.[133]

How far congressmen accepted Collier's vision of Indian home rule and cultural revival can be seen from the Indian Reorganization Act (IRA) as enacted by the two houses. Congress greatly shortened the original bill by eliminating the rhetoric of self-determination and cultural perpetuation and by deleting several crucial parts of Collier's program and toning down others. The declaration of congressional intent to foster Indian cultures and all mention of the federal Indian court went first. To satisfy Indians afraid of the return of their allotted lands to tribal control and White Westerners worried about the expansion of reservations, Congress erected safeguards around the restoration of tribal lands, the transfer of allotments, and the kinds of lands to be added to tribal ownership. Moreover, the number of Indians eligible for the provisions of the act was narrowed through the exemption of certain tribes, increasing the blood quanta from one-quarter to one-half among tribal descendants, and confining the act to reservations in federal trust status. Congress, furthermore, restricted the operation of the act to those tribes that voted by a majority of all adults to accept its benefits in a special election. To receive the actual funding and self-government provisions of the Indian Reorganization Act required another election to adopt a constitution, again with passage by a majority of all adult tribal members. Tribal powers of self-government were reduced from the Collier version and made subject to the approval of the Secretary of Interior. Through these deletions and amendments, congressmen made clear that they subscribed to a very limited ideal of cultural pluralism and self-determination. If Collier hoped to revive old-time tribal community control and culture, Congress at best preferred to stabilize Indian acculturation and assimilation as it was in 1934 without forcing change either forward or backward.[134]

Only presidential pressure and the crisis of the times got congressmen to go even this far toward Collier's dream of reorganizing Indian affairs according to his ideal of the Pueblo countercultural utopia. Although the act fell short of accomplishing all that Collier had recommended originally, it did set as official policy what the title of the law summarized: "to conserve and develop Indian lands and resources; to extend to Indians the right to form business and other organizations; to establish a credit system for Indians; [and] to grant certain rights of home rule to Indians." As administered by Collier, the Indian Reorganization Act sought to better Indian life through what he and others believed was the traditional native attachment to collective landownership and use and to customary tribal government, although these cultural attributes were to be redirected through agencies created by the act to enhance Native American life according to his idea of the Indians' best interests.

Collier's overall program brought forth as enemies those whose interests were violated by the seeming new order of things. Missionaries and their friends accused the new policy of fostering irreligion, that is, native religion, through granting freedom of worship. In their eyes, such a policy repudiated the centuries-long aim of Christian philanthropy. Others saw the encouragement of collective tribal economic and governmental organization and activity as communistic and therefore thoroughly un-American and subversive of United States institutions. Still others feared the program would increase the staff and budget of the Indian Bureau at the expense of the White taxpayer rather than that the bureaucracy would wither away as Indians assimilated into the mainstream of American life, the aim of the old policy. By the end of the so-called first New Deal in 1936, Collier faced increasing opposition to his ideas and program. On the other hand, most anthropologists approved of the policies he administered as consistent with social-science knowledge about native societies and cultural pluralism.[135]

The program never achieved all Collier had hoped or his enemies feared. Increasing congressional reluctance to finance his program soon hindered its effectiveness, especially the purchases of lands to be added to reservations and the management of resources according to good conservation practices. Internally, the entrenched attitudes and rigidity of the large Indian Service bureaucracy often sabotaged Collier's basic goals. To get personnel sufficiently trained in new attitudes and cross-cultural approaches proved difficult. Although Collier sought advice from tribal congresses after drafting his bill, the Indian Reorganization Act, in the end, represented, as did his whole program, his idea of what was best for Indians, and not always what Native Americans in their diverse circumstances thought best for themselves. In this sense, all Indians became Pueblos in his vision, regardless of where or how they lived and regardless of Collier's belief that his program allowed for the multiplicity of tribal cultures and conditions. Although over two-thirds of the eligible tribes voted to come under the IRA, this represented only 40 percent of the individual Indians voting in the special elections. Furthermore, only half of those tribes voting to come under the IRA ever went on to accept constitutions and organize governments according to Collier's plan. Many fewer established tribal economic corporations to develop their resources.[136]

No matter what Native Americans did under the IRA, funding of tribal welfare and economic programs depended upon the federal government as always, and so the decisions of the reorganized tribal governments rested for final authority upon the approval of the Indian Bureau. IRA goals encouraged the ends of progressive factions in the tribes, and that faction often supported and staffed the newly created government at the expense or the opposition of the traditional members and leadership in a tribe. These traditionalists felt quite rightly that the new tribal governments with their written constitutions, elections, and formalized legislative procedures resembled White more than native ways of running their affairs. Official tribal councils under the IRA functioned as the instrumentalities of the Indian service and the progressive factions among Native American groups, and the governments therefore exhibited a high degree of "democratic centralism" and little community control, as one Indian member of the Tribal Organization Division of the BIA noted.[137] In spite of these defects in Collier's program and the IRA, most later commentators feel that native autonomy and interests were better represented under the Indian New Deal than ever before in the history of United States policy—and perhaps subsequently as well.[138]

The Modern Period:
Historic Reversal or Reversion?

MOUNTING CONGRESSIONAL OPPOSITION to the explicit goals of the Collier program and suspicion about its implications forced a reversion to earlier aims of rapid assimilation after World War Two. Collier had always justified his program in terms of the ultimate integration of the Indian into American society, but his pluralistic vision that such incorporation be upon native as well as White terms appeared to many congressmen an outright denial of assimilation and certainly a prolongation of the Indians' special wardship status with its concomitant expense. By early 1945, Collier's enemies in Congress had gained sufficient influence to force his resignation after the longest tenure of any Commissioner of Indian Affairs. In response to a congressional request, his successor drew up a list of tribes according to their readiness for termination of federal services and wardship status. Ten tribes were declared ready for immediate termination of all federal responsibilities and trusteeship; another twenty tribes within five to ten years; and all the remainder of Indian tribes prepared in ten to twenty-five years. Thus once again the desire for assimilation provided grounds for the belief that all Indians could be completely incorporated into American society within a generation.

That termination of federal wardship and services was the official intention of both houses of Congress was declared in House Concurrent Resolution 108 adopted in mid-1953. Although without the force of law as such, the resolution expressed the design of Congress to free the Indian of the guardianship of the general government and give him the full responsibilities as well as the privileges of the ordinary citizen as soon as possible. In line with the resolution, ten termination bills were introduced in the next session of Congress, of which six passed. Essentially the laws provided for the ending of all special federal services, the termination of federal trusteeship over tribal and individuals' lands, resources, and funds, and the withdrawal of all other wardship and federal obligations signifying a special status for Indians. Once termination was completed and proclaimed, the tribal members became subject to the same state laws and jurisdiction as other citizens, with corresponding duties and responsibilities as well as rights and privileges. In the eyes of the main proponent of the policy, Senator Arthur Watkins of Utah, the Indian was at long last set free of the federal government. In words echoing those hailing the passage of the General Allotment Act, Watkins summarized the significance of the policy: "Following in the footsteps of the Emancipation Proclamation . . . I see the following words emblazoned in letters of fire above the heads of Indians—THESE PEOPLE SHALL BE FREE!"[139]

In freeing the Indian of the government, the proponents of termination also hoped to free the federal government of the Indian after so many years, and therefore policies and acts long advocated in an earlier period but only adopted after World War Two became associated with the termination policy. Although the Meriam Report and the Collier bill urged the settlement of long-standing claims against the federal government through the creation of a special court, Congress did not pass an Indian Claims Commission Act until 1946, when many congressmen saw the law as a way of settling Native American grievances prior to termination of federal wardship over them. The act established a three-man board to hear and determine claims for the recovery of financial damages for various categories of grievances against the United States government. Prior to the passage of the act, restitution for such tribal claims came only through special act of Congress as with any other foreign nation rather than through the normal channel of the United States Court of Claims, from which such cases had been specifically excluded shortly after it was created in 1856. As a way of providing economic opportunity for the rapidly growing Native American population in the postwar prosperity, the BIA aided through finances and services the voluntary relocation of Indians from poverty-stricken reservations to urban areas around the country. Again the policy had been advocated by both the Meriam Report and Collier's staff, but the practice at this time was supported by congressmen as part of the whole trend to federal termination of services and wardship for reservation Indians.

The Hoover Commission for the reorganization of the executive branch recommended in 1949 the transfer to the states of social programs for Indians, and once again a policy advanced and practiced under the Collier regime became part of the trend to federal disengagement. Congress voted in 1954 to transfer Indian health programs from the BIA to the United States Public Health Service, and the bureau continued the old policy of placing more and more native children in local public schools. In accord with the general policy of withdrawal of federal wardship, Congress also passed in 1953 Public Law 280, which brought Indians in certain states under the criminal and civil jurisdiction of those states and relieved the federal government of law-enforcement duties in those places. Most symbolic of all, perhaps, was the repeal in 1953 of the century-old law prohibiting the sale of liquor to Indians, so that here too Native Americans joined the ranks of American citizens at last.[140]

The termination policy lost the interest of congressmen and the executive branch within a decade of its official declaration but not before twelve tribes were forced down the road to withdrawal of federal services and trusteeship. Termination was often foisted upon a tribe over the objection of its members, and Indian leaders saw the whole program as just another attempt of the American people to repudiate their promises made through treaty. In their eyes, federal trusteeship and services were legitimate obligations incurred by the

United States government in return for cessions of lands by the tribes. In practice, furthermore, termination affected tribal territory and resources in the same manner as allotment—the rapid transfer of tribal lands to White hands and control, as the Menominee and Klamath soon discovered.[141] President Nixon immediately after his inauguration in 1969 declared the policy of the executive to be self-determination for Indians without termination of federal services or trusteeship and called upon Congress to repudiate further intention to terminate the special federal relationship with Indians embodied in the reservation. Many Whites had come to oppose termination not because they were against acculturation and assimilation or the elimination of the special trust relationship but because they thought the program premature or too expensive for the states assuming the burdens the federal government sloughed off on them. How long this reprieve from traditional assimilative policy would last Native American leaders may well wonder, given the customary fluctuation of executive and congressional decision making on Indian affairs.

Perhaps the most significant development in recent decades for the future of United States Indian policy lay not in the trend to termination or self-determination on the part of the federal government but in the formation of Native American political organizations, both tribal and intertribal (or pan-Indian), that can exert pressures through the American system of brokerage politics. Although this phase of native political association was foreshadowed in the Society of American Indians, which lasted from 1911 to the mid-1920s, the modern era dates from the governments formed under the IRA, and from the National Congress of American Indians (NCAI) founded in 1944. From its initial aim of watching closely congressional Indian legislation and BIA activities, the NCAI soon turned to lobbying in Washington for policies and laws favorable to Indians as its members saw Native American interests. Since so many of its members represented tribes with lands in federal trust status, the NCAI particularly opposed the whole termination policy. While it fought the BIA to benefit Indians, however, it sought their welfare through close association with the bureau.

Objection to this association of the IRA tribal governments, the NCAI, and the BIA on reservation and in Washington led college-educated Indian youth, alienated alike from general American society and from the "Uncle Tomahawks" on the reservations and the "colonial office," as they termed the BIA, to organize the National Indian Youth Council (NIYC) in 1960. These youths brought new tactics and new rhetoric as well as a new organization to the Indian cause as they defined it. Their activist tactics and rhetoric on behalf of Native Americans caused their movement to be labeled "Red Power" in analogy to the Black movement of the time. Urban Indians also formed political organizations in the 1960s, and perhaps best known from the mass media was the American Indian Movement (AIM).

Hoping not only to catch the attention of the Whites they believed apathetic to Native American welfare and rights but also trying to redefine priorities for official tribal leaders, the NIYC, AIM, and other Indian activist groups advanced from Pacific Northwest coast fish-ins (with Marlon Brando as an attention getter) to the occupation of Alcatraz Island, the takeover of the BIA building in Washington, and the "second battle of Wounded Knee." Apparently the liberalism of the 1960s encouraged some Native Americans like their White liberal allies to hope for the drastic modification of American Indian policy along with the transformation of American society. Red Power may mean a whole new era of Native American political influence as Indians. Then again, Native American activism to the extent that it brings traditional leaders and followers into mainstream American politics, regardless of the reason, may signify the final phase of assimilation into the larger society.[142]

While the millennium Red and White radicals hoped for never arrived, the federal government increasingly allowed a changing parity of power between the tribal societies and itself. From the New Deal of Franklin D. Roosevelt to the Great Society of Lyndon B. Johnson and the New Federalism of Richard M. Nixon, Indian self-determination and political autonomy advanced. If Native Americans did not achieve as much home rule and freedom as their leaders sought under the slogan of tribal sovereignty, they escaped from the highly subordinated status of the classic reservation to gain official governments with hired lawyers and lobbyists and national Indian organizations. Although Native American factionalism continued, all sides of the native political spectrum gained some voice, if not their will, in policy making. That the factions disagree over the exact nature of the tribal sovereignty—espoused by radical, traditionalist, progressive, and "Uncle Tomahawk" alike—indicates at least that Native Americans think they have gained some crumbs of political autonomy worth fighting over. All sides see some sort of trust relationship and special homeland existing in the future even though they argue over its control and funding. In short, Native Americans differ among themselves over what their desired future is, but most of their leaders see Indianness continuing to be separate from mainstream Americanism. To the extent that Native Americans see their separateness as a whole from Americans and organize to protect that separateness, then they themselves have created a reality for the image of the Indian invented so long ago by the Whites.

In the end, however, Native American politics and leadership operate within limits imposed by White attitudes and government. Many of the basic issues facing Native American peoples today depend as in the past upon what White Americans want and Congress legislates. Can Indian Americans achieve self-determination without White Americans' acquiescence? Will Congress permit the spending of federal funds without specifying how the monies are used? Since Congress has not allowed federally recognized tribes to determine the basic framework of their own destiny in the past, why should we expect any fundamental change in the future? Even the experience of home rule so recently permitted tribespeople comes from federal impetus, exists under its guidelines, and often receives funds from the federal treasury. The Indian Reorganization Act spurred the formation of many a tribal government either directly or indirectly, and the use of lawyers to give added voice to the tribe stemmed in many instances from the aegis first of the Indian Claims Act and later from the funding and activities of the Office of Economic Opportunity during the 1960s. The nature of tribal government, even its very existence, depends upon the sufferance and discretion of Congress. Surely Native Americans possess a greater say today in their fate as Indians than during the classic reservation era, but that say is as much circumscribed in the final analysis as ever in regard to tribal administration and welfare. Only abandonment of their status as tribal Indians frees Native Americans from the paternalism of the BIA and the supervision of Congress.[143]

Ultimately, tribal self-determination and the right to be Indian depends upon the attitudes of White Americans as much as upon the desires, shrewdness, and perseverance of Native American leaders and their followers. Although many White liberals may think that the nation has entered a new era of cultural pluralism and tolerance of ethnic differences, most native leaders are far from sure that such professions of idealism are anything more than the passing fancy of a few alienated Whites who talk one way while their many fellow Whites think and act quite another way. White individuals and governments upon all levels still seek Indian lands and resources as ardently as ever, but now the justification assumes the form of the pleas for water for thirsty cities and agricultural irrigation; lands, lakes, and rivers for recreation, tourism, wilderness preservation, or nature study; the necessity of oil and minerals to make the nation independent of foreign energy supplies or raw materials; conservation and land-management practices in the name of ecology; or just about any use but an Indian one.[144] In the conflict between Indian uses and White uses, Native Americans are certain that the supposedly new "higher uses" of the Whites will prevail over tribal necessity or treaty obligation just as the old ones did.

In most Americans' minds, the Indian constitutes "America's unfinished business," as the subtitle of a 1960s foundation report on the Indian "problem" put it.[145] All too often White policy makers and philanthropists would like to solve the now classic problems of health, welfare, education, and economic development through policies that would lead to further assimilation in the view of Native Americans. To many White Americans, tribalism, while it may seem quaint to a tourist, still appears opposed to American individualism when viewed economically or politically. The whole policy of termination and relocation in the 1950s, like allotment in the 1890s, was directed at destroying the physical and legal separateness of Native Americans. As a result of this long-time thrust of United States policy, no wonder Native American leaders today suspect the new policy of turning over the administration of federal services to tribal direction in the name of self-determination as just another plan aimed at terminating all services. Still other leaders see giving tribal members the same civil rights possessed by all other Americans as just another way of destroying the communal authority of the tribal government. In the end, White Americans generally wish to help the "poor Indian" as always by helping themselves to his land and resources in the name of higher uses and economic individualism, by eliminating the special services and costs of federal trusteeship and wardship in the name of self-determination and home rule, and through bettering the conditions of Indians according to their understanding of his problems rather than as Native Americans understand their problems—of which the Whites constitute a large part in their opinion. Far too many Whites still see an "Indian problem" rather than Native Americans with problems as a result of the long-time White image of the Indian.

Paradox still lies at the heart of many White policies after two centuries. Congress in the name of self-determination determines the limits of home rule through legislation and funding. Most Americans would still free the tribal Indian to be like them, in the name of individualism. Although Native Americans possess a greater voice in their destiny as Indians, still most policy makers believe they know better in the end what the Indian needs and wants. Both those who desire native lands and resources for reasons of national energy independence or the economic welfare of the country as a whole and those who advocate conservation and wilderness preservation feel that their uses should supersede Indian ones for the welfare of the whole nation, of which Indians are citizens. Self-proclaimed friends of the Indian all too often would help their objects of philanthropy according to their image of the Indian rather than through any understanding of Native Americans as people(s). Both counterculturists and assimilationists, therefore, share the urge to reform the Indian according to their desires rather than to help Native Americans on their own terms.

Perhaps the greatest paradox of all in United States policy is the heritage of its failure and success. Native Americans are hindered from helping themselves through the very success of United States policy in divesting them of lands and resources. At the same time the policy was never successful in stamping out Indianness. While Native Americans no longer live as they once did, their values and communities live on, separate from mainstream America. If the United States government had spent more money and effort in ruthless suppression of tribal cultures and expropriation of tribal resources, the Indian problem would indeed have disappeared. Thus humanitarian sentiment prevented the suppression of Indian life at the same time that economic individualism drastically reduced Native Americans' resources to support such separateness without further aid from White government. Only colonization of native enclaves allowed the continuance of these contradictory policies into the present. Only repudiation of old policies can prevent the continuation of that contradiction into the future.

To the extent that United States policy both failed and succeeded in the past, Native Americans continue to exist as Indians. The uniformity and the persistence of basic American Indian policy provides common grounds for Native Americans, so diverse in cultural backgrounds and present-day circumstances, to unite to the extent they do as Indians. The persisting White image of the Indian both forces and permits Native Americans to remain Indians, in spite of the White policies based on that image.

All anyone who surveys the two centuries of United States Indian policy can be certain of for the future is that the Native American will continue to pose an Indian problem in White policy makers' minds. Legislators, social scientists, and philanthropists will study the Indians' condition in the hopes of exposing the root problem of the Native American as Indian, so long as Native Americans persist in living their separate ways. In fact as United States policy enters its third century, Congress has established a brand-new commission to produce yet another comprehensive report on Indian affairs. New policies will be proclaimed to solve old problems, but outside observers like Native American leaders will wonder whether the consequences bode any better for Native American welfare than previous ones or just how long the new policies will command the attention of Congress and the executive. Just as surely these new studies and solutions will be superseded by still newer reports and policies. So long as Native Americans remain Indians in White eyes, then so long will White policy makers treat them as a problem and seek to bring them into the mainstream of United States society. Whether Native Americans themselves must and can unite as "Indians" organizationally and politically to protect their right to be different remains to be seen.

Epilogue

F ROM THIS SURVEY of the idea of the Indian over time, two dramatic historic trends emerge. What began as reality for the Europeans ended as image and stereotype for Whites, and what began as
an image alien to Native Americans became a reality for them. For
Native Americans the power of the Whites all too often forced them
to be the Indians Whites said they were regardless of their original
social and cultural diversity. To the extent that the resulting discrimination and oppression produced *indigenismo*, Red Power, or another
political movement, then Native American leaders in a sense have
given a political reality to the original White image of the Indian as a
separate but single collectivity. The success of such a movement depends, however, on the ability of the leaders to convince their followers that Native Americans are indeed a single entity as much as
on changing White ideas of justice and the parity of power between
the White and Red peoples.

That the idea of the Indian originated and continues up to the
present as a White image poses major dilemmas for modern Whites
as well as for Native Americans. Through continued use of the term
Indian, does the present-day White still subscribe to past stereotype?
Does the imagery of today, even if revised in accordance with
modern beliefs and values, still conceal Native American lifestyles and
thoughts from the understanding of today's Whites as much as the
historic stereotype did from past Whites? Can the "reality" of Native
American life ever be penetrated behind the screen of White ideology
and imagination no matter how benevolent those conceptions? In a
sense, these questions are so fundamental to cross-cultural understanding that they involve the very epistemology of race and minority
relations.

At first glance these problems would seem easily resolved by
making the simple but important distinction that lies at the heart of

modern understanding: the distinction between Native Americans and Indians, which in scientific terms can be designated as the ethnographic as opposed to the ideological image of the first Americans. Even though Whites once used the idea of the Indian to stereotype the manifold lives of Native Americans, they could now accept the concept of cultural pluralism and the judgment of moral relativity to understand the present and past of Native Americans—and even of their own stereotype. If at one time Whites employed ideology to understand the ethnography of Indians, they could now apply ethnography to separate White ideology from present and past White images to discover the real Native Americans.

Or will they still find the Indian? In light of the history of White Indian imagery, it seems certain that the term and the idea of Indian otherness will continue into the future. Partly such a prediction seems warranted by the continued usefulness of that otherness and the moral judgments on it for so many groups in the White population. Countercultural and pro-societal uses alike for White polemicists, policy makers, media people, and artists dictate the persistence of the idea of the Indian into the future just as they did in the past. Moreover, some Native American leaders' success in consolidating their own political influence depends upon their ability to persuade their followers to see themselves as Indians as opposed to individual tribespeople. Even as these leaders do so, they must play upon the White image of Indian otherness to achieve their own ends for their followers in the larger society. Mostly, however, the history of the White images of the Indian leads one to cynicism about the ability of one people to understand another in mutually acceptable terms.

Both politics and culture militate against such a compromise of power and ideation. To the extent that the way different ethnic groups see each other is not purely a function of the power relationships prevailing among them, then the conceptual and ideological screens of their own cultures must still interpose between the observer and the observed to color the "reality" of mutual perceptions. Although the modern concept of culture carries with it as intellectual and moral baggage the ideas of relativity and pluralism, it also postulates the intermediation of ideological preconception between seeing the world and responding to it. So long as the modern understanding of human actions assumes some sort of cultural influence between stimulus and response, then the future of the Indian as image must be determined by the preconceptions of White cultural premises. The great question, given contemporary understanding, then becomes: To what extent can new meaning be infused into the old term to cancel old prejudices and invent a new evaluative image? At the moment, Native American leaders and scholars as well as liberal Whites are directing their efforts to this transformation. Their success will depend as much on the future intellectual trends in Western, perhaps world, cultures as in the balance of power among peoples.

Notes

PART ONE

1. Especially informative upon early European perceptions of America are J. H. Elliot, *The Old World and the New, 1492–1650* (Cambridge, Eng.: Cambridge University Press, 1970); and Fredi Chiapelli, Michael J. B. Allen, and Robert L. Benson, eds., *First Images of America: The Impact of the New World on the Old* (Berkeley: University of California Press, 1976), 2 vols. Bois Penrose provides a good introduction to the travel literature of the period in *Travel and Discovery in the Renaissance, 1420–1620* (Cambridge: Harvard University Press, 1952). See also the provocative arguments of Edmundo O'Gorman, *The Invention of America: An Inquiry into the Historical Nature of the New World and the Meaning of Its History* (Bloomington: University of Indiana Press, 1961). Needless to say, O'Gorman's title and thesis inspired my title for this part.

2. In the Spanish edition of the letter reprinted in Cecil Jane, ed., *Select Documents Illustrating the Four Voyages of Columbus* (London: Hakluyt Society, 1930), p. 3. See also pp. 5 and 17 for the term. He also uses *gente*, pp. 7, 11; *personas*, p. 17; and *como bestias*, p. 9. Regrettably, this point is unclear from his journal, since all we have today is the copy made by Bartolomé de Las Casas, and the first use of the word is by Las Casas himself in a parenthetical aside.

3. On this broad use of *Indies* and *India*, see Donald R. Lach, *Asia in the Making of Europe: The Century of Discovery* (Chicago, University of Chicago Press, 1965), vol. 1, book 1, p. 4; Samuel E. Morison, *The European Discovery of America, The Southern Voyages, A.D. 1492–1616* (New York: Oxford University Press, 1974), pp. 26n., 30. Compare Wilcomb Washburn, "The Meaning of 'Discovery' in the Fifteenth and Sixteenth Centuries," *American Historical Review*, LXVIII (Oct. 1962), pp. 1–2, 15–18; Gustav H. Blanke, *Amerika in Englischen Schriftum des 16. und 17. Jahrhunderts*, Beitrage zur Englischen Philologie, XLVI (Bochum-Langendreer: Heinrich Poppinghaus, 1962), pp. 68–70.

4. In Richard Eden's translation of 1555 from Edward Arber, ed., *The First Three English Books on America* (Birmingham, Eng.: Author, 1885), p. 242. For a later use of *Indian* as a general designation for all American natives regardless of level of social organization, see chapter titles in José de Acosta,

The Natural and Moral History of the Indies, trans. Clements R. Markham (London: Hakluyt Society, 1880), series 1, vols. 60–61.

5. A good facsimile edition is Giovanni B. Ramusio, *Delle navigationi et viaggi* (Amsterdam: Theatrum Orbis Terrarum, Ltd., 1970). What knowledge of the Americas was available to the educated European in the 1520s is examined by Lawrence C. Wroth, ed., *The Voyages of Giovanni da Verrazano, 1524–1528* (New Haven and London: Yale University Press, 1970), pp. 27–34.

6. Richard Eden's reprints are compiled by Arber in *First Three English Books*. A good guide to English travel literature in the early period is provided by John Parker, *Books to Build an Empire: A Bibliographical History of English Overseas Interests to 1620* (Amsterdam: N. Israel, 1965).

7. In the Cecil Jane translation revised by L. A. Vigneras, *The Journal of Christopher Columbus* (London: Hakluyt Society, 1960), pp. 194–200. Compare the translation of Samuel E. Morison in his *Journals and Other Documents on the Life and Voyages of Christopher Columbus* (New York: The Heritage Press, 1963), pp. 183–85. On the various editions of the letter, consult *ibid.*, pp. 180–81.

8. Jane and Vigneras, *Journal of Christopher Columbus*, p. 200. Compare again the Morison translation cited in preceding note, p. 185.

9. Morison, *Southern Voyages*, pp. 276–97, 304–12, offers a brief guide to the whole controversy and the literature it has spawned.

10. *Mundus Novus Albericus Vespucius Laurentio Petri de Medicis salutem plurimam dicit* appears as *Vespucci Reprints, Texts, and Studies*, vol. 5, trans. George T. Northrup (Princeton: Princeton University Press, 1916). Compare his even more exotic description in the letter to Piero Soderini dated September 4, 1504, published as *Lettera di Amerigo Vespucci delle isole novamente trovate in quattro suoi viaggi*, in facsimile in the series cited above, vol. 2, and translated by Northrup in vol. 4. Still another description of the Brazilian Indians by Vespucci is contained in his so-called Bartolozzi letter translated by Morison, *Southern Voyages*, pp. 284–86.

11. For a list of pictorial representations of Indians from discovery to 1598, consult William C. Sturtevant, "First Visual Images of Native America," in Chiapelli *et al.*, eds., *First Images of America*, vol. 2, pp. 417–54. Hugh Honour provides both early pictures and a discussion of them in *The European Vision of America* (Cleveland: Cleveland Museum of Art, 1975), chaps. 1, 4, 6–7; and *The New Golden Land: European Images of America from the Discoveries to the Present Time* (New York: Pantheon, 1975), chaps. 1, 3–4.

12. Reprinted in Arber, *First Three English Books*, p. xxvii. Parker, *Books to Build an Empire*, pp. 21–22, discusses the dates of publication and authorship.

13. After a survey of European thought from 1550 to 1600, Benjamin Keen reaches this conclusion in *The Aztec Image in Western Thought* (New Brunswick, N.J.: Rutgers University Press, 1971), p. 172. John H. Elliot, "Discovery of America and the Discovery of Man," *Proceedings of the British Academy*, LVIII (1972), pp. 101–25, argues that the Spanish had a common view of the Indian in spite of their knowledge of different tribes and in spite of their own diverse interests and occupations.

14. Keen, *Aztec Image in Western Thought*, chap. 2.

15. Quoted in Lewis Hanke, *The First Social Experiments in America: A Study in the Development of Spanish Indian Policy in the Sixteenth Century* (Cambridge: Harvard University Press, 1935), p. 20.

16. Quoted in Lewis Hanke, *All Mankind Is One: A Study of the Disputation Between Bartolomé de Las Casas and Juan Ginés de Sepúlveda in 1550 on the Intellectual and Religious Capacity of the American Indians* (DeKalb: Northern Illinois University Press, 1974), p. 85. On the whole debate, see, in addition to this and the book by Hanke cited in the previous note, two other books by the same author, *The Spanish Struggle for Justice in the Conquest of America* (Philadelphia: University of Pennsylvania Press, 1949), and *Aristotle and the American Indians: A Study in Race Prejudice in the Modern World* (London: Hollis and Carter, 1959); plus Keen, *Aztec Image in Western Thought*, chaps. 4–5; Juan Friede and Benjamin Keen, eds., *Bartolomé de Las Casas: Toward an Understanding of the Man and His Work* (DeKalb: Northern Illinois University Press, 1971). Las Casas' own treatise in the debate has been translated and annotated by Stafford Poole under the title *In Defense of the Indians: The Defense of the Most Reverend Lord, Don Fray Bartolomé de Las Casas, of the order of Preachers, Late Bishop of Chiapa, Against the Persecutors and Slanderers of the Peoples of the New World Discovered Across the Seas* (DeKalb: Northern Illinois University Press, 1974).

17. Early French thought on Native Americans may be followed in Gilbert Chinard, *L'exotisme américain dans la littérature française au XVIᵉ siècle* (Paris: Hachette, 1911); Geoffrey Atkinson, *Les nouveaux horizons de la renaissance française* (Paris: E. Droz, 1935); Cornelius J. Jaenen, *Friend and Foe: Aspects of French-Amerindian Cultural Contact in the Sixteenth and Seventeenth Centuries* (New York: Columbia University Press, 1976), chap. 1, and *passim*. Early English imagery may be found in Robert R. Cawley, *The Voyagers and Elizabethan Drama* (Boston: D.C. Heath and Co., 1938), pp. 344–95; Blanke, *Amerika in Englische Schriftum*, pp. 186–282; Gary B. Nash, "The Image of the Indian in the Southern Colonial Mind," in Edward Dudley and Maximilian E. Novak, eds., *The Wild Man Within: An Image in Western Thought from the Renaissance to Romanticism* (Pittsburgh: University of Pittsburgh Press, 1972), pp. 55–86.

18. In Richard Hakluyt's translation, *The Principal Navigations, Voyages, Traffiques, and Discoveries of the English Nation* (Glasgow: James MacLehose and Sons, 1903–1905), vol. 8, pp. 201–2.

19. Compare my interpretation with that of Frances Jennings, *The Invasion of America: Indians, Colonialism, and the Cant of Conquest* (Chapel Hill: University of North Carolina Press, 1975), pp. 73–79.

20. Richard Bernheimer, *Wild Men in the Middle Ages: A Study in Art, Sentiment, and Demonology* (Cambridge: Harvard University Press, 1952), pp. 19–20. In addition to this authority, see the interesting essay by Hayden White, "The Forms of Wildness: Archaeology of an Idea," in Dudley and Novak, eds., *Wild Man Within*, pp. 3–38.

21. In the translation of Thomas Hackett of André Thévet, *The New Found World, or Anarcticke* (London: Henrie Bynneman for author, 1568), fol. 26. According to Samuel E. Morison, *The European Discovery of America: The Northern Voyages, A.D. 500–1600* (New York: Oxford University

Press, 1971), p. 428, the French in the early period always called Indians *sauvages*, later used *peaux rouges* and sometimes *indigènes*.

22. *Encyclopédie, ou dictionnaire raisonné des sciences, des artes et des métiers, par une société de gens de lettres*, vol. 14 (Neufchâtel: Samuel Faulches, 1765), p. 729.

23. For the actual translations, see Arber, *First Three English Books*. On Eden, consult Franklin T. McCann, *English Discovery of America to 1585* (New York: King's Crown Press, 1952), pp. 112–37; Parker, *Books to Build an Empire*, pp. 36–53.

24. A standard modern edition is the twelve-volume one issued in Glasgow and cited in note 18. Vols. 7–11 reprint the original third volume, on America.

25. See, for example, the accounts of Ralph Lane and John White in David B. Quinn, ed., *The Roanoke Voyages, 1584–1590: Documents to Illustrate the English Voyages to North America Under the Patent Granted to Walter Raleigh in 1584* (London: Hakluyt Society, 1955), series 2, vols. 104–105, pp. 255–94, 598–622; and of George Percy in Philip L. Barbour, ed., *The Jamestown Voyages Under the First Charter, 1606–1609* (Cambridge, Eng.: Cambridge University Press for Hakluyt Society, 1969), series 2, vol. 136, pp. 129–46.

26. For example, John Davis's account of his second voyage in Hakluyt, *Principal Navigations*, vol. 7, pp. 393–407; and Arthur Barlowe and Thomas Hariot in Quinn, ed., *Roanoke Voyages*, pp. 91–115, 368–82.

27. Smith provides a detailed political geography of the region in his tracts of 1608 and 1612, which are edited by Barbour in his *Jamestown Voyages*, vol. 136, pp. 165–208, vol. 137, pp. 327–464.

28. The second part of William Wood, *New Englands Prospect, A True, Lively, and Experimental Description of That Part of America, Commonly Called New England*, originally published in London in 1634 (facsimile, Amsterdam and New York: Theatrum Orbis Terrarum, Ltd., and Da Capo Press, 1968), presents an early description of New England tribes comparable to the above-mentioned works of Smith.

29. Edited by John Teunissen and Evelyn J. Hinz (Detroit: Wayne State University Press, 1973), pp. 84–85.

30. See dated definitions of "nation" in *The Oxford English Dictionary*, vol. 7 (London: Oxford University Press, 1933), pp. 30–31. Compare the somewhat comparable argument for calling chiefs *kings* of Jennings, *Invasion of America*, pp. 114–15.

31. According to John Rowe, "Ethnography and Ethnology in the Sixteenth Century," *Kroeber Anthropological Society Papers*, no. 30 (Berkeley, Calif., 1964), pp. 5–7. Also see W. R. Jones, "The Image of Barbarians in Medieval Europe," *Comparative Studies in Society and History*, XIII (Oct. 1971), pp. 376–401.

32. Gilbert Chinard in his pioneering *L'exotisme américain dans la littérature française au XVIᵉ siècle* concluded that early French descriptions of Indians could be classified as favorable or unfavorable in their estimate of Indian character, customs, and values.

33. Scholars who have studied accounts of English explorers in the sixteenth century or of settlers and travelers in the succeeding century generally

divide their analyses of Indian imagery into the two basic evaluations. In addition to the authorities on England cited in note 17 above, see Howard M. Jones, *O Strange New World; American Culture: The Formative Years* (New York: Viking, 1964), chaps. 1–2. Compare, however, the approach of Henry Bausum, "Edenic Images of the Western World: A Reappraisal," *South Atlantic Quarterly*, LXVII (Autumn 1968), pp. 672–87, with the one taken by me in this chapter.

34. Hakluyt, *Principal Voyages*, vol. 7, p. 227.

35. *Ibid.*, p. 220.

36. The quotations appear in *ibid.*, vol. 8, pp. 300, 305, 306, respectively.

37. Quoted in Quinn, ed., *Roanoke Voyages*, vol. 104, p. 108. The primitivistic imagery employed here is examined on pages 71–80.

38. Except for Jacques Le Moyne in Florida and Jean de Lery in Brazil according to the opinion of Paul Hulton and David Quinn, eds., *The American Drawings of John White, 1577–1590, with Drawings of European and Oriental Subjects* (London and Chapel Hill: Trustees of the British Museum and University of North Carolina Press, 1964), vol. 1, pp. 25–36. Also see the authorities cited in note 11 above.

39. The best collation of the various editions of the Hariot tract is by Quinn, ed., *The Roanoke Voyages*, vol. 104, pp. 317–87. The best reproduction of the White drawings is in Hulton and Quinn, cited in preceding note. The De Bry edition of Hariot's *Briefe and True Report* has been issued in facsimile by Dover Publications, Inc., of New York, 1972, with an introduction by Paul Hulton.

40. On English perceptions and conceptions, see Nash, "The Image of the Indian in the Southern Colonial Mind." Nancy O. Lurie, "Indian Cultural Adjustment to European Civilization," in James M. Smith, ed., *Seventeenth-Century America: Essays in Colonial History* (Chapel Hill: University of North Carolina Press, 1959), pp. 33–60, suggests Native American attitudes and approaches to the English. Nicholas P. Canny, "The Ideology of English Colonization: From Ireland to America," *William and Mary Quarterly*, XXX (Oct. 1973), pp. 575–98, treats the implications of earlier efforts at Irish colonization for New World settlement by the English.

41. Walter Cope to Lord Salisbury, August 12, 1607, in Barbour, ed., *Jamestown Voyages*, vol. 136, p. 110.

42. In *ibid.*, vol. 137, p. 354.

43. See again the references cited in note 27 above.

44. Alexander Whitaker, *Good Newes from Virginia* (London: Felix Kyngston for William Welby, 1613), pp. 24–27. A drastically edited version of the pamphlet was included by Samuel Purchas in his great travel collection, *Hakluytus Posthumus or Purchas His Pilgrimes*, 20 vols. (Glasgow: James MacLehose and Sons, 1905–1907), vol. 19, pp. 110–16.

45. Christopher Brooke, *A Poem on the Late Massacre in Virginia, With Particular Mention of Those Men of Note That Suffered in That Disaster* (London: G. Eld for Robert Mylbourne, 1622), pp. 22–23.

46. In "Virginia's Verger: Or a Discourse shewing the benefits which may grow to this kingdome from American English Plantations . . . ," in *Hakluytus Posthumus*, vol. 19, p. 231. Compare William Bradford's preconcep-

tion of the Indian as given in his *Of Plymouth Plantation, 1620–1647*, ed. Samuel E. Morison (New York: Alfred A. Knopf, 1952), pp. 25–26.

47. *Leviathan, Or the Matter, Forme, & Power of a Common-wealth Eccleasiasticall and Civill*, ed. Crawford B. MacPherson (Baltimore: Penguin Books, 1968), pp. 186, 187. His italics. The impact of descriptions of Indians and other primitive peoples on Hobbes's thought is suggested by Richard Ashcraft, "Leviathan Triumphant: Thomas Hobbes and the Politics of Wild Men," in Dudley and Novak, eds., *Wild Man Within*, pp. 141–81.

48. The quoted words are from *Two Treatises of Government*, ed. Peter Laslett (Cambridge, Eng.: Cambridge University Press, 1960), p. 319, and appear in a somewhat different context than suggested here. Arthur J. Slavin, "The American Principle from More to Locke," in Chiapelli *et al.*, eds., *First Images of America*, vol. 1, pp. 139–64, stresses the similarities between Locke and Hobbes in comparison to Thomas More.

49. Washburn, "The Meaning of 'Discovery,' " pp. 2–4.

50. Honour, *New Golden Land*, chap. 4, and *European Vision of America*, chaps. 6–9, covers allegorical representations of America in pictures and pageants during the period. A beginning reference for the changing conceptions and images of Europe is Denys Hay, *Europe—The Emergence of an Idea* (Edinburgh: Edinburgh University Press, 1957). White self-references in relation to Blacks are covered by Winthrop Jordan, *White Over Black: American Attitudes Toward the Negro, 1550–1812* (Chapel Hill: University of North Carolina Press, 1968), pp. 93–95.

51. Leo Marx, *The Machine in the Garden: Technology and the Pastoral Ideal in America* (New York: Oxford University Press, 1964), pp. 34–72, treats Shakespearian New World imagery. Cumberland Clark, *Shakespeare and National Character: A Study of Shakespeare's Knowledge and Dramatic and Literary Use of the Distinctive Racial Characteristics of Different Peoples of the World* (London: Hamlin Publishing Co., 1932), provides a cursory introduction to the topic of its title, while Eldred D. Jones, *Othello's Countrymen: The African in English Renaissance Drama* (London: Oxford University Press for the University of Sierra Leone, 1965), offers material for comparison with Indian imagery.

William C. Sturtevant of the Smithsonian Institution suggests in a personal communication that the introduction of a new distinction at a level intermediate between all humans in general and specific nations and ethnic groups need not result in stereotyping and serves a useful taxonomic purpose if such labels are used carefully.

52. Similar White treatment of other peoples they considered primitive is covered in Katherine George, "The Civilized West Looks at Primitive Africa, 1400–1800," *Isis*, XLIX (March 1958), pp. 62–72. On the other hand, I agree with Jordan, *White Over Black*, pp. 239–52, that European conceptions of the African and the Indian differed in some fundamental aspects, particularly in regard to color symbolism.

The tawny or red hue of the Indian, although remarked by Europeans, did not arouse the intrinsic prejudice in White minds that the blackness of the Africans did, with its suggestion of evil and impurity. In fact, most observers of this period thought that Indian children were born white and turned red as they grew. For this reason, I have not attached special significance to the appellation *Red Skin*. Surely it was a name Whites commonly gave Native Americans, but it did not carry, in my opinion, the immense symbolic weight that Black did for Afro-Americans, nor did it possess a significance different from other terms applied by Whites to the Indian.

53. Rowe, "Ethnography and Ethnology in the Sixteenth Century," excepts Juan de Lery from this generalization, and perhaps John White's drawings should be excepted also.

54. For instance, John Adair, *The History of the American Indians* (London: Edward and Charles Dilly, 1775).

55. This is also the main point of T. D. Stewart and Marshall T. Newman, "An Historical Résumé of the Concept of Differences in Indian Types," *American Anthropologist*, LIII (Jan.–March 1951), pp. 19–36, and D'Arcy McNickle, "American Indians Who Never Were," *Indian Historian*, III (Jan. 1970), pp. 4–7.

56. For example, Maurice M. Wasserman, "The American Indian as Seen by Seventeenth Century Chroniclers" (Unpub. Ph.D. dissertation, University of Pennsylvania, 1954); Richard Slotkin, *Regeneration Through Violence: The Mythology of the American Frontier, 1600–1860* (Middletown, Conn.: Wesleyan University Press, 1973), particularly pp. 42–56.

57. This was true of European descriptions of other cultures and societies as well, particularly Africa. In addition to George, "The Civilized West Looks at Primitive Africa," and Jordan, *White Over Black*, see Margaret T. Hodgen, *Early Anthropology in the Sixteenth and Seventeenth Centuries* (Philadelphia: University of Pennsylvania Press, 1964), especially pp. 194–201, and Richard G. Cole, "Sixteenth-Century Travel Books as a Source of European Attitudes Toward Non-White and Non-Western Culture," *Proceedings of the American Philosophical Society*, CXVI (Feb. 1972), pp. 59–67.

58. The point of Murray L. Wax and Rosalie H. Wax, "Cultural Deprivation as an Educational Ideology," *Journal of American Indian Education*, III (Jan. 1964), pp. 15–18.

59. Roy H. Pearce, *Savagism and Civilization: A Study of the Indian and the American Mind* (2nd ed., Baltimore: Johns Hopkins University Press, 1965).

60. A basic approach of Bernard Sheehan, *Seeds of Extinction: Jeffersonian Philanthropy and the American Indian* (Chapel Hill: University of North Carolina Press, 1973).

61. As argued by James G. Meade, "The 'Westerns' of the East: Narratives of Indian Captivity from Jeremiad to Gothic Novel" (Unpub. Ph.D. dissertation, Northwestern University, 1971); Neal Salisbury, "Conquest of the 'Savage': Puritan Missionaries and Indians, 1620–1680" (Unpub. Ph.D. dissertation, University of California at Los Angeles, 1972); and Slotkin, *Regeneration Through Violence*. A variant version of this argument for the later period appears in Michael P. Rogin, *Fathers and Children: Andrew Jackson and the Subjugation of the American Indian* (New York: Alfred A. Knopf, 1975).

62. These basic positions are generally designated by authors as the noble and ignoble, good and bad, or favorable and unfavorable images for short. In addition to Chinard, *L'exotisme américain*; Cawley, *Voyagers and Elizabethan*

Drama; Blanke, *Amerika in Englischen Schriftum;* and Jones, *O Strange New World* already cited on this theme, see among many other books organized along these same lines or drawing the same conclusion: John H. Kennedy, *Jesuit and Savage in New France* (New Haven: Yale University Press, 1950); George E. Jones, "The American Indian in the American Novel (1875–1950)" (Unpub. Ph.D. dissertation, New York University, 1958); Pearce, *Savagism and Civilization;* Lewis O. Saum, *The Fur Trader and the Indian* (Seattle: University of Washington Press, 1965); Priscilla Shames, "The Long Hope: A Study of American Indian Stereotypes in American Popular Fiction, 1890–1950" (Unpub. Ph.D. dissertation, University of California at Los Angeles, 1969); Louise K. Barnett, *The Ignoble Savage: American Literary Racism, 1790–1890* (Westport: Greenwood, 1975), chap. 3; Sheehan, *Seeds of Extinction.* Two anthologies based on the same principle are Jack D. Forbes, ed., *The Indian in America's Past* (Englewood Cliffs, N.J.: Prentice-Hall, 1964), and Giuliano Gliozzi, *La scoperta dei selvaggi: anthropologia e colonialisme da Columbo a Diderot* (Milan: Principato, 1971).

63. Murray Wax condemns modern anthropology textbooks for this approach in a brief review article, "The White Man's Burdensome Business," *Social Problems,* XVI (Summer 1968), pp. 106–13.

64. A question repeatedly asked in Rupert Costo, ed., and Jeannette Henry, *Textbooks and the American Indian* (San Francisco: Indian Historian Press, 1970).

65. The special theme of Brian W. Dippie, "The Vanishing American: Popular Attitudes and American Indian Policy in the Nineteenth Century (Unpub. Ph.D. dissertation, University of Texas, 1970), but also see Sheehan, *Seeds of Extinction,* and Pearce, *Savagism and Civilization.*

66. With the possible exception of Keen, *Aztec Image in Western Thought,* and the portions devoted to the Indian in Dwight W. Hoover, *The Red and the Black* (Chicago: Rand McNally, 1976), which appeared after my initial draft of this book.

PART TWO

1. As a result of this problem, historians of anthropology trace the beginnings of their subject to quite different periods. For varying opinions about the beginnings of anthropology arranged approximately in order of their dating, see among others Annemarie de Waal Malefijt, *Images of Man: A History of Anthropological Thought* (New York: Alfred A. Knopf, 1974); Margaret T. Hodgen, *Early Anthropology in the Sixteenth and Seventeenth Centuries* (Philadelphia: University of Pennsylvania Press, 1964); John H. Rowe, "The Renaissance Foundations of Anthropology," *American Anthropologist,* LXVII (Feb. 1965), pp. 1–20; Fred W. Voget, *A History of Ethnology* (New York: Holt, Rinehart and Winston, 1975); Paul Honigsheim, "The Philosophical Background of European Anthropology," *American Anthropologist,* XLIV (July–Sept. 1942), pp. 376–87; Marvin Harris, *The Rise of Anthropological*

Theory: A History of Theories of Culture (New York: Thomas Y. Crowell Co., 1968), pp. 8–52; Robert H. Lowie, *The History of Ethnological Theory* (New York: Rinehart and Co., 1937); H. R. Hays, *From Ape to Angel: An Informal History of Social Anthropology* (New York: Alfred A. Knopf, 1965); Regna Darnell, *Readings in the History of Anthropology* (New York: Harper & Row, 1974), esp. pp. 11–18, 169–79. Compare Sol Tax, "From Lafitau to Radcliffe-Brown. A Short History of the Study of Social Organization," in Fred Eggan, ed., *Social Anthropology of North American Indian Tribes* (2nd ed., Chicago: University of Chicago Press, 1955), pp. 445–81.

2. Arriving at the same conclusion for different eras are Paul Honigsheim, "The American Indian in the Philosophy of the Enlightenment," *Osiris*, X (1952), pp. 91–108; Benjamin Keen, *The Aztec Image in Western Thought* (New Brunswick, N.J.: Rutgers University Press, 1971), pp. 252–57; Robert E. Bieder, "The American Indian and the Development of Anthropological Thought in the United States, 1780–1851" (Unpub. Ph.D. dissertation, University of Minnesota, 1972), pp. 419–20. For the earlier period, see Geoffrey Atkinson, *Les nouveaux horizons de la renaissance française* (Paris: E. Droz, 1935).

3. Thus I agree with Winthrop Jordan, *White Over Black: American Attitudes Toward the Negro, 1550–1812* (Chapel Hill: University of North Carolina Press, 1968), in his oft-stated position on this point.

4. The best authorities upon speculation about Indian origins in the early period are Lee E. Huddleston, *Origins of the American Indians: European Concepts, 1492–1729* (Austin: University of Texas Press, 1967); Hodgen, *Early Anthropology*, pp. 207–53; Don C. Allen, *The Legend of Noah: Renaissance Rationalism in Art, Science, and Letters*, Illinois Studies in Language and Literature, XXXIII (1949), nos. 3–4; Maurice M. Wasserman, "The American Indian as Seen by Seventeenth Century Chroniclers" (Unpub. Ph.D. dissertation, University of Pennsylvania, 1954), pp. 456–68.

5. The conclusion of Huddleston, *Origins of the American Indians.*

6. Quoted in Roy H. Pearce, *Savagism and Civilization: A Study of the Indian and the American Mind* (2nd ed., Baltimore: Johns Hopkins University Press, 1965), p. 29.

7. John J. Teunissen and Evelyn J. Hinz, eds., *A Key into the Language of America* (Detroit: Wayne State University Press, 1973), p. 200.

8. Hodgen, *Early Anthropology*, chap. 7, summarizes thinking on diffusion, degeneration, and environmentalism in this period.

9. For the example of Henry Rowe Schoolcraft in the nineteenth century, see Bieder, "The American Indian and the Development of Anthropological Thought," pp. 230, 237–39, 250, and in general, John F. Freeman, "Religion and Personality in the Anthropology of Henry Schoolcraft," *Journal of the History of the Behavioral Sciences*, I (Jan. 1965), pp. 301–12.

10. How religious commitment informed the works of a leader in English anthropology during the first half of the nineteenth century can be seen from the excellent analysis of George W. Stocking, Jr., in his introduction to James Cowles Prichard, *Researches into the Physical History of Man* (Chicago: University of Chicago Press, 1973), pp. xxxiii–c.

The question of Indian origins remains to this day an intriguing problem to scholars and lay persons alike. Proposed solutions over the centuries since 1700 can be followed in Arthur R. Buntin, "The Indian in American Literature, 1680–1760" (Unpub. Ph.D. dissertation, University of Washington, 1961), pp. 354–61; Daniel J. Boorstin, *The Lost World of Thomas Jefferson* (New York: Henry Holt and Co., 1948), pp. 68–80; Bernard Sheehan, *Seeds of Extinction: Jeffersonian Philanthropy and the American Indian* (Chapel Hill: University of North Carolina Press, 1973), pp. 45–65; Samuel F. Haven, "Archaeology of the United States, or Sketches, Historical and Bibliographical, of the Progress of Information and Opinion Respecting Vestiges of Antiquity in the United States," *Smithsonian Contributions to Knowledge*, VIII (Washington, D.C., 1856); Justin Winsor, "The Progress of Opinion Respecting the Origin and Antiquity of Man in America," in Winsor, ed., *Narrative and Critical History of America* (Boston and New York: Houghton Mifflin, 1889), pp. 369–412; John S. Haller, Jr., *Outcasts from Evolution: Scientific Attitudes of Racial Inferiority, 1859–1900* (Urbana: University of Illinois Press, 1971), pp. 69–94; Robert Wauchope, *Lost Tribes and Sunken Continents: Myth and Method in the Study of American Indians* (Chicago: University of Chicago Press, 1962).

11. A good general history of environmental theory to 1800 is Clarence J. Glacken, *Traces on the Rhodian Shore: Nature and Culture in Western Thought from Ancient Times to the End of the Eighteenth Century* (Berkeley: University of California Press, 1967). Such thinking in the new United States is covered by Sheehan, *Seeds of Extinction*, pp. 1–44; Pearce, *Savagism and Civilization*, esp. pp. 76–104; and Bieder, "The American Indian and Anthropological Thought," pp. 1–22.

12. Gladys Bryson, *Man and Society: The Scottish Inquiry of the Eighteenth Century* (Princeton: Princeton University Press, 1945), analyzes the general assumptions of the period.

13. Carl von Linné, *Systema naturae per regna tria naturae* (10th ed., Holmiae: Laurentie Salvie, 1758), vol. 1, p. 21. Compare the translations in Earl W. Count, ed., *This Is Race: An Anthology Selected from the International Literature on the Races of Man* (New York: Henry Schuman, 1950), p. 356, and James S. Slotkin, ed., *Readings in the History of Early Anthropology*, Viking Fund Publications (New York: Wenner-Gren Foundation, 1965), p. 177.

14. Noah Webster, *An American Dictionary of the English Language* (New York: S. Converse, 1828), vol. 2, sig. 77, p. 3, col. 1. On the concept of species in the eighteenth century, see appropriate essays in Bentley Glass, Owsei Temkin, and William L. Straus, Jr., eds., *Forerunners of Darwin, 1745–1859* (Baltimore: Johns Hopkins University Press, 1959); and John C. Greene, *The Death of Adam: Evolution and Its Impact on Western Thought* (Ames: Iowa State University Press, 1959), pp. 129–74.

15. Edited by Winthrop Jordan (Cambridge: Harvard University Press, 1965), pp. 149–50.

16. *Ibid.*, p. 215.

17. Quoted in Jordan, *White Over Black*, p. 287.

18. Quoted in Antonello Gerbi, *The Dispute of the New World: The History of a Polemic, 1750–1900*, trans. Jeremy Moyle (Pittsburgh: University

of Pittsburgh Press, 1973), p. 261. On actions as well as ideas, see among many Jordan, *White Over Black*, pp. 429–541; Frederick M. Binder, *The Color Problem in Early National America as Viewed by John Adams, Jefferson, and Jackson* (The Hague: Mouton, 1968), pp. 83–119.

19. Quoted in Gilbert Chinard, "Eighteenth Century Theories on America as Human Habitat," *Proceedings of the American Philosophical Society*, XCI (Feb. 1947), p. 31. The whole debate is the subject of Gerbi's book cited in preceding note, but see also the Chinard article just cited and Sheehan, *Seeds of Extinction*, pp. 66–68. Keen, *Aztec Image in Western Thought*, pp. 249–309, treats the dispute in relation to the Aztecs. On Buffon's anthropology, see Michele Duchet, *Anthropologie et histoire au siècle des lumières* (Paris: François Maspero, 1971), pp. 229–80.

20. Edited by William Peden (Chapel Hill: University of North Carolina Press, 1955), esp. pp. 58–64, but see also pp. 199–202 for Charles Thomson's commentary. Compare pp. 92–107. Ralph N. Miller, "American Nationalism as a Theory of Nature," *William and Mary Quarterly*, XII (Jan. 1955), pp. 74–95, discusses other American writers and thinkers refuting the degenerationist argument.

21. Compare the argument of Richard Popkin, "The Philosophical Basis of Eighteenth-Century Racism," in Harold E. Pagliaro, ed., *Racism in the Eighteenth Century, Studies in Eighteenth-Century Culture*, III (Cleveland: Case Western Reserve University Press, 1973), pp. 245–62.

22. In addition to Bryson, *Man and Society*, on the general intellectual background of this period in relation to the "social sciences," consult also Ronald V. Sampson, *Progress in the Age of Reason: The Seventeenth Century to the Present Day* (Cambridge: Harvard University Press, 1956); and Peter Gay, *The Enlightenment: An Interpretation*, 2 vols. (New York: Alfred A. Knopf, 1966–1969).

23. I conclude this from the survey of Honigsheim, "The American Indian in the Philosophy of the Enlightenment," but see Edna Lemay, "L'Amérique et l'enfance des sociétés dans l'ouvrage de Jean-Nicolas Démeunier, précurseur au XVIIIe siècle de l'anthropologie sociale en France," *Cahiers des Amériques Latines*, V (Jan.–June 1970), pp. 75–90.

24. As translated by Hodgen, *Early Anthropology*, p. 348.

25. Frank E. Manuel, *The Eighteenth Century Confronts Its Gods* (Cambridge: Harvard University Press, 1959), covers the development of comparative religious studies at the time.

26. Quoted in John W. Burrow, *Evolution and Society: A Study in Victorian Social Theory* (Cambridge, Eng.: Cambridge University Press, 1966), p. 12.

27. Keen, *Aztec Image in Western Thought*, pp. 94, 112, 182. Compare John H. Rowe, "Ethnography and Ethnology in the Sixteenth Century," *Kroeber Anthropological Society Papers*, no. 30 (Berkeley, Calif., 1964), pp. 1–19, for Acosta.

28. Both Lemay, "L'Amérique et l'enfance des sociétés dans l'ouvrage de Jean-Nicolas Démeunier," and Ronald L. Meek, *Social Science and the Ignoble Savage* (Cambridge, Eng.: Cambridge University Press, 1976), argue

the importance of the idea of the American Indian in eighteenth-century social theorists' formulation of the conception of societal stages and development.

29. William Robertson, *The History of America* (London: Printed for W. Strahan, T. Cadell, and J. Balfour, 1777), vol. 1, pp. 282–83. In general, see E. Adamson Hoebel, "William Robertson: An 18th Century Anthropologist-Historian," *American Anthropologist*, LXII (Aug. 1960), pp. 648–55.

30. See again on Jefferson, Binder, *Color Problem*, pp. 82–119. Compare his friend Benjamin Rush's philosophy as delineated by Stephen Kunitz, "Benjamin Rush on Savagism and Progress," *Ethnohistory*, XVII (Winter–Spring 1970), pp. 31–42.

31. Compare Duchet, *Anthropologie et histoire au siècle des lumières*. For primitivism in European thought, see pages 71–80.

32. I therefore question some of the interpretation of Fred Voget, "Progress, Science, History and Evolution in Eighteenth and Nineteenth Century Anthropology," *Journal of the History of Behavioral Sciences*, III (Apr. 1967), pp. 132–55, but see his "Anthropology in the Age of the Enlightenment: Progress and Utopian Functionalism," *Southwestern Journal of Anthropology*, XXIV (Winter 1968), pp. 321–45, for a more ambiguous view of the matter. Stow Persons, "The Cyclical Theory of History in Eighteenth Century America," *American Quarterly*, VI, no. 2 (Summer 1954), pp. 147–63, clarifies the relation between cyclic and progressive views of history in the thinking of the period.

33. Bieder, "The American Indian and the Development of Anthropological Thought," sees this continuance of older ideas of progress and even degeneration as a major theme of the period he covers. Compare Sheehan, *Seeds of Extinction*, for a similar interpretation.

34. Greene, *Death of Adam*, provides a good guide to the development of evolutionary theories in the various sciences during the nineteenth century.

35. George W. Stocking, Jr., "American Social Scientists and Race Theory: 1890–1915" (Unpub. Ph.D. dissertation, University of Pennsylvania, 1960), chap. 3, outlines the history of the changing idea of species in relation to heredity and environmental change during the nineteenth century.

36. Changing conceptions of time and the earth's age are the subject of Stephen Goodfield and June Goodfield, *The Discovery of Time* (New York: Harper & Row, 1965), pp. 141–246; Francis C. Haber, *The Age of the World: Moses to Darwin* (Baltimore: Johns Hopkins University Press, 1959); Jacob Gruber, "Brixham Cave and the Antiquity of Man," in Melford E. Spiro, ed., *Context and Meaning in Cultural Anthropology* (New York: Free Press, 1965), pp. 373–402.

37. Edward B. Tylor, *Primitive Culture: Researches into the Development of Mythology, Philosophy, Religion, Art and Custom* (London: John Murray, 1871), vol. 1, p. 28.

38. In general: Idus L. Murphree, "The Evolutionary Anthropologists: The Progress of Mankind. The Concepts of Progress and Culture in the Thought of John Lubbock, Edward B. Tylor, and Lewis H. Morgan," *Proceedings of the American Philosophical Society*, CV (June 1961), pp. 265–300; Burrow, *Evolution and Society*. Compare Voget, "Progress, Science, History and Evolution," and Harris, *Rise of Anthropological Theory*, pp. 108–209.

George W. Stocking, Jr., "Some Problems in the Understanding of Nineteenth Century Cultural Evolutionism," in Darnell, *Readings in the History of Anthropology*, pp. 407–25, raises some important issues for the study of evolutionary thought.

39. Rochester: Sage and Brother, Publishers, 1851, p. ix. On Morgan as an individual and as an anthropologist, see Bernard J. Stern, *Lewis Henry Morgan: Social Evolutionist* (Chicago: University of Chicago Press, 1931); Carl Resek, *Lewis Henry Morgan: American Scholar* (Chicago: University of Chicago Press, 1960); and Bieder, "The American Indian and the Development of Anthropological Thought," pp. 367–410.

40. Edited by Leslie White (Cambridge: Harvard University Press, 1964), p. 41.

41. See especially, *ibid.*, pp. 6–7. Compare John Wesley Powell, founder of the Bureau of American Ethnology, as quoted in William C. Darrah, *Powell of Colorado* (Princeton: Princeton University Press, 1957), pp. 255–56. The wider implications of the idea of the vanishing Indian and other primitive peoples for the development of anthropology is suggested by Jacob Gruber, "Ethnographic Salvage and the Shaping of Anthropology," *American Anthropologist*, LXXII (Dec. 1970), pp. 1289–99.

42. Some mention of these new departments may be found in John F. Freeman, "University Anthropology: Early Departments in the United States," *Kroeber Anthropological Society Papers*, no. 32 (Berkeley, Calif., 1965), pp. 78–90.

43. Darrah, *Powell of Colorado*, pp. 255–69; Regna Darnell, "The Development of American Anthropology, 1879–1920: From the Bureau of American Ethnology to Franz Boas" (Unpub. Ph.D. dissertation, University of Pennsylvania, 1969), pp. 1–139; and Curtis M. Hinsley, Jr., "The Development of a Profession: Anthropology in Washington, D.C., 1846–1903" (Unpub. Ph.D. dissertation, University of Wisconsin, 1976), all stress the importance of evolutionary ideas to Powell and others in the Bureau of American Ethnology, but Hinsley suggests some of the variants on the idea among the scholars and even points to some who questioned the whole approach.

44. On racial assumptions of evolutionary anthropologists, see in particular, Harris, *Rise of Anthropological Theory*, pp. 108–41, but also Stocking, "American Social Scientists and Race Theory," pp. 419–68, esp. pp. 443–48, Murphree, "The Evolutionary Anthropologists," and Voget, "Progress, Science, History and Evolution," pp. 143–45.

45. Eric Voegelin, "The Growth of the Race Idea," *Review of Politics*, II (July 1940), pp. 283–317; Dante Puzzo, "Racism and the Western Tradition," *Journal of the History of Ideas*, XXV (Oct.–Dec. 1964), pp. 579–86; and Stocking, "American Social Scientists and Race Theory," and *Race, Culture, and Evolution: Essays on the History of Anthropology* (New York: Free Press, 1968), offer three different views on these issues. Count, *This Is Race*, is a good anthology on racial thought from the eighteenth century to the present.

46. What we know of the etymology of the word *race* is summarized by Stocking, "American Social Scientists and Race Theory," pp. 24–27.

47. T. Bendysshe, "The History of Anthropology," *Memoirs Read Before the Anthropological Society of London*, I (1863–64), pp. 335–458, is still the

standard authority on the history of polygenetic thinking in the early period, but see also Marcel Bataillon, "L'unité du genre humain," in *Mélanges à la mémoire de Jean Sarrailh* (Paris: Centre de Recherches de l'Institut d'Études Hispaniques, 1966), vol. 1, pp. 75–95. Stocking particularly stresses the influence of polygenetic assumptions in what he calls the "dark ages" of the writing of the history of anthropology. See his *Race, Culture, and Evolution, passim,* but especially chap. 3. He argues the relation of ethnology, polygenism, and evolutionism as paradigms of anthropological thought in this period in his introduction to Prichard, *Researches into the Physical History of Man,* pp. c–cx. William Stanton, *The Leopard's Spots: Scientific Attitudes Toward Race in America, 1815–59* (Chicago: University of Chicago Press, 1960), of necessity must treat polygenism in the period of his topic.

48. In general for these developments, see in addition to Stocking and Stanton cited in the preceding note, Greene, *Death of Adam,* pp. 175–248; Harris, *Rise of Anthropological Theory,* pp. 80–141; Haller, *Outcasts from Evolution;* Thomas F. Gossett, *Race: The History of an Idea in America* (Dallas: Southern Methodist University Press, 1963), pp. 32–83; Christine Bolt, *Victorian Attitudes to Race* (London: Routledge and Kegan Paul, 1971).

49. James S. Slotkin, "Racial Classifications of the Seventeenth and Eighteenth Centuries," Wisconsin Academy of Sciences, Arts and Letters, *Transactions,* XXXVI (1944), pp. 459–60; Hodgen, *Early Anthropology,* pp. 418–25.

50. Slotkin, "Racial Classifications," pp. 461–66; Greene, *Death of Adam,* pp. 31–41.

51. On general developments in physical anthropology and raciology: John G. Burke, "The Wild Man's Pedigree: Scientific Method and Racial Anthropology," in Edward Dudley and Maximilian E. Novak, eds., *The Wild Man Within: An Image in Western Thought from the Renaissance to Romanticism* (Pittsburgh: University of Pittsburgh Press, 1972), pp. 259–307; Herbert H. Odom, "Generalizations on Race in Nineteenth-Century Physical Anthropology," *Isis,* LVIII (Spring 1967), pp. 5–18. For such developments in American anthropology: A. Irving Hallowell, "The Beginnings of Anthropology in America," in Frederica de Laguna, ed., *Selected Papers from the American Anthropologist, 1888–1920* (Evanston: Row, Peterson & Co., pp. 58–73; Aleš Hrdlička, "Physical Anthropology in America: A Sketch," *American Anthropologist,* XVI (Oct.–Dec. 1914), pp. 508–54, reprinted in *ibid,* pp. 310–56.

52. Josiah Nott and George R. Gliddon, *Types of Mankind; Or, Ethnological Researches Based Upon the Ancient Monuments, Paintings, Sculptures, and Crania of Races* (6th ed., Philadelphia: Lippincott, Grambo and Co., 1854), p. 461.

53. On the American School and racism in general: Stanton, *Leopard's Spots.* Compare George Frederickson's view in *The Black Image in the White Mind: The Debate on Afro-American Character and Destiny, 1817–1914* (New York: Harper & Row, 1971), chap. 3, that such raciology had important origins in and implications for justifying racial discrimination. On application to Indians in particular, Reginald Horsman, "Scientific Racism and the American Indian in the Mid-Nineteenth Century," *American Quarterly,* XXVII (May 1975), pp. 152–68.

54. The point of Harris, *Rise of Anthropological Theory*, pp. 121, 138, about the two men.

55. Harris, *Rise of Anthropological Theory*, and Haller, *Outcasts from Evolution*, present this view with the strongest thrust, but see Stocking, *Race, Culture, and Evolution*, pp. 110–32. Stocking wants greater discrimination among evolutionary viewpoints to determine more exactly their relationship to racial thinking, "Some Problems in . . . Cultural Evolutionism."

56. New York: N. D. C. Hodges, 1890. The following quotations appear on pp. 18, 51–52, 248, respectively.

57. 2 vols., Bulletin 30 (Washington, D.C.: Government Printing Office, 1907–10). Contrast, however, the article on "Psychology" by Clark Wissler, vol. 1, pp. 311–13.

58. On the later history of the idea, Gossett, *Race*, pp. 339–430.

59. In general on this school: introduction to George W. Stocking, Jr., ed., *The Shaping of American Anthropology, 1883–1911: A Franz Boas Reader* (New York: Basic Books, 1974), pp. 1–20; Stocking, *Race, Culture, and Evolution*, pp. 133–233; Darnell, "Development of American Anthropology"; Harris, *Rise of Anthropological Theory*, pp. 250–372; Charles Erasmus, *Las dimensiones de la cultura: historia de la ethnologie en los Estados Unidos entre 1900 y 1950* (Bogotá, Colombia: Editorial Iqueima, 1953); Robert H. Lowie, *The History of Ethnological Theory* (New York: Rinehart and Co., 1937), pp. 128–55; Panchanana Mitra, *A History of American Anthropology* (Calcutta: University of Calcutta, 1933), pp. 163–82; Voget, *A History of Ethnology*, chaps. 9–12.

60. See the dated definitions in Alfred L. Kroeber and Clyde Kluckhohn, *Culture: A Critical Review of Concepts and Definitions*, Papers of the Peabody Museum of American Archaeology and Ethnology, XLVII, no. 1 (Cambridge: Harvard University Press, 1952).

61. On this point see Stocking, *Race, Culture, and Evolution*, pp. 195–233; Stocking, *Shaping of American Anthropology*, pp. 1–20; Darnell, "Development of American Anthropology." Compare Fred W. Voget, "Man and Culture: An Essay in Changing Anthropological Interpretation," *American Anthropologist*, LXII (Dec. 1960), pp. 946–49. Whether Boas understood the culture concept in the fully modern sense is questioned by Joan Mark, "Frank Hamilton Cushing and an American Science of Anthropology," *Perspectives in American History*, X (1976), pp. 466–74. She argues that although Boas conceived of culture in the plural he never appreciated cultures as integral wholes and that others such as Cushing must be given credit for developing this aspect of the conception as early as the 1890s. She does agree, however, that Boas's students revived this meaning of the concept of culture in the 1920s.

62. On this phrase and its larger intellectual context, F. H. Matthews, "The Revolt Against Americanism: Cultural Pluralism and Cultural Relativism as an Ideology of Liberation," *Canadian Review of American Studies*, I (Spring 1970), pp. 4–31; James H. Powell, "The Concept of Cultural Pluralism in American Social Thought, 1915–1965" (Unpub. Ph.D. dissertation, University of Notre Dame, 1971); J. H. Moore, "The Culture Concept as Ideology," *American Ethnologist*, I (Sept. 1974), pp. 537–49; John Higham, *Send*

These to Me: Jews and Other Immigrants in Urban America (New York: Atheneum, 1975), chap. 10.

63. In his article, "The Superorganic," *American Anthropologist,* XIX (Apr.–June 1917), pp. 163–213.

64. The assumptions of the method are described in Alfred L. Kroeber, "The Culture-Area and Age-Area Concepts of Clark Wissler," in Stuart A. Rice, ed., *Methods in Social Science* (Chicago: University of Chicago Press, 1931), pp. 248–65.

65. Clark Wissler, *The American Indian: An Introduction to the Anthropology of the New World* (New York: Douglas McMurtrie, 1917), p. 334.

66. How Benedict tried to combine scientific objectives with humanistic concerns in this book as well as her own life is the subject of Judith Modell, "Ruth Benedict, Anthropologist: The Reconciliation of Science and Humanism," in Timothy Thoreson, ed., *Toward a Science of Man: Essays in the History of Anthropology* (The Hague: Mouton, 1975), pp. 199–202.

67. Cited in note 60 above. Compare another attempt to clarify the concept of culture at the same time, David Bidney, *Theoretical Anthropology* (New York: Columbia University Press, 1953).

68. Recent developments in anthropology may be followed in Erasmus, *Las dimensiones de la cultura,* pp. 74–146; Wolfgang Rudolph, *Die Amerikanische "Cultural Anthropology" und des Wertproblem,* Forschungen zur Ethnologie und Sozialpsychologie, vol. 3 (Berlin: Duncker and Humblot, 1959); Voget, "Man and Culture"; Eric Wolf, *Anthropology* (Englewood Cliffs, N.J.: Prentice-Hall, 1964); Harris, *Rise of Anthropological Theory,* chaps. 15–23; Voget, *A History of Ethnology,* chaps. 13–19.

One example of the application to the social anthropology of A. R. Radcliffe-Brown to American Indians by those he influenced at the University of Chicago may be found in Fred Eggan, ed., *Social Anthropology of North American Tribes* (1st ed., 1937; rev. ed., Chicago: University of Chicago Press, 1955). The new evolutionary approach to Indians is exemplified by Julian H. Steward, *Theory of Culture Change: The Methodology of Multilinear Evolution* (Urbana: University of Illinois Press, 1955); and Elman R. Service, *Primitive Social Organization: An Evolutionary Perspective* (New York: Random House, 1962). A popularization of the latter school, as suggested by its long title, is Peter Farb, *Man's Rise to Civilization as Shown by the Indians of North America from Primeval Times to the Coming of the Industrial State* (New York: E. P. Dutton and Co., 1968).

69. Compare the conclusion of Stocking, *Shaping of American Anthropology,* pp. 16–20, about the history and implications of modern movements in the field.

70. First ed. (Chicago: University of Chicago Press, 1953). Two later texts stress the ethnographic present even more than Underhill: Harold E. Driver, *Indians of North America* (Chicago: University of Chicago Press, 1961); Robert F. Spencer, Jesse D. Jennings *et al., The Native Americans: Prehistory and Ethnology of the North American Indians* (New York: Harper & Row, 1965).

71. Eleanor B. Leacock and Nancy O. Lurie, eds., *North American Indians in Historical Perspective* (New York: Random House, 1971).

72. If that duration be measured by the publication dates between Ralph Linton, ed., *Acculturation in Seven American Indian Tribes* (New York: D. Appleton-Century, 1940), and Edward Spicer, ed., *Perspectives in American Indian Culture Change* (Chicago: University of Chicago Press, 1961).

73. Eleanor Leacock in Leacock and Lurie, cited in note 71 above, p. 12. Nancy Lurie has particularly stressed the survival of Indianness as well as Indians into the present as part of current Native American political activism: for example, her chapter in *ibid.*, pp. 418–80; her article of famed title, "The Enduring Indian," *Natural History*, LXXV (Sept. 1966), pp. 10–22; and her afterword, "An American Indian Renascence?" in Stuart Levine and Lurie, eds., *The American Indian Today* (Deland, Fla.: Everett/Edwards, Inc., 1968), pp. 187–208.

74. In addition to Matthews and Moore cited in note 62 above on the ideological context of the concept of culture, see Raymond Williams, *Culture and Society, 1780–1950* (London: Chatto and Windus, 1958), and Alfred G. Meyer, "Historical Notes on Ideological Aspects of the Concept of Culture in Germany and Russia," in Kroeber and Kluckhohn, *Culture*, pp. 403–13. Another suggestive work on the larger intellectual context of the concept of culture is Karl J. Weintraub, *Visions of Culture* (Chicago: University of Chicago Press, 1966).

PART THREE

1. Harry Levin, *The Myth of the Golden Age in the Renaissance* (Bloomington: Indiana University Press, 1969), and A. Bartlett Giamatti, *The Earthly Paradise and the Renaissance Epic* (Princeton: Princeton University Press, 1966), provide a good introduction to the idea and uses of primitivism in this period. Arthur O. Lovejoy, Gilbert Chinard, George Boss, and Ronald S. Crane, eds., *A Documentary History of Primitivism and Related Ideas* (Baltimore: Johns Hopkins University Press, 1935), and George Boas, *Essays on Primitivism and Related Ideas in the Middle Ages* (Baltimore; Johns Hopkins University Press, 1948), do the same for the history of the subject until the Renaissance. Compare my interpretation with that of Henry S. Bausum, "Edenic Images of the Western World: A Reappraisal," *South Atlantic Quarterly*, LXVII (Autumn 1968), pp. 672–87. I have not drawn the usual distinction between hard and soft primitivism, because it does not seem particularly relevant to my major points.

2. Loren Baritz, "The Idea of the West," *American Historical Review*, LXVI (April 1961), pp. 618–40, and Charles L. Sanford, *Quest for Paradise: Europe and the American Moral Imagination* (Urbana: University of Illinois Press, 1961), chaps. 3–4, treat the importance of such ideas for the early explorers' perceptions of the Americas.

3. Edmundo O'Gorman, *The Invention of America: An Inquiry into the Historical Nature of the New World and the Meaning of Its History* (Bloomington: University of Indiana Press, 1961), pp. 94–99, suggests that more than paradisaical imagery per se caused Columbus to argue that he might have found the fabled Eden.

4. David B. Quinn, ed., *The Roanoke Voyages, 1584–1590: Documents to Illustrate the English Voyages to North America Under the Patent Granted to Walter Raleigh in 1584* (London: Hakluyt Society, 1955), series 2, vol. 104, p. 108. Interestingly, Hakluyt omitted the last sentence in his edition of Barlowe's account.

5. That Native Americans frequently manifested the virtues attributed to them by the Noble Savage convention and primitivistic faith is the argument of Wilcomb Washburn in "A Moral History of Indian-White Relations," *Ethnohistory*, IV (Winter 1957), pp. 47–61; and "The Clash of Morality in the American Forest," in Fredi Chiapelli, Michael J. B. Allen, and Robert L. Benson, eds., *First Images of America: The Impact of the New World on the Old* (Berkeley: University of California Press, 1976), vol. 1, pp. 335–50.

6. On the role of the artist in sixteenth-century discovery voyages, see Paul Hulton and David B. Quinn, *The American Drawings of John White, 1577–1590, with Drawings of European and Oriental Subjects* (London and Chapel Hill: Trustees of the British Museum and University of North Carolina Press, 1964), vol. 1, pp. 29–36. On the early artistic representations of the Indian, see William C. Sturtevant, "First Visual Images of Native America," in Chiapelli *et al.*, eds., *First Images of America*, vol. 1, pp. 417–54.

7. Henri Baudet, *Paradise on Earth: Some Thoughts on European Images of Non-European Man*, trans. Elizabeth Wenholt (New Haven: Yale University Press, 1965), and Hoxie N. Fairchild, *The Noble Savage: A Study in Romantic Naturalism* (New York: Columbia University Press, 1928), are the standard references on their subject. On the Indian in literature in general for the period as well as the role of primitivism in that story, see Gilbert Chinard, *L'exotisme américain dans la littérature française au XVIe siècle* (Paris: Hachette, 1911); and *L'Amérique et le rêve exotique dans la littérature française au XVIIe et au XVIIIe siècle* (Paris: E. Droz, 1934); Geoffrey Atkinson, *The Extraordinary Voyage in French Literature Before 1700* (New York: Columbia University Press, 1920), *Les relations de voyages du XVIIe siècle et l'évolution des idées: contribution a l'étude de la formation de l'esprit du XVIIIe siècle* (Paris: Édouard Champion, 1924), *Les nouveaux horizons de la renaissance française* (Paris: E. Droz, 1935); Benjamin Bissell, *The American Indian in English Literature of the Eighteenth Century*, Yale Studies in English, LXVIII (New Haven: Yale University Press, 1925); Lois Whitney, *Primitivism and the Idea of Progress in English Popular Literature of the Eighteenth Century* (Baltimore: Johns Hopkins University Press, 1934); Howard M. Jones, *O Strange New World; American Culture: The Formative Years* (New York: Viking Press, 1964), pp. 1–34; Ira O. Wade, *The Intellectual Origins of the French Enlightenment* (Princeton: Princeton University Press, 1971), pp. 361–91; Benjamin Keen, *The Aztec Image in Western Thought* (New Brunswick, N.J.: Rutgers University Press, 1971), pp. 138–248.

8. Chinard, *L'Amérique et le rêve exotique*, pp. 122–87, and John H.

Kennedy, *Jesuit and Savage in New France* (New Haven: Yale University Press, 1950), treat the Jesuit image of the Indian, while George R. Healey, "The French Jesuits and the Idea of the Noble Savage," *William and Mary Quarterly*, 3d series, XV (April 1958), pp. 143–67, suggests the polemical purposes of the image.

9. R. W. Frantz, *The English Traveller and the Movement of Ideas, 1660–1732* (Bison ed., Lincoln: University of Nebraska, 1967), pp. 72–99, 146–53, and J. Ralph Randolph, *British Travelers Among the Southern Indians, 1660–1763* (Norman: University of Oklahoma Press, 1973), cover English accounts of Indians in this period. For three prominent colonists' views, see A. L. Diket, "The Noble Savage Convention as Epitomized in John Lawson's *A New Voyage to Carolina*," *North Carolina Historical Review*, XLIII (Oct. 1966), pp. 413–29; Wilbur R. Jacobs, "Cadwallader Colden's Noble Iroquois Savages," in Lawrence H. Leder, ed., *Historians of Nature and Man's Nature, the Colonial Legacy*, vol. 3 (New York: Harper & Row, 1973), pp. 34–58; Wilcomb Washburn, "James Adair's 'Noble Savages,'" *ibid.*, pp. 91–120. How little Anglican missionaries romanticized Indian life may be seen in Frank Klingberg, "The Noble Savage as Seen by the Missionaries of the Society for the Propagation of the Gospel in Colonial New York, 1702–1750," *Historical Magazine of the Protestant Episcopal Church*, VIII (June 1939), pp. 128–65; and Gerald J. Goodwin, "Christianity, Civilization and the Savage: The Anglican Mission to the American Indian," *ibid.*, XLII (June 1973), pp. 93–110.

Perhaps the disinterest in the Noble Savage among the colonists accounts for the paucity of Indian prints in the colonies before the Revolution. Bradford F. Swan, "Prints of the American Indian, 1670–1775," in *Boston Prints and Printmakers, 1670–1775* (Boston: Published for the Colonial Society of Massachusetts by the University Press of Virginia, 1973), pp. 241–82, traces the genealogy of the few prints that appeared.

10. The influence of the American Indian upon Montaigne's ideas is described by Chinard, *L'exotisme américain dans la littérature française en XVIe siècle*, pp. 193–218; Fairchild, *The Noble Savage*, pp. 15–21; and Keen, *Aztec Image in Western Thought*, pp. 156–62.

11. Gilbert Chinard analyzes the sources and the influence of Lahontan's ideas in his long introduction to *Dialogues curieux entre l'auteur et un sauvage de bon sens qui a voyagé et mémoires de l'Amérique Septentrionale* (Baltimore: Johns Hopkins University Press, 1931). The *philosophes*' use of the Indian is explored in Chinard, *L'Amérique et le rêve exotique*, pp. 341–98; Paul Honigsheim, "Voltaire as Anthropologist," *American Anthropologist*, XLVII (Jan.–March 1945), pp. 104–18; Jean David, "Voltaire et des Indiens d'Amérique," *Modern Language Quarterly*, IX (March 1948), pp. 90–103; Paul Honigsheim, "The American Indian in the Philosophy of the Enlightenment," *Osiris*, X (1952), pp. 91–108; Michèle Duchet, "Bougainville, Raynàl, Diderot et les sauvages du Canada," *Revue d'histoire littéraire de la France*, LXIII (April–June 1963), pp. 228–36, and *Anthropologie et histoire au siècle des lumières* (Paris: François Maspero, 1971); and René Gonnard, *La Légende du bon sauvage: contributions à l'étude des origines du socialisme* (Paris: De Médicis, 1946).

12. Richmond P. Bond, *Queen Anne's American Kings* (Oxford: Claren-

don Press, 1952), gives a detailed account of this visit and its effect on English art and letters.

13. For this transition in English use of the Indian, see once again Fairchild, *The Noble Savage;* Bissell, *American Indian in English Literature of the Eighteenth Century;* and Whitney, *Primitivism and the Idea of Progress in English Popular Literature of the Eighteenth Century,* pp. 7–136.

14. The use of the Indian as part of United States cultural nationalism is told below. Benjamin Franklin employed the American Indian as a polemical and literary device at times. See, for example, Alfred O. Aldridge, "Franklin's Deistical Indians," *Proceedings of the American Philosophical Society,* XCIV (Aug. 1950), pp. 398–410. European artistic representation of the Noble Savage at this time can be studied in Hugh Honour, *The New Golden Land: European Images of America from the Discoveries to the Present Time* (New York: Pantheon, 1975), chaps. 4–5, and *The European Vision of America* (Cleveland: Cleveland Museum of Art, 1975), chaps. 6–9. Compare Elwood Parry, *The Image of the Indian and the Black Man in American Art, 1590–1900* (New York: George Braziller, 1974), chap. 2, and Swan, "Prints of the American Indian," for some colonial American representations during the same era.

15. Arthur O. Lovejoy's article on "The Parallel of Deism and Classicism," reprinted in his *Essays in the History of Ideas* (Baltimore: Johns Hopkins University Press, 1948), pp. 78–98; Gladys Bryson, *Man and Society: The Scottish Inquiry of the Eighteenth Century* (Princeton: Princeton University Press, 1945); and Whitney, *Primitivism and the Idea of Progress in English Popular Literature of the Eighteenth Century,* pp. 7–41, summarize these basic assumptions and criticisms of the time.

16. In addition to the Aldridge article cited in note 14 above, see also Fairchild, *Noble Savage,* pp. 413–40, for the critique of religion according to these premises.

17. William Boyd mentions throughout his book, *The Educational Theory of Jean Jacques Rousseau* (New York: Russell and Russell, 1963), the Indian as an influence on this philosopher's ideas.

18. For example, Rousseau, according to Geoffrey Symcox, "The Wild Man's Return: The Enclosed Vision of Rousseau's *Discourses,*" in Edward Dudley and Maximilian E. Novak, eds., *The Wild Man Within: An Image in Western Thought from the Renaissance to Romanticism* (Pittsburgh: University of Pittsburgh Press, 1972), pp. 223–47. Two of Geoffrey Atkinson's books cited earlier, *Les relations de voyages du XVIIᵉ siècle et l'évolution des idées,* and *Les nouveaux horizons de la renaissance française,* are relevant to the themes of this paragraph. See also René Hubert, *Les sciences sociales dans l'Encyclopédie: la philosophie de l'histoire et la problème des origines sociales* (Paris: Félix Alcan, 1928).

19. The nature of French criticism of colonial administration is analyzed by Duchet, *Anthropologie et histoire au siècle des lumières,* pp. 65–226.

20. In the opinion of Keen, *Aztec Image in Western Thought,* pp. 217–18, and John W. Burrow, *Evolution and Society: A Study in Victorian Social Theory* (Cambridge, Eng.: Cambridge University Press, 1966), pp. 4–6.

21. Fairchild, *Noble Savage,* pp. 327–38.

22. Eugene E. Reed, "The Ignoble Savage," *Modern Language Review,* LIX (Jan. 1964), pp. 53–64.

23. Antonello Gerbi, *The Dispute of the New World: The History of a Polemic, 1750–1900,* trans. Jeremy Moyle (Pittsburgh: University of Pittsburgh Press, 1973), pp. 3–324, may be read from this perspective.

24. Quoted in Fairchild, *Noble Savage,* p. 426.

25. Romantic use of the Noble Savage convention is treated by Fairchild, *Noble Savage;* Chinard, *L'Amérique et le rêve exotique,* esp. pp. 280–312, 399–430; and Peter L. Thorsley, Jr., "The Wild Man's Revenge," in Dudley and Novak, eds., *Wild Man Within,* pp. 281–307.

26. Again see Fairchild, *The Noble Savage,* pp. 258–67, for a brief statement on Cooper.

27. The standard authority upon this aspect of Chateaubriand's thought is still Gilbert Chinard, *L'exotisme américain dans l'oeuvre de Chateaubriand* (Paris: Hachette, 1918), but see also Richard Slotkin, *Regeneration Through Violence: The Mythology of the American Frontier, 1600–1860* (Middletown, Conn.: Wesleyan University Press, 1973), pp. 371–82, for a modern interpretation. The art inspired by Atala is examined briefly in Honour, *Golden Land,* pp. 220–25, and *European Vision of America,* pp. 286–302.

28. The role of Indian imagery in Puritan thought is the subject of Roy H. Pearce, "The 'Ruines' of Mankind: The Indian and the Puritan Mind," *Journal of the History of Ideas,* XIII (April 1952), pp. 200–17.

29. Puritans' perception of their land as a wilderness is covered in Alan Heimert, "Puritanism, the Wilderness, and the Frontier," *New England Quarterly,* XXVI (Sept. 1953), pp. 361–82; Peter N. Carroll, *Puritanism and the Wilderness: The Intellectual Significance of the New England Frontier, 1629–1700* (New York: Columbia University Press, 1969); Roderick Nash, *Wilderness and the American Mind* (2nd ed., New Haven: Yale University Press, 1973), chap. 2.

30. Quoted in Perry Miller and Thomas H. Johnson, eds., *The Puritans* (New York: American Book Company, 1938), p. 163, his italics.

31. Such is the interpretation of James G. Meade, "The 'Westerns' of the East: Narratives of Indian Captivity from Jeremiad to Gothic Novel" (Unpub. Ph.D. dissertation, Northwestern University, 1971); Neal Salisbury, "Conquest of the 'Savage': Puritans, Puritan Missionaries, and Indians, 1620–1680" (Unpub. Ph.D. dissertation, University of California at Los Angeles, 1972); and Slotkin, *Regeneration Through Violence,* pp. 57–179.

32. None more so than Francis Jennings, *The Invasion of America: Indians, Colonialism, and the Cant of Conquest* (Chapel Hill: University of North Carolina Press, 1975), who sees systematic distortion in the documents as conscious manipulation of the written word to dupe the Indians out of their lands.

33. Quoted in Peter Gay, *A Loss of Mastery: Puritan Historians in Colonial America* (Berkeley: University of California Press, 1966), pp. 35–36.

34. The place of the Indian in Puritan historiography may be followed in Jarvis Morse, *American Beginnings: Highlights and Sidelights of the Birth of the New World* (Washington, D.C.: Public Affairs Press, 1952), pp. 105–29; Slotkin, *Regeneration Through Violence,* pp. 57–93. Arthur R. Buntin, "The

Indian in American Literature, 1680–1760" (Unpub. Ph.D. dissertation, University of Washington, 1961), pp. 176–344, covers the Indian in this and the later period in colonial historiography.

35. No complete first edition of this book survives, so references must be to the two second editions of the same year. I have used the edition published in Cambridge by Samuel Green in 1682, pp. iv, 62.

36. This interpretation of the early captivity narrative accords with Meade, "The 'Westerns' of the East," chap. 3, and Slotkin, *Regeneration Through Violence*, pp. 94–115.

37. Or so Frank L. Mott, *Golden Multitudes: The Story of Best Sellers in the United States* (New York: Macmillan, 1947), pp. 20–22, estimates the sales at the time.

38. For the genre in the later colonial period, see Buntin, "The Indian in American Literature," pp. 43–174; Meade, "The 'Westerns' of the East," pp. 58–117. Richard Van Der Beets, ed., *Held Captive by Indians: Selected Narratives, 1642–1836* (Knoxville: University of Tennessee Press, 1973), provides a brief overall history of the literature along with his anthology of some of the more noted accounts. Roy H. Pearce examines the role of the genre in "The Significances of the Captivity Narrative," *American Literature*, XIX (March 1947), pp. 1–20. R. W. G. Vail compiled a list of all colonial captivity narratives in *The Voice of the Old Frontier* (Philadelphia: University of Pennsylvania Press, 1949), pp. 22–61, but see the more complete lists in *Narratives of Captivity Among the Indians of North America: A List of Books and Manuscripts on This Subject in the Edward E. Ayer Collection of the Newberry Library* (Chicago: Newberry Library, 1912); and *Supplement*, I (Chicago: Newberry Library, 1929).

39. Benjamin T. Spencer, *The Quest for Nationality: An American Literary Campaign* (Syracuse: Syracuse University Press, 1957), mentions the Indian as part of his subject. The use of the Indian as pictorial representation of the new American Nation is traced in E. McClung Fleming, "The American Image as Indian Princess, 1765–1783," *Winterthur Portfolio*, II (1965), pp. 65–81, and "From Indian Princess to Greek Goddess: The American Image," *ibid.*, III (1967), pp. 37–66.

40. On American romanticism and the Indian, see among others Fred A. Crane, "The Noble Savage in America, 1815–1860: Concepts of the Indian with Special Reference to the Writers of the Northeast" (Unpub. Ph.D. dissertation, Yale University, 1952); Paul R. Cox, "The Characterization of the American Indian in American Indian Plays, 1800–1860, as a Reflection of the American Romantic Movement" (Unpub. Ph.D. dissertation, New York University, 1970); and, in spite of the dates in the title, Louise K. Barnett, *The Ignoble Savage: American Literary Racism, 1790–1890* (Westport: Greenwood, 1975). Compare the attitude toward the wilderness as presented by Nash, *Wilderness and the American Mind*, chaps. 3–4.

41. Jefferson's version of the speech was published in his *Notes on the State of Virginia*, ed. William Peden (Chapel Hill: University of North Carolina Press, 1955), pp. 62–63. The controversy over its authenticity is summarized by Ray H. Sandefur, "Logan's Oration—How Authentic?" *Quarterly Journal of Speech*, XLVI (Oct. 1960), pp. 289–96. Buntin, "The Indian in

American Literature," pp. 521–99, surveys the treaty proceedings of the eighteenth century, while Lawrence C. Wroth, "The Indian Treaty as Literature," *Yale Review*, new series, XVII (July 1928), pp. 749–66; A. M. Drummond and Richard Moody, "Indian Treaties: The First American Dramas," *Quarterly Journal of Speech*, XXXIX (Feb. 1953), pp. 15–24; and Louis T. Jones, *Aboriginal American Oratory: The Tradition of Eloquence Among the Indians of the United States* (Los Angeles: Southwest Museum, 1965), all offer an appreciation of the form. Compare, however, Edna C. Sorber, "The Noble Eloquent Savage," *Ethnohistory*, XIX (Summer 1972), pp. 227–36.

42. Roy H. Pearce, *Savagism and Civilization: A Study of the Indian and the American Mind* (2nd ed., Baltimore: Johns Hopkins University Press, 1965), pp. 135–46; Diket, "The Noble Savage Convention as Epitomized in John Lawson's *A New Voyage to Carolina*"; Bernard Sheehan, *Seeds of Extinction: Jeffersonian Philanthropy and the American Indian* (Chapel Hill: University of North Carolina Press, 1973), pp. 89–116; Lewis O. Saum, *The Fur Trader and the Indian* (Seattle: University of Washington Press, 1965), pp. 108–109; Klingberg, "The Noble Savage as Seen by the Missionaries of the Society for the Propagation of the Gospel in Colonial New York," discuss these exceptions.

43. For example, Albert Keiser, *The Indian in American Literature* (New York: Oxford University Press, 1933), p. 293; Crane, "The Noble Savage in America," pp. 39, 83, 372.

44. George Catlin, *North American Indians, Being Letters and Notes on Their Manners, Customs, Written During Eight Years' Travel Amongst the Wildest Tribes of Indians in America* (Edinburgh: John Grant, 1841), vol. 1, p. 293.

45. On these artists, see Harold McCracken, *George Catlin and the Old Frontier* (New York: Dial Press, 1959); Lloyd Haberly, *Pursuit of the Horizon: A Life of George Catlin, Painter and Recorder of the American Indian* (New York: Macmillan, 1944); John F. McDermott, *Seth Eastman: Pictorial Historian of the Indian* (Norman: University of Oklahoma Press, 1961); David I. Bushman, Jr., *Seth Eastman: The Master Painter of the North American Indian*, Smithsonian Miscellaneous Collections (Washington, D.C.: Government Printing Office, 1932), vol. 87, no. 3.

46. Frank Weitenkamp, "How Indians Were Pictured in Earlier Days," *New York Historical Quarterly*, XXXIII (Oct. 1949), pp. 213–22; "Early Pictures of North American Indians: A Question of Ethnology," *Bulletin of the New York Public Library*, LIII (Nov. 1949), pp. 591–614; John C. Ewers, "An Anthropologist Looks at Early Pictures of North American Indians," *New York Historical Quarterly*, XXXIII (Oct. 1949), pp. 223–34; and "Fact and Fiction in the Documentary Art of the American West," in John F. McDermott, ed., *The Frontier Re-examined* (Urbana: University of Illinois Press, 1967), pp. 79–95, discuss ethnographic accuracy of these painters as well as of earlier artists.

47. Rena N. Coen, "The Indian as the Noble Savage in Nineteenth Century Art" (Unpub. Ph.D. dissertation, University of Minnesota, 1969), throws valuable light upon the evolution of the Noble Savage image in art from De Bry to the romantics of the nineteenth century, while John C. Ewers, "The

Emergence of the Plains Indian as the Symbol of the North American Indian," *Annual Report of the Smithsonian Institution for 1964* (Washington, D.C.: Government Printing Office, 1965), pp. 531–45, documents the new image. Some European pictures of the period are presented in Honour, *European Vision of America*, chap. 16. Compare Parry, *Image of the Indian and the Black Man in American Art*, chaps. 3–4, for a somewhat different interpretation than mine of this period.

48. Jay B. Hubbell, "The Smith-Pocahontas Literary Legend," in his *South and Southwest: Literary Essays and Reminiscences* (Durham: Duke University Press, 1965), pp. 175–204, and Philip Young, "The Mother of Us All; Pocahontas Reconsidered," *Kenyon Review*, XXIV (Summer 1962), pp. 391–415, place this story in its larger historical and literary context.

49. Recent discussions of Irving's Indian imagery are Robert L. Hough, "Washington Irving, Indians, and the West," *South Dakota Review*, VI (Winter 1968–69), pp. 27–39, and Per Seyersted, "The Indian in Knickerbocker's New Amsterdam," *The Indian Historian* (Summer 1974), pp. 14–28.

50. On the literary Indian of this period in general, see Pearce, *Savagism and Civilization*, pp. 169–236; Crane, "The Noble Savage in America"; Keiser, *Indian in American Literature*, pp. 21–97. Some indication of plays about the Indian at this time may be gleaned from Cox, "The Characterization of the American Indian in American Indian Plays."

51. The tension resulting from ambivalent imagery and competing models of Indians and pioneers in this period is the theme of Pearce, *Savagism and Civilization;* Slotkin, *Regeneration Through Violence*, pp. 268–565; Barnett, *Ignoble Savage*. Ernest Redekop, "The Redmen: Some Representations of Indians in American Literature," *Canadian Association of American Studies Bulletin*, III (Winter 1968), pp. 1–44; and Joseph Slate, *The Impact of Darwinian Thought on American Life and Culture* (Austin: University of Texas Press, 1959), pp. 73–83, see much less ambivalence about White American choices in the period than the preceding scholars.

52. Ruth Elson, *Guardians of Tradition: American Schoolbooks of the Nineteenth Century* (Lincoln: University of Nebraska Press, 1964), pp. 71–81, covers in brief this aspect of White schooling at the time.

53. What might be done with Indian sculpture is suggested by Coen, "The Indian as the Noble Savage in Nineteenth Century American Art," pp. 133–45. See also the brief article by William Gerdts, "The Marble Savage," *Art in America*, LXII (July–Aug. 1974), pp. 64–70.

54. The landmark book in exploring the larger imagery of the frontier was Henry N. Smith, *Virgin Land: The American West as Symbol and Myth* (Cambridge: Harvard University Press, 1950), but consult also Arthur K. Moore, *The Frontier Mind: A Cultural Analysis of the Kentucky Frontiersman* (Lexington: University of Kentucky Press, 1957).

55. The opinion of F. C. Ten Kate, "The Indian in Literature," *Annual Report of the Smithsonian Institution for 1921* (Washington, D.C.: Government Printing Office, 1922), pp. 509–14.

56. In his introduction to the revised edition of *The Last of the Mohicans* (1850), quoted in Pearce, *Savagism and Civilization*, p. 203.

57. Both Arthur C. Parker, "Sources and Range of Cooper's Indian Lore,"

New York History, XXXV (Oct. 1954), pp. 447–56, and Paul Wallace, "Cooper's Indians," *ibid.,* pp. 423–46, discuss the author's knowledge and sources for his Indian imagery with somewhat different conclusions.

58. *The Last of the Mohicans: A Narrative of 1757* (Philadelphia: H. C. Carey and I. Lea, 1826), vol. 1, pp. 70–71.

59. Crane, "The Noble Savage in America," pp. 114–81; Keiser, *Indian in American Literature,* pp. 101–43; and Kay Seymour House, *Cooper's Americans* (Columbus: Ohio State University Press, 1965), chap. 2, examine Cooper's Indian imagery in general. Wallace, "Cooper's Indians," and John T. Frederick, "Cooper's Eloquent Indians," *Publications of the Modern Language Association,* LXXXI (Dec. 1956), pp. 1004–17, defend the author's portrayal of the Indian against his critics then and subsequently. Cooper's influence upon writers overseas is studied in Margaret Murray Gibb, *Le roman de Bas-de-Cuir: étude sur Fenimore Cooper et son influence en France* (Paris: Libraire Ancienne Honoré Champion, 1927), and Willard Thorpe, "Cooper Beyond America," *New York History,* XXXV (Oct. 1954), pp. 522–39.

60. Pearce, *Savagism and Civilization,* pp. 244–51, offers a brief but perceptive analysis of Melville's ideas on this subject. Compare Barnett, *Ignoble Savage,* chap. 7. On the subgenre of Indian-hater fiction in general, see *ibid.,* chap. 5.

61. Crane, "The Noble Savage in America," pp. 223–25, 326–29, 387.

62. How these historians used Indian imagery is described by Pearce, *Savagism and Civilization,* pp. 162–68; David Levin, *History as Romantic Art: Bancroft, Prescott, Motley, and Parkman* (Stanford: Stanford University Press, 1959), *passim,* but especially pp. 133–41; Richard C. Vitzhum, *The American Compromise: Theme and Method in the Histories of Bancroft, Parkman, and Adams* (Norman: University of Oklahoma Press, 1974), *passim.* A different view of the Indian is ascribed to another historian of the time in Richard Hammond, "The Maverick and the Red Man: Richard Hildreth Views the American Indian," *The History Teacher,* VII (Nov. 1973), pp. 37–47.

63. This reconstruction of Parkman's original text depends upon E. N. Feldskog's edition of *The Oregon Trail* (Madison: University of Wisconsin Press, 1969), pp. 292–93, 627.

64. Mason Wade, *Francis Parkman, Heroic Historian* (New York: Viking Press, 1942), and Robert L. Gale, *Francis Parkman* (New York: Twayne Publishers, 1973), mention Indians throughout these biographies of the historian. Parkman's Indian imagery and sources are investigated in Francis Jennings, "A Vanishing Indian: Francis Parkman Views His Sources," *Pennsylvania Magazine of History and Biography,* LXXXVII (July 1963), pp. 306–23; Russell B. Nye, "Parkman, Red Fate, and White Civilization," in Clarence Gohdes, ed., *Essays on American Literature in Honor of Jay B. Hubbell* (Durham: Duke University Press, 1967), pp. 152–63; Wilbur Jacobs, *Dispossessing the American Indian: Indians and Whites on the Colonial Frontier* (New York: Charles Scribner's Sons, 1972), chap. 8; Robert Shulman, "Parkman's Indians and American Violence," *The Massachusetts Review,* XII (Spring 1971), pp. 221–39.

65. Russell B. Nye, *The Unembarrassed Muse: The Popular Arts in Amer-*

ica (New York: The Dial Press, 1970), provides a brief history of the popular arts in the United States. On the Indian in popular and folk art, see the forthcoming article by Rena Green in vol. 4 of the *Handbook of North American Indians* to be published by the Smithsonian Institution.

66. A standard analysis of the Western formula is John G. Cawelti, *The Six-Gun Mystique* (Bowling Green, Ohio: Bowling Green University Press, 1971), but he relies heavily on Smith, *Virgin Land*. Compare, however, Will Wright, *Six Guns and Society: A Structural Study of the Western* (Berkeley: University of California Press, 1975); Ralph Brauer and Donna Brauer, *The Horse, the Gun and the Piece of Property: Changing Images of the TV Western* (Bowling Green, Ohio: Bowling Green University Press, 1975); James K. Folsom, *The American Western Novel* (New Haven: Yale University Press, 1966).

67. Van Der Beets, *Held Captive by Indians;* Slotkin, *Regeneration Through Violence;* and Jules Zanger, "The Frontiersman in Popular Fiction, 1820–60," in John McDermott, ed., *The Frontier Re-examined* (Urbana: University of Illinois Press, 1968), pp. 141–53, examine some of the literary and mythical traditions that became the source of cheap literature themes.

68. The Indian as a subject for popular authors is not particularly stressed by the authorities on cheap literature after the Civil War, but see the text and pictures in Edmund Pearson, *Dime Novels or, Following an Old Trail in Popular Literature* (Boston: Little Brown, 1929), and Albert Johannsen, *The House of Beadle and Adams and Its Dime and Nickel Novels: The Story of a Vanished Literature* (Norman: University of Oklahoma Press, 1950–62), 3 vols. Also see on the genre, Merle Curti, "Dime Novels and the American Tradition," *Yale Review*, XXVI (June 1937), pp. 761–78, and Mary Noel, *Villains Galore: The Heyday of the Popular Story Weekly* (New York: Macmillan, 1954).

69. Quoted in Nye, *Unembarrassed Muse*, p. 207.

70. The increasing wildness of the dime-novel hero and heroine is the theme of Smith, *Virgin Land*, chaps. 9–10.

71. Henry B. Sell and Victor Weybright, *Buffalo Bill and the Wild West* (New York: Oxford University Press, 1955), pp. 125–260, describe the creation and the contents of the show over time.

72. Gibb, *Le roman de Bas-de-Cuir;* Thorpe, "Cooper Beyond America." The influence of domestic and external sources of imagery on European artistic representations of Indians during the late nineteenth century is the subject of Roxanna Barry, "Rousseau and Buffalo Bill and the European Image of the American Indian," *Art News*, LXXIV (Dec. 1975), pp. 58–61.

73. Although there is a vast literature on May and his German predecessors, little seems directly relevant to an understanding of his use of Indian imagery except Hans Plischke, *Von Cooper bis Karl May: Eine Geschichte des volkerkundlichen Reise- und Abenteurromans* (Düsseldorf: Droste, 1951); George E. Brooks, "The American Frontier in German Fiction," in McDermott, ed., *The Frontier Re-examined*, pp. 155–67; Richard H. Cracroft, "The American West of Karl May," *American Quarterly*, XIX (Summer 1967), pp. 249–58. Honour, *New Golden Land*, pp. 242–43, reproduces some of the illustrations for the covers of May's books.

74. Morton Cronon, "Currier and Ives: A Content Analysis," *American Quarterly*, IV (Winter 1952), pp. 329–30.

75. Harold McCracken, *Frederic Remington: Artist of the Old West* (Philadelphia: J. B. Lippincott, 1947), mentions Indian imagery of the artist incidental to his biography, as does G. Edward White, *The Eastern Establishment and the Western Experience: The West of Frederic Remington, Theodore Roosevelt, and Owen Wister* (New Haven: Yale University Press, 1968), pp. 94–121. Peter H. Hassrick, *Frederic Remington: Paintings, Drawings, and Sculpture in the Amon Carter Museum and the Sid W. Richardson Collections* (New York: Abrams, 1973), is a sumptuous edition of the artist's drawings, oils, and bronzes. Some idea of the Indian in the art of the period can be obtained from Coen, "The Indian as Noble Savage in Nineteenth Century Art," pp. 121–31, while Parry, *Image of the Indian and the Black Man in American Art*, pp. 115–16, 120–27, 131–32, 137–39, 143–48, 156–63, provides a brief but broader survey of pictorial representations of the Indian in the period.

76. Edward Curtis's photographs appeared under the title *The North American Indian: Being a Series of Volumes Picturing and Describing the Indians of the United States and Alaska* (Seattle and Cambridge: E. S. Curtis and University Press, 1907–30). A selection of these photographs with an introduction to his biography and imagery is presented by A. D. Coleman and T. C. McLuhan, *Portraits from North American Indian Life: Edward S. Curtis* (New York: Promontory Press, 1972). Robert Taft, *Photography and the American Scene: A Social History 1839–1889* (New York: Macmillan, 1938), chaps. 14–15, discusses frontier photographers in general. Martin F. Schmitt and Dee Brown, *Fighting Indians of the West* (New York: Charles Scribner's Sons, 1948), presents an interesting selection of photographs by the leading frontier lensmen.

77. On the Indian and the Western movie, see Ralph E. Friar and Natasha A. Friar, *The Only Good Indian . . . The Hollywood Gospel* (New York: Drama Book Specialists, 1972); John A. Price, "The Stereotyping of North American Indians in Motion Pictures," *Ethnohistory*, XX (Spring 1973), pp. 153–71; and George N. Fenin and William K. Everson, *The Western: From Silents to the Seventies* (New York: Grossman, 1973).

78. See Nye, *Unembarrassed Muse*, pp. 390–418, for the story of radio and television in general, and Horace Newcomb, *TV: The Most Popular Art* (Garden City, N.Y.: Anchor Books, 1974), pp. 59–82, on Westerns on that medium. Brauers, *The Horse, the Gun and the Piece of Property*, pp. 177–85, specifically discuss Indians on the tube.

79. In addition to the works cited in note 77 above, see also Philip French, *Westerns: Aspects of a Movie Genre* (London: Secker and Warburg, 1973), pp. 76–93, and Dan Georgakas, "They Have Not Spoken: American Indians in the Film," *Film Quarterly*, XXV (Spring 1972), pp. 26–32, for recent film treatment of the Indian. Friar and Friar (note 77 above) accuse well-intentioned countercultural movie directors of lack of knowledge and therefore a real concern for the Indian when in *Little Big Man* they used Crow as Sioux and in *A Man Called Horse* employed Catlin pictures to authenticate their costumes and artifacts but for the wrong tribe.

80. A more radical interpretation of the history and use of American Indian imagery by White Americans is advanced by Leslie Fiedler, *The Return of the Vanishing American* (New York: Stein and Day, 1968), and Elémire Zolla, *The Writer and the Shaman: A Morphology of the American Indian,* trans. Raymond Rosenthal (New York: Harcourt Brace Jovanovich, 1973), who in their own way exemplify the modern countercultural use of Indian imagery.

81. So conclude George E. Jones, "The American Indian in the American Novel (1875–1950)" (Unpub. Ph.D. dissertation, New York University, 1958), and Priscilla Shames, "The Long Hope: A Study of American Indian Stereotypes in American Popular Fiction, 1890–1950" (Unpub. Ph.D. dissertation, University of California at Los Angeles, 1969), after a survey of their respective subjects.

82. As, for example, Jones, "The American Indian in the American Novel," does to some degree for literature (and Fenin and Everson, *The Western,* do for motion pictures).

83. So Shames, "The Long Hope," argues for literature, and Friar and Friar, *Only Good Indian,* and Georgakas, "They Have Not Spoken," for the movies.

84. Samuel L. Clemens, *Roughing It* (Hartford: American Publishing Co., 1872), pp. 146–47, 149.

85. Joaquin Miller, *Songs of the Sierras* (Boston: Roberts Brothers, 1871), p. 122. For a brief analysis of Miller's Indian imagery, see Keiser, *Indian in American Literature,* pp. 232–48.

86. In addition to Keiser in preceding note, pp. 249–52, Ruth Odell, *Helen Hunt Jackson* (New York: D. Appleton-Century, 1939), pp. 153–211, 224–26, traces the life and books of H. H., as she so often signed her pieces, in regard to Native Americans. On another author in this period, see Owen J. Reamer, "Hamlin Garland and the Indians," *New Mexico Quarterly,* XXXIV (Autumn 1964), pp. 257–80. That authors of children's books used the same Indian imagery as writers for an adult audience in the period is the point of Brenda Berkman, "The Vanishing Race: Conflicting Images of the American Indian in Children's Literature, 1880–1930," *North Dakota Quarterly,* XLIV (Spring 1976), pp. 31–40.

87. Brief introductions to Bandelier and others living in the Southwest who wrote about Indians can be found in Keiser, *Indian in American Literature,* pp. 253–60, and Zolla, *Writer and the Shaman,* pp. 166–72, 185–99. Perhaps the most important result of this school was the outlook gained by D. H. Lawrence while visiting the Luhan colony at Taos and the sojourn there for a time of John Collier, who later became Commissioner of Indian Affairs under Franklin D. Roosevelt (see pages 176–86).

88. Most biographies mention *Laughing Boy* and La Farge's attitudes toward and work with American Indians: Everett A. Gillis, *Oliver La Farge* (Austin: Stock-Vaughan, 1967); D'Arcy McNickle, *Indian Man: A Life of Oliver La Farge* (Bloomington: Indiana University Press, 1971); Thomas M. Pearce, *Oliver La Farge* (New York: Twayne, 1972). Franz Schulz, *Der nordamerikanische Indianer und seine Welt in den Werken von Ernest Hem-*

ingway und Oliver La Farge (Munich: Max Hueber, 1964), offers a literary analysis of this author's work.

89. On these authors, consult Shames, "The Long Hope," pp. 192–253.

90. Fred H. Matthews, "The Revolt Against Americanization: Cultural Pluralism and Cultural Relativism as an Ideology of Liberation," *Canadian Review of American Studies*, I (Spring 1970), pp. 4–31.

91. Shames, "The Long Hope," pp. 254–307.

92. On Hemingway, see Schulz, *Der nordamerikanische Indianer*, and for other modern authors, Zolla, *Writer and the Shaman*, chap. 10.

93. John Caughey, *Hubert Howe Bancroft: Historian of the West* (Berkeley: University of California Press, 1946); Brian W. Dippie, "The Vanishing American: Popular Attitudes and American Indian Policy in the Nineteenth Century" (Unpub. Ph.D. dissertation, University of Texas, 1970), pp. 123–28.

94. Ronald M. Benson, "Ignoble Savage: Edward Eggleston and the American Indian," *Illinois Quarterly*, XXXV (Feb. 1973), pp. 41–51.

95. David A. Nichols, "Civilization over Savage: Frederick Jackson Turner and the Indian," *South Dakota History*, II (Fall 1972), pp. 383–405, discusses Turner's views of the Indian in the context of his evolutionary assumptions. For other analyses of his general intellectual framework, see Smith, *Virgin Land*, pp. 291–305, and Robert F. Berkhofer, Jr., "Space, Time, Culture and the New Frontier," *Agricultural History*, XXXVIII (Jan. 1964), pp. 21–30. That the so-called Imperial School of historians lacked interest in the Indians when it did not stereotype them is the theme of Richard L. Haan, "Another Example of Stereotypes on the Early American Frontier: The Imperialist Historians and the American Indian," *Ethnohistory*, XX (Spring 1973), pp. 143–52.

96. Meade, "The 'Westerns' of the East," Salisbury, "Conquest of the 'Savage,' " Slotkin, *Regeneration Through Violence*.

97. For this society's critique of White historians' treatment of the Native American past and some possible alternatives, see its journal, *The Indian Historian*, and Rupert Costo, ed., and Jeannette Henry, *Textbooks and the American Indian* (San Francisco: Indian Historian Press, 1970).

98. In order of publication: *The Teachings of Don Juan: A Yaqui Way of Knowledge* (Berkeley: University of California Press, 1968); *A Separate Reality: Further Conversations with Don Juan* (New York: Simon & Schuster, 1971); *Journey to Ixtlan: The Lessons of Don Juan* (New York: Simon & Schuster, 1972); *Tales of Power* (New York: Simon & Schuster, 1974).

PART FOUR

1. The role of ideals and moral judgment in writing about motives in past Indian policy is discussed by Wilcomb Washburn in several articles: "A Moral History of Indian-White Relations," *Ethnohistory*, IV (Winter 1957), pp. 47–61; "Indian Removal Policy: Administrative, Historical and Moral Criteria

for Judging Its Success or Failure," *ibid.*, XII (Summer 1965), pp. 274–78; and "The Writing of American Indian History: A Status Report," *Pacific Historical Review*, XL (Aug. 1971), pp. 263–68. Bernard Sheehan, "Indian-White Relations in Early America: A Review Essay," *William and Mary Quarterly*, XXVI (April 1969), pp. 267–86, offers another perspective on this problem.

2. Francis Parkman, *The Jesuits in North America in the Seventeenth Century* (Boston: Little, Brown, 1867), vol. 1, p. 131. This sentence is ambiguous in context and seems, in fact, a *non sequitur* at the end of a paragraph.

3. Charles Gibson, *Spain in America* (New York: Harper & Row, 1966), pp. 43–47, provides a brief history of the Black Legend, with references, and Benjamin Keen, "The Black Legend Revisited: Assumptions and Realities," *Hispanic American Historical Review*, XLIX (Nov. 1969), pp. 703–19, expands upon the theme.

4. See the interesting analysis of James Axtell in "The White Indians of Colonial America," *William and Mary Quarterly*, XXXII (Jan. 1975), pp. 55–88; and "The Scholastic Philosophy of the Wilderness," *ibid.*, XXIX (July 1972), pp. 335–66.

5. I believe that this argument holds for the Portuguese, Dutch, and, at times, Swedish policies and results in the Western Hemisphere, if, for example, one reads with this thesis in mind: Dauril Alden, "Black Robes Versus White Settlers: The Struggle for 'Freedom of the Indians' in Colonial Brazil," in Howard Peckham and Charles Gibson, eds., *Attitudes of the Colonial Powers Toward the American Indian* (Salt Lake City: University of Utah Press, 1969), pp. 19–45; Allen W. Trelease, "Dutch Treatment of the American Indian, With Particular Reference to New Netherland," in *ibid.*, pp. 47–59.

My approach was inspired by Elman R. Service, "Indian-European Relations in Colonial Latin America," *American Anthropologist*, LVII (June 1955), pp. 411–25; Charles Wagley and Marvin Harris, *Minorities in the New World: Six Case Studies* (New York: Columbia University Press, 1958), pp. 15–86; and Marvin Harris, *Patterns of Race in the Americas* (New York: Walker, 1964).

6. For example, Hubert Deschamps, *Méthodes et doctrines coloniales de la France (du XVIᵉ siècle à nos jours)* (Paris: Armand Colin, 1953), for the French, and Loren Pennington, "The Origins of English Promotional Literature for America, 1553–1625" (Unpub. Ph.D. dissertation, University of Michigan, 1962), for the English.

7. Much literature has been published on Spanish and English aims and theories of empire. For the Spanish, see among many John H. Parry, *The Spanish Theory of Empire in the Sixteenth Century* (Cambridge, Eng.: Cambridge University Press, 1961), and *The Spanish Seaborne Empire* (New York: Alfred A. Knopf, 1966); Silvio Zavala, *The Political Philosophy of the Conquest of Empire* (Mexico City: Cultura, 1953); and the relevant portions of Benjamin Keen, *The Aztec Image in Western Thought* (New Brunswick, N.J.: Rutgers University Press, 1971). For the English see among many in addition to Pennington cited in the preceding note: Louis B. Wright, *Religion and Empire: The Alliance Between Piety and Commerce in English Expansion, 1558–1625* (Chapel Hill: University of North Carolina Press, 1943), *The Colonial Search for a Southern Eden* (Birmingham [?]: University of Alabama Press, 1953), and *The Dream of Prosperity in Colonial America* (New

York: New York University Press, 1965); Perry Miller, *Errand into the Wilderness* (Cambridge: Harvard University Press, 1956), chap. 4; Howard Mumford Jones, *O Strange New World; American Culture: The Formative Years* (New York: Viking, 1964), chap. 5; Norman Lewis, "English Missionary Interest in the Indians of North America, 1578–1700" (Unpub. Ph.D. dissertation, University of Washington, 1968); Maxwell F. Taylor, Jr., "The Influence of Religion on White Attitudes Toward Indians in the Early Settlement of Virginia" (Unpub. Ph.D. dissertation, Emory University, 1961). French aims and theories seem to be less explored, but consult in addition to Deschamps cited in preceding note: J. Chailly-Bert, *Les Compagnies de colonisation sous l'ancien régime* ([Paris, 1898] New York: Burt Franklin, 1968); John H. Kennedy, *Jesuit and Savage in New France* (New Haven: Yale University Press, 1950); Mason Wade, "The French and the Indians," in Peckham and Gibson, eds., *Attitudes of Colonial Powers Toward the American Indian*, pp. 61–80.

8. From his *A True Reporte of the Late Discoveries*, reprinted in David B. Quinn, ed., *The Voyages and Colonising Enterprises of Sir Humphrey Gilbert* (London: Hakluyt Society, 1940), series 2, vol. 84, p. 450.

9. *Ibid.*, p. 438.

10. Quoted in Parry, *Spanish Theory of Empire*, p. 41.

11. *A True Declaration of the Estate of the Colonie in Virginia* (London: for William Barret, 1610), p. 9. Fred M. Kimmey, "Christianity and Indian Lands," *Ethnohistory*, VII (Winter 1960), pp. 44–60, examines the use of this rationale by the English.

12. His own words quoted by Las Casas in entry for October 12, 1492, *The Journal of Christopher Columbus*, trans. Cecil Jane and revised by L. A. Vigneras (London: Hakluyt Society, 1960), p. 24.

13. So conclude Benjamin Bissell, *The American Indian in English Literature of the Eighteenth Century*, Yale Studies in English, LXVIII (New Haven, 1925), p. 3; and Hoxie N. Fairchild, *The Noble Savage: A Study in Romantic Naturalism* (New York: Columbia University Press, 1928), p. 13.

14. Keen, *Aztec Image in Western Thought*, chaps. 4–5, analyzes the debate in these terms.

15. *Hakluytus Posthumus or Purchas His Pilgrimes*, vol. 19 (Glasgow: James MacLehose and Sons, 1906), p. 231.

16. *Winthrop Papers* (Boston, Massachusetts, Historical Society, 1931), vol. 2, p. 141. Chester E. Eisinger, "The Puritans' Justification for Taking the Land," Essex Institute, *Historical Collections*, LXXXIV (April 1948), pp. 131–43, examines New Englanders' employment of the *vacuum domicilium* rationale.

17. Francis Jennings, *The Invasion of America: Indians, Colonialism, and the Cant of Conquest* (Chapel Hill: University of North Carolina Press, 1975), stresses how Puritans and other English colonists rigged rationales as well as procedures to favor themselves in land dealings.

18. I follow John T. Juricek, "English Claims to North America to 1660: A Study in Legal and Constitutional History" (Unpub. Ph.D. dissertation, University of Chicago, 1970), on this matter as in so much else in this section.

19. *Journal of Christopher Columbus*, p. 94.

20. In addition to Juricek, "English Claims to North America," pp. 109–46, see Arthur S. Keller, Oliver J. Lissitzyn, and Frederick J. Mann, *Creation of Rights of Sovereignty Through Symbolic Acts, 1400–1800* (New York: Columbia University Press, 1938), on the practice of symbolic possession.

21. Captain John Smith recounts the diplomatic maneuvers on both sides surrounding the coronation of Powhatan in *A Map of Virginia* (1612), in Philip L. Barbour, ed., *The Jamestown Voyages Under the First Charter, 1606–1609* (Cambridge, Eng.: Hakluyt Society, 1969), series 2, vol. 137, pp. 410–14.

22. Quoted in Charles Gibson, ed., *The Spanish Tradition in America* (New York: Harper & Row, 1968), pp. 59–60.

23. My interpretation of the ultimate meaning of Spanish opposition to forceful conquest and enslavement is based upon my reading of Parry, *Spanish Theory of Empire;* Lewis Hanke, *The Spanish Struggle for Justice in the Conquest of America* (Philadelphia: University of Pennsylvania Press, 1949); and Bernice Hamilton, *Political Thought in Sixteenth-Century Spain: A Study of Political Ideas of Vitoria, De Soto, Suarez, and Molina* (Oxford: Clarendon Press, 1963), chap. 6.

24. In Quinn, ed., *The Voyages and Colonising Enterprises of Sir Humphrey Gilbert,* p. 450.

25. Especially book II, chap. 13, of *De jure belli ac pacis libri tres,* trans. Francis W. Kelsey and others ([1625], Oxford: Clarendon Press, 1925), vol. 2, pp. 196–200.

26. Introductions to Spanish colonization in general may be found in Carl Sauer, *The Early Spanish Main* (Berkeley: University of California Press, 1966); Gibson, *Spain in America;* Parry, *Spanish Seaborne Empire.*

27. I depend primarily upon the scholarship of Charles Gibson, *The Aztecs Under Spanish Rule: A History of the Indians of the Valley of Mexico, 1519–1810* (Stanford: Stanford University Press, 1964), for this paragraph, but see also, for missionary activity among the Indians, Robert Ricard, *The Spiritual Conquest of Mexico: An Essay on the Apostolate and Evangelizing Methods of the Mendicant Orders in New Spain, 1523–1572,* trans. Leslie B. Simpson (Berkeley: University of California Press, 1966); and Ursula Lamb, "Religious Conflicts in the Conquest of Mexico," *Journal of the History of Ideas,* XVII (Oct. 1956), pp. 526–39.

28. William J. Eccles, *The Canadian Frontier, 1534–1760* (New York: Holt, Rinehart and Winston, 1969), is valuable on French colonization in general. The importance of geographical factors in the settlement of New France is stressed by historical geographers: in general, Richard C. Harris and John Warkentin, *Canada Before Confederation: A Study in Historical Geography* (New York: Oxford University Press, 1974), chaps. 1–2, and in greater detail, Richard C. Harris, *The Seigneurial System in Early Canada* (Madison: University of Wisconsin Press, 1966), and Andrew H. Clark, *The Geography of Early Nova Scotia to 1760* (Madison: University of Wisconsin Press, 1968).

29. Kennedy, *Jesuit and Savage in New France,* deals with the former, while G. F. G. Stanley, "The First Indian 'Reserves' in Canada," *Revue d'histoire de l'Amérique française,* IV (Sept. 1950), pp. 178–210, and James P.

Ronda, "The Sillery Experiment: A Jesuit-Indian Village in New France, 1637–1663," unpub. ms., discuss the latter.

30. G. F. G. Stanley, "The Policy of 'Francization' as Applied to the Indians During the Ancien Regime," *Revue d'histoire de l'Amérique française*, III (Dec. 1949), pp. 333–48, and James P. Ronda, "The European Indian: Jesuit Civilization Planning in New France," *Church History*, XLI (Sept. 1972), pp. 385–95, both stress the connection between civilization and religion in French missionary work. Compare Micheline Dumont Johnson, *Apôtres ou agitateurs: la france missionaire en Acadie* (Trois Rivières: Le Boréal Express, 1970), for a later period.

31. Brief mention of the conflict between French legal proceedings and tribal justice may be found in Alfred G. Bailey, *The Conflict of European and Eastern Algonkian Cultures, 1504–1700: A Study in Canadian Civilization* (2nd ed., Toronto: University of Toronto Press, 1969), pp. 93–94; Eccles, *Canadian Frontier*, pp. 77–78. Unfortunately, we know too little of efforts to mesh tribal and French sovereignty or exactly how land title was transferred. Modern scholars are investigating, however, French missionary activity and results. See particularly, in addition to the works cited in the two preceding notes, Cornelius Jaenen, "Problems of Assimilation in New France, 1603–1645," *French Historical Studies*, IV (Spring 1966), pp. 265–89; "The Frenchification and Evangelization of the Amerindians in Seventeenth Century New France," Canadian Catholic Historical Association, *Study Sessions, 1968*, XXXV (1969), pp. 57–72; "The Meeting of the French and Amerindians in the Seventeenth Century," *Revue de l'université d'Ottawa*, XLIII (Jan.–March 1973), pp. 128–44; and "Amerindian Views of Seventeenth Century French Culture," *Canadian Historical Review*, LV (Sept. 1974), pp. 261–91. Jaenen's book, *Friend and Foe: Aspects of French-Amerindian Cultural Contact in the Sixteenth and Seventeenth Centuries* (New York: Columbia University Press, 1976), appeared after this chapter was completed. See also Peter G. Le Blanc, "Indian-Missionary Contact in Huronia, 1615–1649," *Ontario History*, LX (Sept. 1968), pp. 133–46. Of Bruce G. Trigger's many articles on Huronia, "The French Presence in Huronia: The Structure of Franco-Huron Relations in the First Half of the Seventeenth Century," *Canadian Historical Review*, XLIX (June 1968), is relevant to this topic.

32. Bruce G. Trigger, "The Jesuits and the Fur Trade," *Ethnohistory*, XII (Winter 1965), pp. 30–53; Harold Hickerson, "Fur Trade Colonialism and the North American Indians," *Journal of Ethnic Studies*, I (Summer 1973), pp. 15–44; Arthur J. Ray, *Indians in Fur Trade: Their Role as Trappers, Hunters, and Middlemen in the Lands Southwest of Hudson Bay, 1660–1870* (Toronto: University of Toronto Press, 1974); and John McManus, "An Economic Analysis of Indian Behavior in the North American Fur Trade," *Journal of Economic History*, XXXII (March 1972), pp. 36–53, all offer interesting perspectives on the fur trade and Native American societies.

33. The opinion of Eccles, *Canadian Frontier*, p. 6. Bailey, *Conflict of European and Eastern Algonkian Cultures*, seems to confirm for the early period, while the Natchez uprising in eighteenth-century Louisiana suggests as much for the later period according to the analysis of Andrew C. Albrecht,

"Indian-French Relations at Natchez," *American Anthropologist,* XLVIII (July–Sept. 1946), pp. 321–54.

34. Or so concludes Lewis Saum, *The Fur Trade and the Indian* (Seattle: University of Washington Press, 1965), chap. 4, based upon data from a later era as much as from the colonial period.

35. Population estimates for Virginia and Massachusetts in 1650 and 1700 are given in *Historical Statistics of the United States: Colonial Times to 1957* (Washington, D.C.: Government Printing Office, 1960), p. 756, and for Canada in Jacques Henripin, *La population canadienne au début du XVIIIᵉ siècle,* Publications de l'institut national d'études démographiques, cahier 22 (Paris: Presses Universitaires de France, 1954), p. 3; Marcel Trudel, *La population du Canada en 1663* (Montreal: Fides, 1973).

36. Even W. Stitt Robinson, Jr., "Indian Policy of Colonial Virginia" (Unpub. Ph.D. dissertation, University of Virginia, 1950), pp. 16–25, is not entirely clear on this matter, but chaps. 1–4 provide a detailed description of the subject of his title for the seventeenth century. See also Wesley F. Craven, "Indian Policy in Early Virginia," *William and Mary Quarterly,* 3d series, I (Jan. 1944), pp. 65–82.

37. Nancy O. Lurie, "Indian Cultural Adjustment to European Civilization," in James M. Smith, ed., *Seventeenth-Century America: Essays in Colonial History* (Chapel Hill: University of North Carolina Press, 1959), pp. 33–60, remains the best discussion of English relations with the Powhatan Confederacy and other Virginia tribes in the seventeenth century from another than white-centered viewpoint. Edmund Morgan, "The Labor Problem at Jamestown, 1607–18," *American Historical Review,* LXXVI (June 1971), pp. 587–600, writes of English hopes of repeating Spanish success in their own colonization, particularly in Virginia.

38. Compare Alden T. Vaughan, *New England Frontier: Puritans and Indians, 1620–1675* (Boston: Little, Brown, 1965), pp. 104–114; Wilcomb Washburn, *The Indian in America* (New York: Harper & Row, 1975), pp. 83–84; Jennings, *Invasion of America,* chap. 8, for varying views on the origins of cession through purchase.

39. Marshall Harris, *Origins of the Land Tenure System in the United States* (Ames: Iowa State College Press, 1953), summarizes the land-tenure system in the thirteen colonies, with chap. 11 devoted to the methods of acquiring Indian lands. This book should be used with caution, however, and each topic checked against other authorities. Georgiana C. Nammack, *Fraud, Politics, and the Dispossession of the Indians: The Iroquois Land Frontier in the Colonial Period* (Norman: University of Oklahoma Press, 1969), and Francis Jennings, "The Scandalous Indian Policy of William Penn's Sons: Deeds and Documents of the Walking Purchase," *Pennsylvania History,* XXXVII (Jan. 1970), pp. 306–23, expose examples of later land deals.

40. Quoted in John L. Myres, "The Influence of Anthropology on the Course of Political Science," *University of California Publications in History* (Berkeley, 1916), vol. 4, no. 1, p. 29n.

41. Still standard on the White enslavement of Indians in this period is Almon W. Lauber, "Indian Slavery in Colonial Times Within the Present

Limits of the United States," *Columbia University Studies in History*, no. 14 (New York, 1913).

42. This paragraph draws on the conclusions of W. Stitt Robinson, Jr., "The Legal Status of the Indian in Colonial Virginia," *The Virginia Magazine of History and Biography*, LXI (July 1953), pp. 247–59; Vaughan, *New England Frontier*, chap. 7; Yasuhide Kawashima, "Jurisdiction of the Colonial Courts Over the Indians in Massachusetts, 1689–1763," *New England Quarterly*, XLII (Dec. 1969), pp. 532–50, and "Indians and Southern Colonial Statutes," *Indian Historian*, VII (Winter 1974), pp. 10–16; James P. Ronda, "Red and White at the Bench: Indians and the Law in Plymouth Colony, 1620–1691," Essex Institute, *Historical Collections*, CX (July 1974), pp. 200–15.

43. Quoted in R. Pierce Beaver, "Methods in American Missions to the Indians in the Seventeenth and Eighteenth Centuries: Calvinist Models for Protestant Foreign Missions," *Journal of Presbyterian History*, XLVII (June 1969), p. 135.

44. For varying assessments of the English missionaries' purposes, motives, and accomplishments, see Vaughan, *New England Frontier*, chaps. 9–11; R. Pierce Beaver, in addition to citation in preceding note, "American Missionary Motivation Before the Revolution," *Church History*, XXXI (June 1962), pp. 216–26, and *Church, State, and the American Indians: Two and a Half Centuries of Partnership in Missions Between Protestant Churches and Government* (St. Louis: Concordia Publishing House, 1966), chap. 1; Ola E. Winslow, *John Eliot, Apostle to the Indians* (Boston: Houghton Mifflin, 1968); William Kellaway, *The New England Company, 1649–1776: Missionary Society to the American Indians* (London: Longmans, Green, 1961); W. Stitt Robinson, Jr., "Indian Education and Missions in Colonial Virginia," *Journal of Southern History*, XVIII (May 1952), pp. 152–68; Taylor, "Influence of Religion on White Attitudes Towards Indians"; Lewis, "The English Missionary Interest in the Indians of North America," especially chaps. 6–10; Norman E. Tanis, "Education in John Eliot's Indian Utopias, 1646–1675," *History of Education Quarterly*, X (Fall 1970), pp. 308–23; Neal Salisbury, "Conquest of the 'Savage': Puritans, Puritan Missionaries, and Indians, 1620–1680" (Unpub. Ph.D. dissertation, University of California at Los Angeles, 1972), and "Red Puritans: The 'Praying Indians' of Massachusetts Bay and John Eliot," *William and Mary Quarterly*, XXXI (Jan. 1974), pp. 27–54; Francis Jennings, "Goals and Functions of Puritan Missions to the Indians," *Ethnohistory*, XVIII (Sept. 1971), pp. 197–212, and *Invasion of America*, especially chaps. 4, 14.

45. James Axtell, " 'To Reduce Them to Civility': The Educational Contest for North America," an abridged version of which appeared as "The European Failure to Convert the Indians: An Autopsy," *National Museum of Man Mercury Series*, Canadian Ethnology Service Paper No. 23 (Ottawa, 1974), pp. 274–90, provides a judicious appraisal of these factors for the French and English colonies. That Puritan prejudice and practice amounted to racism is argued by G. E. Thomas, "Puritans, Indians, and the Concept of Race," *New England Quarterly*, XLVIII (March 1975), pp. 3–27. Discrimination by the French is suggested in Jaenen, "Problems of Assimilation in New France," and "The Frenchification and Evangelization of the Amerindians."

46. In addition to the works cited in the preceding two notes, see also

Ricard, *Spiritual Conquest of Mexico*, chap. 16, and Lamb, "Religious Conflicts in the Conquest of Mexico," pp. 534–39, for overall results.

47. For a discussion of this important issue, see the citations in note 1 above.

48. To discuss policy aims and methods in terms of a fundamental ideology of Americanism as I do here is not to dismiss all differences among groups as varying interpretations of the same ideals. Different groups do have different interests and these are shown in opposing policies. Rather I would like to show that both situations prevail in the formulation and execution of United States Indian policy.

49. John Higham, *Send These to Me: Jews and Other Immigrants in Urban America* (New York: Atheneum, 1975), particularly chap. 6, stresses the larger nativist strain in American history that differentiates "them" from "us" by ethnicity and race. Compare David B. Davis, "Some Themes of Counter-Subversion: An Analysis of Anti-Masonic, Anti-Catholic, and Anti-Mormon Literature," *Mississippi Valley Historical Review*, XLVII (Sept. 1960), pp. 205–24, and "Some Ideological Functions of Prejudice in Ante-Bellum America," *American Quarterly*, XV (Summer 1963), pp. 115–25, for a more specific linkage of nativism and Americanism.

50. As the reader no doubt realized, I have begun to use the term *American* to designate White Americans only, and usually of Anglo-Saxon heritage.

51. This paragraph synthesizes interpretations presented by Bernard Bailyn, *Ideological Origins of the American Revolution* (Cambridge: Harvard University Press, 1967), chaps. 5–6; Gordon S. Wood, *The Creation of the American Republic, 1776–1787* (Chapel Hill: University of North Carolina Press, 1969); Paul Conkin, *Self-Evident Truths: Being a Discourse on the Origins and Development of the First Principles of American Government— Popular Sovereignty, Natural Rights and Balance of Powers* (Bloomington: University of Indiana Press, 1974); and Sidney E. Mead, *The Lively Experiment: The Shaping of Christianity in America* (New York: Harper & Row, 1963), pp. 16–71. Foreign views of the symbolic importance of the new United States are given in Durand Echeverria, *Mirage in the West: A History of the French Image of American Society to 1815* (Princeton: Princeton University Press, 1957), and Robert R. Palmer, *The Age of Democratic Revolution: The Challenge* (Princeton: Princeton University Press, 1959), chap. 9. Compare Cushing Strout, *The American Image of the Old World* (New York: Harper & Row, 1963), chaps. 1–3, for the same views from the early United States in evaluating Europe's institutions and peoples.

52. In letter of Thomas Jefferson to Francis Hopkinson, May 3, 1784, in *Papers of Thomas Jefferson*, ed. Julian P. Boyd et al. (Princeton: Princeton University Press, 1950–), vol. 7, p. 206.

53. See, for example, the comments of George Washington in his Circular to the States, June 8, 1783, in *The Writings of George Washington from the Original Manuscript Sources, 1745–1799*, ed. John C. Fitzpatrick (Washington, D.C.: Government Printing Office, 1931–44), vol. 26, pp. 484–85.

54. Paul C. Nagel, *One Nation Indivisible: The Union in American Thought, 1776–1861* (New York: Oxford University Press, 1964), passim; Ernest L. Tuveson, *Redeemer Nation: The Idea of America's Millennial Role*

(Chicago: University of Chicago Press, 1968), *passim;* and Rutherford E. Delmage, "The American Idea of Progress, 1750–1800," *Proceedings of the American Philosophical Society,* XCI (Oct. 1947), pp. 307–14, examine the subjects of their titles for the period.

55. In John W. Thornton, ed., *Pulpit of the American Revolution: Or, the Political Sermons of the Period of 1776* (Boston: Gould and Lincoln, 1860), p. 415.

56. Henry N. Smith, *Virgin Land: The American West as Symbol and Myth* (Cambridge: Harvard University Press, 1950), chaps. 11–12, discusses agrarianism and the yeoman farmer concept in the early republic and cites the standard references.

57. Quoted in Lynn H. Parsons, "'A Perpetual Harrow upon My Feelings': John Quincy Adams and the American Indian," *The New England Quarterly,* XLVI (Sept. 1973), p. 343.

58. *The American Geography* (Elizabethtown, N.J.: Shepard Kollock, 1789), p. 469.

59. Specifically on the subject of this paragraph see Reginald Horsman, "American Indian Policy and the Origins of Manifest Destiny," *University of Birmingham Historical Journal,* XI (Dec. 1968), pp. 128–40. Richard W. Van Alstyne, *The Rising American Empire* (New York: Oxford University Press, 1960), chaps. 1–3, and *Genesis of American Nationalism* (Waltham, Mass.: Blaisdell, 1970), discusses the conception of American empire in relation to American nationality. Nationality and Manifest Destiny are the subject of Paul C. Nagel, *This Sacred Trust: American Nationality, 1798–1898* (New York: Oxford University Press, 1971), chaps. 1–2, as well as his *One Nation Indivisible.* On continuity and change in conceptions of Manifest Destiny, see Albert K. Weinberg, *Manifest Destiny: A Study of Nationalist Expansion in American History* (Baltimore: Johns Hopkins University Press, 1935), chaps. 1–7; Frederick Merk, *Manifest Destiny and Mission in American History* (New York: Alfred A. Knopf, 1963); Edward M. Burns, *The American Idea of Mission: Concepts of National Purpose and Destiny* (New Brunswick, N.J.: Rutgers University Press, 1957); Tuveson, *Redeemer Nation,* especially chap. 4. Yehosua Arielli, *Individualism and Nationalism in American Ideology* (Cambridge: Harvard University Press, 1964), provides valuable context upon the subjects of the preceding paragraphs.

As indicative as the rhetoric of the relationship between the ideology of Americanism and the idea of the Indian was the rapid transformation of the symbolic or iconographic representation of America from the Indian princess traditionally used in the colonial period and derived from the European symbolization of the continent into the Greek goddess to proclaim the glories of the new republic in neoclassic fashion. See E. McClung Fleming, "From Indian Princess to Greek Goddess: The American Image, 1783–1815," *Winterthur Portfolio,* III (1967), pp. 37–66.

60. Edmund C. Burnett, *The Continental Congress* (New York: Macmillan, 1941), provides a narrative history of the context and interconnection among these problems and policies. But see also Merrill Jensen, *The Articles of Confederation: An Interpretation of the Socio-Constitutional History of the American Revolution, 1774–1781* (Madison: University of Wisconsin Press,

1940), and *The New Nation: A History of the United States During the Confederation, 1781–1789* (New York: Alfred A. Knopf, 1950). Jack M. Sosin, *The Revolutionary Frontier, 1763–1783* (New York: Holt, Rinehart and Winston, 1967), and Reginald Horsman, *The Frontier in the Formative Years, 1783–1815* (New York: Holt, Rinehart and Winston, 1970), focus more narrowly upon policies and outcomes in the West for the periods covered in their titles.

61. William D. Pattison, *Beginnings of the American Rectangular Land Survey System, 1784–1800* (Chicago: Rand McNally, 1957), traces the evolution of the ordinance and its early transformations. Payson J. Treat, *The National Land System, 1785–1820* (New York: E. B. Treat, 1910), remains a standard reference on its subject, but see also Malcolm Rohrbaugh, *The Land Office Business: The Settlement and Administration of American Public Lands, 1789–1837* (New York: Oxford University Press, 1968).

62. This interpretation of the Northwest Ordinance is presented in my articles "Jefferson, The Ordinance of 1784, and the Origins of the American Territorial System," *William and Mary Quarterly*, XXIX (April 1972), pp. 231–62, and "The Northwest Ordinance and the Principle of Territorial Evolution," in John P. Bloom, ed., *The American Territorial System* (Athens: Ohio University Press, 1973), pp. 45–55. See also the interpretations of Arthur Bestor, "Constitutionalism and the Settlement of the West: The Attainment of Consensus, 1754–1784," in *ibid.*, pp. 13–44, and Jack E. Eblen, *The First and Second United States Empires: Governors and Territorial Government, 1784–1912* (Pittsburgh: University of Pittsburgh Press, 1968), chaps. 1–2.

63. Francis P. Prucha, *American Indian Policy in the Formative Years: The Indian Trade and Intercourse Acts, 1790–1834* (Cambridge: Harvard University Press, 1962), chaps. 1–3, and Reginald Horsman, *Expansionism and American Indian Policy, 1783–1812* (East Lansing: Michigan State University Press, 1967), chaps. 1–3, provide brief surveys of Indian policy in the Revolutionary era, and Walter H. Mohr, *Federal Indian Relations, 1774–1788* (Philadelphia: University of Pennsylvania Press, 1933), offers an expanded treatment of the subject.

64. Report of June 15, 1789, *American State Papers: Indian Affairs*, vol. 1 (Washington, D.C.: Gales and Seaton, 1832), p. 13.

65. Report of July 7, 1789, in *ibid.*, p. 53.

66. *Ibid.*

67. Compare my interpretation of Knox with Horsman, *Expansionism and American Indian Policy*, chap. 4.

68. The evolution of the trade and intercourse acts until 1834 is the main subject of Prucha, *American Indian Policy*. For the working out of these policies, see also Horsman, *Expansionism and American Indian Policy*, chaps. 5–10, and George D. Harmon, *Sixty Years of Indian Affairs, 1789–1850* (Chapel Hill: University of North Carolina Press, 1941).

69. Although modern historians refer to the Bureau of Indian Affairs, people during the nineteenth century generally called it the Office of Indian Affairs. The former term was not formally adopted until 1947, but I shall follow historians' custom by employing Bureau of Indian Affairs or BIA to refer to the agency throughout its entire existence.

70. Quoted in Prucha, *American Indian Policy*, p. 51.

71. *Ibid.*, chap. 4; Ronald N. Satz, *American Indian Policy in the Jacksonian Era* (Lincoln: University of Nebraska Press, 1975), chaps. 6–7; and Alban W. Hoopes, *Indian Affairs and Their Administration, with Special Reference to the Far West, 1849–60* (Philadelphia: University of Pennsylvania Press, 1932), chap. 2, carry the story of the administrative structure of the BIA up to 1860. The standard older reference on the evolution of the administrative structure of the bureau is Laurence F. Schmeckebier, *The Office of Indian Affairs: Its History, Activities and Organization*, Service Monographs of the United States Government, no. 48 (Baltimore: Johns Hopkins University Press, 1927). The biography of the first superintendent of Indian affairs by Herman J. Viola, *Thomas L. McKenney: Architect of America's Indian Policy, 1816–1830* (Chicago: Swallow Press, 1974), offers insights into the administration of Indian affairs during the period of its coverage. Eblen, *First and Second Empires,* chap. 8, and William M. Neil, "The Territorial Governor as Indian Superintendent in the Trans-Mississippi West," *Mississippi Valley Historical Review,* XLIII (Sept. 1956), pp. 213–37, treat the territorial governor as Indian superintendent.

72. Francis P. Prucha, *The Sword of the Republic: The United States Army on the Frontier, 1783–1846* (New York: Macmillan, 1969), and Robert M. Utley, *Frontiersmen in Blue: The United States Army and the Indian, 1848–1865* (New York: Macmillan, 1967), and *Frontier Regulars: The United States Army and the Indian, 1866–1891* (New York: Macmillan, 1973), constitute an exception to military histories failing to mention the Indian wars in relation to army organization and history as a whole. Leo E. Oliva, "The Army and the Indian," *Military Affairs,* XXXVIII (Oct. 1974), pp. 117–19, reviews these and other books relevant to the topic, but most of the items he mentions concern the story after the Civil War, for which see below.

73. Letter of John Sevier to James Ore, May 12, 1798, quoted in Prucha, *American Indian Policy*, p. 143.

74. Although no detailed, quantitative studies exist of the correlation among party affiliation, geographical location, and congressional voting on Indian policy during the nineteenth century, historians generally assume that there is a positive connection between the frontier and harsh policies and between the East and a philanthropic and more enlightened approach. William T. Hagan phrases the principle succinctly in his *American Indians* (Chicago: University of Chicago Press, 1961), p. 70: "As usual, moral indignation over the plight of the red man varied with the distance from him." Although I follow this approach in this and the next two sections, such an assumption is no substitute for the rigorous quantitative analyses that would sustain or deny the premise. Since writing these words, the dissertation of Frederick E. Hoxie, "Beyond Savagery: The Campaign to Assimilate the American Indian, 1880–1920" (Unpub. Ph.D. dissertation, Brandeis University, 1977), has come to hand, in which just such analyses of congressional voting blocs are given as I call for in this note.

75. The appendix to Robert F. Berkhofer, Jr., "Protestant Missionaries and American Indians, 1787–1862" (Unpub. Ph.D. dissertation, Cornell University,

1960), chronicles the development of Indian mission work from the Revolution to the Civil War.

76. The story of collaboration between missionary societies and the federal government in the nineteenth century is the theme of Beaver, *Church, State, and the American Indians,* chaps. 2–5. The standard work on its topic, Evelyn C. Adams, *American Indian Education: Government Schools and Economic Progress* (Morningside Heights, N.Y.: King's Crown Press, 1946), is too brief and error-filled to be of any value. Better is Martha E. Laymen, "A History of Indian Education in the United States" (Unpub. Ph. D. dissertation, University of Minnesota, 1942), but we need a good survey of the subject.

77. To most leading Americans of the time, Protestantism was assumed to be more compatible with the freedom and individuality of American values and institutions, but in the decades after, the federal government supported increasing numbers of Catholic missions among the Indians. No overall survey of Catholic missions to the Indians exists but see Gilbert J. Garraghan, *The Jesuits of the Middle United States* (New York: America Press, 1938), 3 vols., chaps. 12–13, 23–30, and Hiram M. Chittenden and Alfred T. Richardson, eds., *Life, Letters, and Travels of Father Pierre-Jean De Smet, S.J., 1801–1873* (New York: Francis P. Harper, 1905), 4 vols.

78. The evolution of the idea of the manual labor boarding school is traced in Robert F. Berkhofer, Jr., "Model Zions for the American Indians," *American Quarterly,* XV (Summer 1963), pp. 176–90.

79. Robert F. Berkhofer, Jr., *Salvation and the Savage: An Analysis of Protestant Missions and American Indian Response, 1787–1862* (Lexington: University of Kentucky Press, 1965), stresses the role, techniques, and goals of Protestant missionaries in promulgating their brand of Christian civilization before the Civil War. Compare for the later period Howard L. Harrod, *Mission Among the Blackfeet* (Norman: University of Oklahoma Press, 1971).

80. Statement of the Board of Managers of the United Foreign Missionary Society, May 5, 1823, quoted in Berkhofer, *Salvation and the Savage,* pp. 10–11.

81. Berkhofer, "Protestant Missionaries and American Indians," chap. 3, details the funding and size of missionary establishments for Indians from 1819 to 1862.

82. In letter of Stephen Riggs to David Green, April 29, 1846, quoted in Berkhofer, *Salvation and the Savage.* His italics.

83. Bernard Sheehan, *Seeds of Extinction: Jeffersonian Philanthropy and the American Indian* (Chapel Hill: University of North Carolina Press, 1973), particularly emphasizes the use and decline of Enlightenment ideals and environmental theory in Indian policy in the early decades of the nineteenth century. James F. Cox III, "The Selfish Savage: Protestant Missionaries and Nez Percé and Cayuse Indians, 1835–1847" (Unpub. Ph.D. dissertation, University of Michigan, 1975), suggests the effects of the transition from environmental and millennial assumptions to racial views on the policy of the largest missionary society among the Indians before the Civil War. Satz, *American Indian Policy in the Jacksonian Era,* chap. 9, treats missionaries in this period. The anthropologists covered by Robert E. Bieder, "The American Indian and the Development of Anthropological Thought in the United States, 1780–1851"

(Unpub. Ph.D. dissertation, University of Minnesota, 1972), especially pp. 415–18, all believed in the desirability of Indian acculturation through the means available at the time.

84. Published originally in 1835 and translated in 1838, the book contains a section entitled "The Present and Probable Future Condition of the Indian Tribes Which Inhabit the Territory Possessed by the Union" (in vol. 1, chap. 18), in which de Tocqueville discusses the nature of the Indian and the removal program under Andrew Jackson. What de Tocqueville and other European visitors to the United States thought of American-Indian relations is examined in Gary C. Stein, " 'And the Strife Never Ends': Indian-White Hostility as Seen by European Travellers in America, 1800–1860," *Ethnohistory*, XX (Spring 1973), pp. 173–87.

85. Of the many books and articles on American democracy and liberalism, I have found particularly helpful John W. Ward, "Jacksonian Democratic Thought: 'A Natural Charter of Privilege,' " in Stanley Coben and Lorman Ratner, eds., *The Development of an American Culture* (Englewood Cliffs, N.J.: Prentice-Hall, 1970), pp. 44–64; and Arielli, *Individualism and Nationalism in American Ideology*. See, however, Louis Hartz, *The Liberal Tradition in America: An Interpretation of American Political Thought Since the Revolution* (New York: Harcourt, Brace and World, 1955), chaps. 1, 4–5.

86. Mary E. Young, "The West and American Cultural Identity: Old Themes and New Variations," *Western Historical Quarterly*, I (April 1970), pp. 137–60, suggests the relation between the ideology of liberalism and the conception of the frontier in the nineteenth century, while in her "Congress Looks West: Liberal Ideology and Public Land Policy in the Nineteenth Century," in David M. Ellis *et al.*, eds., *The Frontier in American Development: Essays in Honor of Paul Wallace Gates* (Ithaca: Cornell University Press, 1969), pp. 74–112, she examines the use of liberal ideology as a rationale for United States land policy. Michael P. Rogin gives a psychohistorical basis to liberal ideology in its role in Jacksonian Indian policy in his *Fathers and Children: Andrew Jackson and the Subjugation of the American Indian* (New York: Alfred A. Knopf, 1975).

87. The changing image of the frontiersmen can be followed in Rush Welter, "The Frontier West as Image of American Society: Conservative Attitudes Before the Civil War," *Mississippi Valley Historical Review*, XLVI (March 1960), pp. 593–614, and "The Frontier West as Image of American Society, 1776–1860," *Pacific Northwest Quarterly*, LII (Jan. 1961), pp. 1–6; and Henry N. Smith, *Virgin Land: The American West as Symbol and Myth* (Cambridge: Harvard University Press, 1950).

88. Frederick Merk, *Manifest Destiny and Mission in American History*, chap. 7, covers the debate over the annexation of Mexico and its Indian population. Compare anti-Black prejudice on the frontier in Eugene H. Berwanger, *The Frontier Against Slavery: Western Anti-Negro Prejudice and the Slavery Extension Controversy* (Urbana: University of Illinois Press, 1967). Eric Foner, *Free Soil, Free Labor, Free Men: The Ideology of the Republican Party Before the Civil War* (New York: Oxford University Press, 1970), particularly pp. 1–39, 261–317, discusses the connection between liberal ideology, the race issue, and antebellum westward expansion. Klaus J. Hansen, "The Millennium,

the West, and Race in the Antebellum American Mind," *Western Historical Quarterly*, III (Oct. 1972), pp. 373–90, surveys the literature on his themes. The doctrine of Anglo-Saxonism as a rationale for expansion is not well treated in the secondary literature on the period before the Civil War, but see the scattered references in Weinberg, *Manifest Destiny*. Once again see the article by Horsman, "American Indian Policy and the Origins of Manifest Destiny," on the topic of this paragraph.

89. Sheehan, *Seeds of Extinction*, pp. 174–80, and Loring B. Priest, *Uncle Sam's Stepchildren: The Reformation of United States Indian Policy* (New Brunswick, N.J.: Rutgers University Press, 1942), p. 147, mention some of the few Whites who did advocate miscegenation as a solution to the Indian problem. White prejudice was probably greatest against persons of mixed Indian-Black ancestry. A recent article on Red-Black relationships with references is William G. McLaughlin, "Red Indians, Black Slavery and White Racism: America's Slaveholding Indians," *American Quarterly*, XXVI (Oct. 1974), pp. 366–85.

90. On the importance of improved methods of transportation for the expansion of the market system, see George R. Taylor, *The Transportation Revolution, 1815–1860, The Economic History of the United States*, vol. 4 (New York: Rinehart and Co., 1951). The speed and area of White Western settlement may be followed in Ray A. Billington, *Westward Expansion: A History of the American Frontier* (4th ed., New York: Macmillan, 1974).

91. I follow Ronald P. Formisano, "Deferential-Participant Politics: The Early Republic's Political Culture, 1789–1840," *American Political Science Review*, LXVIII (June 1974), pp. 473–87, in arguing that the so-called first party system was not a true political party system in the modern sense. Richard Hofstadter, *The Idea of the Party System: The Rise of Legitimate Opposition in the United States, 1780–1840* (Berkeley: University of California Press, 1969), clarifies the evolution of the concept of political party conflict.

92. Winthrop D. Jordan, *White Over Black: American Attitudes Toward the Negro, 1550–1812* (Chapel Hill: University of North Carolina Press, 1968), chap. 15, treats Jefferson's opinions on this matter in their larger context.

93. In a special message to Congress, January 27, 1825, in James D. Richardson, ed., *A Compilation of the Messages and Papers of the Presidents, 1789–1902* (Washington, D.C.: Bureau of National Literature and Art, 1905), vol. 2, p. 282.

94. Still standard on the history of removal policy before Jackson is Annie H. Abel, "The History of Events Resulting in Indian Consolidation West of the Mississippi," *Annual Report of the American Historical Association for the Year 1906* (Washington, D.C.: Government Printing Office, 1908), vol. 1, chaps. 1–7; but see also Prucha, *American Indian Policy*, pp. 224–33, and Sheehan, *Seeds of Extinction*, chap. 9. Paul W. Gates, "Indian Allotments Preceding the Dawes Act," in John G. Clark, ed., *The Frontier Challenge: Responses to the Trans-Mississippi West* (Lawrence: University Press of Kansas, 1971), pp. 141–70, and Mary E. Young, *Redskins, Ruffleshirts, and Rednecks: Indian Land Allotments in Alabama and Mississippi, 1830–1860* (Norman: University of Oklahoma Press, 1961), *passim*, discuss the nature, function, and results of Indian land allotments in this period. That the United

States Senate never intended to grant Indians land in fee simple is the argument of Robert W. McCluggage, "The Senate and Indian Land Titles, 1800–1825," *Western Historical Quarterly*, I (Oct. 1970), pp. 415–25.

95. Quoted in a speech by Congressman Henry Storrs of New York during debate in the House of Representatives, May 15, 1830, *Register of Debates in Congress*, 21 Cong., 1 sess. (Washington: Gales and Seaton, 1830), vol. 6, p. 996.

96. Richardson, *Compilation of the Messages and Papers of the Presidents*, vol. 2, p. 459. For a psychohistorical interpretation of Jackson's attitudes and policies, see Rogin, *Fathers and Children*. More orthodox in interpretation is Ronald N. Satz, *American Indian Policy in the Jacksonian Era*, chap. 1.

97. Speech before the Senate, April 9, 1830, *Register of Debates in Congress*, 21 Cong., 1 sess., vol. 6, p. 315.

98. Quoted in Weinberg, *Manifest Destiny*, p. 83.

99. Satz, *American Indian Policy in the Jacksonian Era*, chaps. 1–2, stresses partisan affiliation in the positions taken in the removal debates. The role of missionary societies and missionaries in the removal debates and the subsequent emigration is treated in Beaver, *Church, State, and the American Indians*, chap. 3. The leading missionary advocating removal is the subject of George A. Schultz, *An Indian Canaan: Isaac McCoy and the Vision of an Indian State* (Norman: University of Oklahoma Press, 1972), but see also Robert F. Berkhofer, Jr., introduction to Isaac McCoy, *History of Baptist Indian Missions* (1840, New York: Johnson Reprint Corp., 1970), pp. v–xxvii. No modern biography of Jeremiah Evarts, who led the missionary society opposition to removal, exists, but see J. Orin Oliphant, ed., *Through the South and West with Jeremiah Evarts in 1826* (Lewisburg, Pa.: Bucknell University Press, 1956), pp. 1–62. Francis P. Prucha, "Thomas L. McKenney and the New York Indian Board," *Mississippi Valley Historical Review*, XLVIII (March 1962), pp. 635–55, shows how McKenney tried to mobilize public opinion in favor of removal through ministerial support.

100. The arguments for the extension of state law over members of the Five Civilized Tribes and the effects of such laws for their landholdings is the theme of Mary E. Young, "Indian Removal and Land Allotment: The Civilized Tribes and Jacksonian Justice," *American Historical Review*, LXIV (Oct. 1958), pp. 31–45; *Redskins, Ruffleshirts, and Rednecks*.

101. *Cherokee Nation v. The State of Georgia*, 5 Peters 15–17. Compare, however, the dissent of Justice Smith Thompson, 5 Peters 49, and Marshall's decision in *Worcester v. The State of Georgia*, 6 Peters 515 (1832). For previous Supreme Court decisions on Indian title and sovereignty, see *Fletcher v. Peck*, 6 Cranch 87 (1810), and *Johnson and Graham's Lessee v. McIntosh*, 8 Wheaton 543 (1823). Compare the interpretation of McCluggage, "The Senate and Indian Land Titles," with these Court decisions.

102. The United States had denied the request of England to include the Indians as party to the peace treaty between the two nations after the War of 1812 on the grounds that the Indians were subjects of the United States and therefore their status was not negotiable with a foreign power. See Parsons, "'A Perpetual Harrow upon My Feelings,'" pp. 344–46, for this story in relation to John Quincy Adams as an American negotiator.

103. In addition to Annie H. Abel, "Proposals for an Indian State, 1778–1878," *Annual Report of the American Historical Association for the Year 1907* (Washington, D.C.: Government Printing Office, 1908), vol. 1, pp. 87–104, see Prucha, *American Indian Policy*, pp. 269–75, and Satz, *American Indian Policy in the Jacksonian Era*, chaps. 5, 8. Isaac McCoy hoped to create an Indian state of which he was head: Schultz, *An Indian Canaan*, and Berkhofer, intro. to McCoy, *History of Baptist Missions*. What did pass in 1834 were trade and intercourse acts codifying previous practice and a law setting up the Indian office, for which see Prucha, *American Indian Policy*, chap. 10.

104. On policy in the 1840s and 1850s, Robert A. Trennert, Jr., *Alternative to Extinction: Federal Indian Policy and the Beginnings of the Reservation System, 1846–51* (Philadelphia: Temple University Press, 1975); and Prucha, "American Indian Policy in the 1840s," supersede the older, standard references: Hoopes, *Indian Affairs and Their Administration*, and James C. Malin, "Indian Policy and Westward Expansion," *Bulletin of the University of Kansas*, vol. 22, no. 17 (Lawrence, 1921). On army policy in regard to Indians, consult Prucha, *Sword of the Republic*, chaps. 17–18; Utley, *Frontiersmen in Blue*. The effects of these policies upon the Indians of California is the subject of Robert F. Heizer and Alan J. Almquist, *The Other Californians: Prejudice and Discrimination under Spain, Mexico, and the United States to 1920* (Berkeley: University of California Press, 1971), chaps. 2–3.

105. On Civil War policy itself, see Edward J. Danziger, Jr., *Indians and Bureaucrats: Administering the Reservation Policy During the Civil War* (Urbana: University of Illinois Press, 1974); Minnie Thomas Bailey, *Reconstruction in Indian Territory: A Study of Avarice, Discrimination, and Opportunism* (Port Washington, N.Y.: Kennikat Press, 1972); Sammy David Buice, "The Civil War and the Five Civilized Tribes: A Study of Federal-Indian Relations" (Unpub. Ph.D. dissertation, University of Oklahoma, 1970); William E. Unrau, "The Role of the Indian Agent in the Settlement of the South Central Plains, 1861–1868" (Unpub. Ph.D. dissertation, University of Colorado, 1963); and the older three volumes by Annie H. Abel, all published by Arthur H. Clark Co.: *The American Indian as Slave-holder and Secessionist: An Omitted Chapter in the Diplomatic History of the Southern Confederacy* (1915); *The American Indian as Participant in the Civil War* (1919); *The American Indian Under Reconstruction* (1925). Linda K. Kerber, "The Abolitionist Perception of the Indian," *Journal of American History*, LXII (Sept. 1975), pp. 271–95, examines the views of those reformers before and after the Civil War.

106. The transfer issue is the major subject of Donald J. D'Elia, "The Argument Over Civilian or Military Control, 1865–1880," *The Historian*, XXIV (Feb. 1962), pp. 207–25, and Henry J. Waltmann, "The Interior Department, War Department, and Indian Policy, 1865–1887" (Unpub. Ph.D. dissertation, University of Nebraska, 1962), while Utley, *Frontier Regulars*, provides the military history of the period. That army opinion was not unanimous and many officers rejected a policy of extermination is the point of Robert G. Athearn, "War Paint Against Brass: The Army and the Plains Indians," *Montana: The Magazine of Western History*, VI (Summer 1956), pp. 11–22; Richard N. Ellis, "The Humanitarian Soldiers," *Journal of Arizona*

History, X (Summer 1969), pp. 53–66; and "The Humanitarian Generals," *Western Historical Quarterly,* III (April 1972), pp. 169–78; Thomas C. Leonard, "Red, White and Army Blue: Empathy and Anger in the American West," *American Quarterly,* XXVI (May 1974), pp. 176–90; Robert M. Utley, "The Frontier Army: John Ford or Arthur Penn?" in Jane F. Smith and Robert M. Kvasnicka, eds., *Indian-White Relations: A Persistent Paradox* (Washington, D.C.: Howard University Press, 1976), pp. 133–45; and for the earlier period, William B. Skelton, "Army Officers' Attitudes Towards Indians, 1830–1860," *Pacific Northwest Quarterly,* LXVII (July 1976), pp. 113–24. Billington, *Westward Expansion,* chaps. 28–33, describes the movement of the White frontiers after the Civil War.

107. William E. Unrau, "The Civilian as Indian Agent: Villain or Victim," *Western Historical Quarterly,* III (Oct. 1972), pp. 405–20, argues that the charges of corruption against Indian agents may have resulted from the growth of federal bureaucracy in the period as much as from their handling of finances and rations.

108. The best general references on postwar Indian policy, including the Peace Policy, are Loring B. Priest, *Uncle Sam's Stepchildren;* Henry E. Fritz, *The Movement for Indian Assimilation, 1860–1890* (Philadelphia: University of Pennsylvania Press, 1963); Robert W. Mardock, *The Reformers and the American Indian* (Columbia: University of Missouri Press, 1971); and Hoxie, "Beyond Savagery," part one. As was mentioned earlier, this latter work was completed too late to influence my writing of this section. On specific religious denominations and the Peace Policy, see Peter J. Rahill, *The Catholic Indian Missions and Grant's Peace Policy, 1870–1884* (Washington, D.C.: Catholic University of America Press, 1953); Robert H. Keller, Jr., "The Protestant Churches and Grant's Peace Policy: A Study in Church-State Relations" (Unpub. Ph.D. dissertation, University of Chicago, 1967); Beaver, *Church, State, and the American Indians,* chap. 4; Joseph E. Illick, " 'Some of Our Best Indians are Friends . . .': Quaker Attitudes and Actions Regarding the Western Indians During the Grant Administration," *Western Historical Quarterly,* II (July 1971), pp. 283–94; Henry G. Waltmann, "Presbyterian and Reformed Participation in the Indian 'Peace Policy' of the 1870s," *Transactions of the Conference Group for Social and Administrative History,* V (April 1974), pp. 8–23. In addition to the above, see Robert M. Utley, "The Celebrated Peace Policy of General Grant," *North Dakota History,* XX (July 1953), pp. 121–42, and Henry G. Waltmann, "Circumstantial Reformer: President Grant and the Indian Problem," *Arizona and the West,* XIII (Winter 1971), pp. 323–42, for the debate about the actual initiators of the policy. Henry E. Fritz, "The Board of Indian Commissioners and Ethnocentric Reform, 1878–1893," in Smith and Kvasnicka, eds., *Indian-White Relations,* pp. 57–78, assesses the role of that religious coordinating body. I wonder whether there would have been any difference in the results for Native Americans in the end if either the army or the missionaries had had full responsibility for Indian policy.

109. Columbus Delano, Secretary of the Interior, *Annual Report,* in *Executive Documents, 1873–74* (Washington, D.C.: Government Printing Office, 1874), vol. 4, pp. iii–iv.

11c. Whether the actual power structure and informal organization of the Indian Bureau and reservations really coincided with official policy is quite another matter. On the idea and practice of the reservation, see Priest, *Uncle Sam's Stepchildren*, chap. 10; Wilcomb Washburn, *Indian in America*, chap. 10; William T. Hagan, "Indian Policy After the Civil War: The Reservation Experience," in Indiana Historical Society, *Lectures, 1970–1971* (Indianapolis: Indiana Historical Society, 1971), pp. 20–36; "Kiowas, Comanches, and Cattlemen, 1867–1906: A Case Study of the Failure of U.S. Reservation Policy," *Pacific Historical Review*, XL (Aug. 1971), pp. 333–55; "The Reservation Policy: Too Little and Too Late," in Smith and Kvasnicka, eds., *Indian-White Relations*, pp. 157–69; and Ray H. Mattison, "The Indian Reservation System on the Upper Missouri, 1865–1890," *Nebraska History*, XXXVI (Sept. 1955), pp. 141–72. Interesting perspectives on the "theory" of the reservation are Henry F. Dobyns, "Therapeutic Experience of Responsible Democracy," in Stuart Levine and Nancy O. Lurie, eds., *The American Indian Today* (Baltimore: Penguin Books, 1968), pp. 268–91; George P. Castille, "Federal Indian Policy and the Sustained Enclave: An Anthropological Perspective," *Human Organization*, XXXIII (Fall 1974), pp. 219–28; Joseph G. Jorgensen, *The Sun Dance Religion: Power for the Powerless* (Chicago: University of Chicago Press, 1972), pp. 89–173, and his "Indians and the Metropolis," in Jack O. Waddell and O. Michael Watson, eds., *The American Indian in Urban Society* (Boston: Little, Brown, 1971), pp. 67–113.

111. For examples of such optimism, see Fritz, *Movement for Indian Assimilation*, p. 120; Mardock, *Reformers and the American Indian*, p. 80.

112. Anthropological opinion on acculturation is mentioned by Bieder, "The American Indian and the Development of Anthropological Thought in the United States," pp. 399–401; Brian W. Dippie, "The Vanishing Indian: Popular Attitudes and American Indian Policy in the Nineteenth Century" (Unpub. Ph.D. dissertation, University of Texas, 1970), pp. 205–13; Mardock, *Reformers and the American Indian*, p. 183; Washburn, *Indian in America*, pp. 244–45; Hoxie, "Beyond Savagery," chap. 2.

113. George Sinkler, *The Racial Attitudes of American Presidents from Abraham Lincoln to Theodore Roosevelt* (New York: Doubleday, 1971), briefly mentions opinions toward Indians as part of the coverage of his topic.

114. Commissioner of Indian Affairs, *Annual Report*, in *Executive Documents, 1869–70* (Washington, D.C.: Government Printing Office, 1870), vol. 3, p. 448. Perhaps Parker felt strongly about the legal status of the Indian and the seeming duplicity of treaty diplomacy as a result of his earlier opposition to the Ogden Land Company during the successful fight to retain the reservation of his own people, the Tonawanda Seneca.

115. Actually some of the executive agreements made subsequent to this date resembled treaties in effect. Priest, *Uncle Sam's Stepchildren*, chap. 8; Laurence F. Schmeckebier, *Office of Indian Affairs*, pp. 58–66, mention the end of treaty making. G. E. E. Lindquist, "Indian Treaty-Making," *Chronicles of Oklahoma*, XXVI (Winter 1948–49), pp. 416–48, summarizes the nature of the United States treaties with the Indians, while the standard reference on land cessions over time is Charles C. Royce, "Indian Land Cessions in the United

States," *Eighteenth Annual Report of the Bureau of American Ethnology, 1896–97* (Washington, D.C.: Government Printing Office, 1899), part 2.

116. William T. Hagan, *Indian Police and Judges* (New Haven: Yale University Press, 1966), covers this topic with his usual thoroughness.

117. Everett A. Gilcreast, "Richard Henry Pratt and American Indian Policy, 1877–1906: A Study of the Assimilation Movement" (Unpub. Ph.D. dissertation, Yale University, 1967), discusses Pratt's biography in light of his attitudes, policies, and politics, while Carmelita S. Ryan, "The History of the Carlisle Indian Industrial School" (Unpub. Ph.D. dissertation, Georgetown University, 1962), covers the curriculum and methods of his school.

118. Adams, *American Indian Education*, chap. 4, discusses briefly the topic in this period, but Layman, *A History of Indian Education in the United States*, chap. 8, and Hoxie, "Beyond Savagery," chap. 5, are better. See also Delos S. Otis, *The Dawes Act and the Allotment of Indian Lands*, ed. Francis P. Prucha (Norman: University of Oklahoma Press, 1973), chap. 6. That the tendency to centralization of administration and bureaucratization was common to the educational systems of the time, partly as an effort to Americanize immigrants and Blacks, can be seen from David B. Tyack, *The One Best System: A History of American Urban Education* (Cambridge: Harvard University Press, 1974).

119. The introduction and selections in Francis P. Prucha, ed., *Americanizing the American Indians: Writings by the "Friends of the Indian," 1880–1900* (Cambridge: Harvard University Press, 1973), present the program of the reformers of the period. More critical of these reformers is Wilbert H. Ahern, "Assimilationist Racism: The Case of the 'Friends of the Indian,'" *Journal of Ethnic Studies*, IV (Summer 1976), pp. 23–32. On the formation of the reform organizations at the time, see the concluding chapters of Fritz, *Movement for Indian Assimilation*, and Mardock, *Reformers and the American Indian*. Larry E. Burgess, "The Lake Mohonk Conferences on the Indian, 1883–1916" (Unpub. Ph.D. dissertation, Claremont Graduate School, 1972), presents a chronological history of the activities of that group from its published proceedings.

120. Presidential address by Merrill E. Gates, *Proceedings of the Fourteenth Annual Meeting of the Lake Mohonk Conference of Friends of the Indian* (Lake Mohonk: Lake Mohonk Conference, 1896), pp. 11–12. Compare William T. Hagan, "Private Property, The Indian's Door to Civilization," *Ethnohistory*, III (Spring 1956), pp. 126–37, and Berkhofer, *Salvation and the Savage*, pp. 81–82, for perspective on such thinking.

121. Otis, *Dawes Act and the Allotment of Indian Lands;* Priest, *Uncle Sam's Stepchildren*, chaps. 14–15, 17–18; Mardock, *Reformers and the American Indian*, chap. 12; Washburn, *Indian in America*, chap. 11; Dippie, "The Vanishing American," chap. 11; Burgess, "The Lake Mohonk Conference," chap. 3; J. P. Kinney, *A Continent Lost—A Civilization Won: Indian Land Tenure in America* (Baltimore: Johns Hopkins University Press, 1937); and Hoxie, "Beyond Savagery," chap. 6, all present their versions of the Dawes Act and allotment. On earlier allotment and its results, see once again Gates, "Indian Allotment Preceding the Dawes Act," and Young, *Redskins, Ruffleshirts, and Rednecks*.

122. Under pressure to open Oklahoma to White settlement and to admit the territory to statehood, Congress from 1893 to 1906 incorporated the Indian Territory into Oklahoma, dissolved tribal governments, and forced allotment upon the Five Civilized Tribes and other Indians of the territory.

123. Only after court decisions in 1948 in Arizona and 1962 in New Mexico did those states finally extend the franchise to Indian residents. Not until the Naturalization Act of 1940 were foreign-born Indians eligible for naturalization.

Priest, *Uncle Sam's Stepchildren*, chap. 16, tells the story for the period after the Civil War, while Hoxie, "Beyond Savagery," chaps. 6, 12, carries the story forward to the eve of the citizenship act. Gary C. Stein, "The Indian Citizenship Act of 1924," *New Mexico Historical Review*, XLVII (July 1972), pp. 257–74, discusses the reasons for the passage of the act by Congress. Felix Cohen, *Handbook of Federal Indian Law* (Washington, D.C.: Government Printing Office, 1941), pp. 153–59, discusses Indian citizenship until date of publication. See also Helen L. Peterson, "American Indian Political Participation," *Annals of the American Academy of Political and Social Science*, CCCXI (May 1957), pp. 116–26, for the more recent period.

124. The best introduction to racial thinking, immigration restriction, and Americanization in this period is John Higham, *Strangers in the Land: Patterns of American Nativism, 1860–1925* (rev. ed., New Brunswick, N.J.: Rutgers University Press, 1955), chaps. 6–11, but see also Maldwyn A. Jones, *American Immigration* (Chicago: University of Chicago Press, 1960), chap. 9; and Thomas F. Gossett, *Race: The History of an Idea in America* (Dallas: Southern Methodist University Press, 1963), chaps. 12–15. Hoxie, "Beyond Savagery," part two, treats the implications of early twentieth-century racial assumptions for Indian policy making. He argues that the virulent racism of the period caused policy makers to relegate the Indian to a fixed subordinate position in the economic, political, and intellectual life of the nation. Moreover, he asserts that as Americans came to accept the diversity of Indians and their cultures, they gave up any effort to integrate Native Americans into American society upon a level equal to Whites. Assimilation measures were to lead to separate but unequal institutions for Indians as for Blacks.

125. Fred H. Matthews, "The Revolt Against Americanism: Cultural Pluralism and Cultural Relativism as an Ideology of Liberation," *The Canadian Review of American Studies*, I (Spring 1970), pp. 4–31; James H. Powell, "The Concept of Cultural Pluralism in American Social Thought, 1915–1965" (Unpub. Ph.D. dissertation, University of Notre Dame, 1971), chaps. 1–2.

126. John Collier, *From Every Zenith: A Memoir and Some Essays on Life and Thought* (Denver: Sage Books, 1963), p. 126.

127. In addition to his autobiography, see on Collier's thought: Kenneth R. Philp, "John Collier and the American Indian, 1920–1945" (Unpub. Ph.D. dissertation, Michigan State University, 1968), *passim;* and "John Collier and the American Indian, 1920–1945," in Leon B. Blair, ed., *Essays on Radicalism in Contemporary America* (Austin: University of Texas Press, 1972), pp. 63–80; Stephen Kunitz, "The Social Philosophy of John Collier," *Ethnohistory*, XVIII (Summer 1971), pp. 213–29. His activities in the 1920s are the subject of two articles by Philp, "Albert B. Fall and the Protest from the Pueblos," *Arizona*

and the West, XII (Autumn 1970), pp. 237–54; "John Collier and the Crusade to Protect Indian Religious Freedom," *Journal of Ethnic Studies,* I (Spring 1973), pp. 22–38.

128. On the development of social work as a profession and the changing conception of social problems, see Robert H. Bremner, *From the Depths: The Discovery of Poverty in the United States* (New York: New York University Press, 1956); Clarke Chambers, *Seedtime of Reform: America's Social Services and Social Action, 1918–1933* (Minneapolis: University of Minnesota Press, 1963); Roy Lubove, *The Professional Altruist: The Emergence of Social Work as a Career, 1880–1930* (Cambridge: Harvard University Press, 1965).

129. Lewis Meriam *et al., The Problem of Indian Administration* (Baltimore: Johns Hopkins University Press, 1928), p. 21.

130. *Ibid.,* pp. 22–23.

131. *Ibid.,* p. 51. The institute issued at the same time the study by Laurence F. Schmeckebier, cited in note 71.

132. Kenneth R. Philp, "Herbert Hoover's New Era: A False Dawn for the American Indian, 1929–1932," *Rocky Mountain Social Science Journal,* IX (April 1972), pp. 53–60; Randolph C. Downes, "A Crusade for Indian Reform, 1922–1934," *Mississippi Valley Historical Review,* XXXII (Dec. 1945), pp. 331–54; S. Lyman Tyler, *Indian Affairs: A Study of the Changes in Policy of the United States Toward Indians* (Provo, Utah: Brigham Young University Press, 1964), chap. 3; Margaret Szasz, *Education and the American Indian: The Road to Self-Determination, 1928–1973* (Albuquerque: University of New Mexico Press, 1974), chap. 3, offer interpretations of Indian affairs under the Hoover administration.

133. The bill and a long memorandum from Collier are printed as part of the hearings before the House of Representatives Committee on Indian Affairs, *Readjustment of Indian Affairs,* 73 Cong., 2 sess. (Washington, D.C.: Government Printing Office, 1934), pp. 1–29. The credit fund amendment is printed in the hearings before the Senate Committee on Indian Affairs, *To Grant to Indians Living Under Federal Tutelage the Freedom to Organize for Purposes of Local Self-Government and Economic Enterprise,* 73 Cong., 2 sess. (Washington, D.C.: Government Printing Office, 1934), pp. 15–16.

134. On the story of the bill and its amendments in Congress, see Philp, "John Collier and the American Indian," chap. 4; "John Collier and the Controversy Over the Wheeler-Howard Bill," in Smith and Kvasnicka, eds., *Indian-White Relations,* pp. 171–200; and John L. Freeman, Jr., "The New Deal for the Indian: A Study in Bureau-Committee Relations in American Government" (Unpub. Ph.D. dissertation, Princeton University, 1952).

135. Graham D. Taylor, "Anthropologists, Reformers, and the Indian New Deal," *Prologue,* VII (Fall 1975), pp. 151–62, discusses and evaluates Collier's use of anthropologists in his program, while Tyler, *Indian Affairs,* pp. 73–101, *passim;* Freeman, "The New Deal for the Indian," chaps. 5–6; and Philp, "John Collier and the American Indian," chap. 5, mention the opposition to the commissioner's program. The adjustments made in Collier's plans to meet the needs and opposition of the allotted Indians of Oklahoma and those who spoke for them is the subject of Peter M. Wright, "John Collier and the

Oklahoma Indian Welfare Act of 1936," *Chronicles of Oklahoma*, L (Autumn 1972), pp. 347–71.

136. Lawrence C. Kelly, "The Indian Reorganization Act: The Dream and the Reality," *Pacific Historical Review*, XLIV (Aug. 1975), pp. 291–312, is valuable on its subject but provides particular clarification on the actual numbers of tribes and persons voting for and against the IRA.

137. Graham D. Taylor, "The Tribal Alternative to Bureaucracy: The Indian's New Deal, 1933–1945," *Journal of the West*, XIII (Jan. 1974), pp. 128–42, throws light on the problems of achieving grass-roots support for a centralized program. Robert F. Berkhofer, Jr., "Persisting Problems of American Indian Leadership," in John Higham, ed., *The Leadership of American Ethnic Groups*, to be published by the Johns Hopkins University Press, provides the larger historical context in terms of Native American factionalism for this issue.

138. For the working out of the program and variant assessments of its success, see in addition to the above authorities on the Indian New Deal, Szasz, *Education and the American Indian*, chaps. 6–8; Lawrence C. Kelly, *The Navajo Indians and Federal Indian Policy, 1900–1935* (Tucson: University of Arizona Press, 1968), chaps. 9–11; Donald L. Parman, *The Navajos and the New Deal* (New Haven: Yale University Press, 1976); and William H. Kelly, ed., *Indian Affairs and the Indian Reorganization Act: The Twenty-Year Record* (Tucson: University of Arizona Press, 1954). The latter is a symposium featuring Collier and others prominent in the Indian New Deal.

139. From his article "Termination of Federal Supervision: Removal of Restrictions Over Indian Property and Person," *Annals of the American Academy of Political and Social Science*, CCCXI (May 1957), p. 55, his emphasis, but see the whole article. See also the articles by William Zimmerman, Jr., "The Role of the Bureau of Indian Affairs Since 1933," and Oliver La Farge, "Termination of Federal Supervision: Disintegration and the American Indians," in the same special issue of the *Annals* devoted to the American Indian, pp. 31–46. Tyler, *Indian Affairs*, pp. 109–58, and *Indian Affairs: A Work Paper on Termination: With an Attempt to Show Its Antecedents* (Provo, Utah: Brigham Young University Press, 1964), chronicles the background and passage of the termination resolution and bills. The relationship between federal termination policy and state services to Indians is a major theme of Theodore W. Taylor, *The States and Their Indian Citizens* (Washington, D.C.: Government Printing Office, 1972).

140. Szasz, *Education and the American Indian*, chaps. 9–14; Hagan, *American Indians*, pp. 158–71; James E. Officer, "The American Indian and Federal Policy," in Jack O. Waddell and O. Michael Watson, eds., *The American Indian in Urban Society* (Boston: Little, Brown, 1971), pp. 44–58; Ralph A. Barney, "Legal Problems Peculiar to Indian Claims Litigation," *Ethnohistory*, II (Fall 1955), pp. 315–24; Nancy O. Lurie, "The Indian Claims Commission Act," *Annals of the American Academy of Political and Social Science*, CCCXI (May 1957), pp. 56–70; Thomas LeDuc, "The Work of the Indian Claims Commission Under the Act of 1946," *Pacific Historical Review*, XXVI (Feb. 1957), pp. 1–16; Wilcomb Washburn, *Red Man's Land/White Man's Law: A Study of the Past and Present Status of the American Indian* (New

York: Charles Scribner's Sons, 1971), pp. 80–108, all provide information on the policies since World War Two mentioned in this and the preceding paragraphs. Washburn offers a survey of the present status of the Indian in his *Red Man's Land/White Man's Law*, parts 2–3.

141. How termination worked out for one tribe is the subject of Gary Orfield, *A Study of Termination Policy* (Denver: National Congress of American Indians, 1964), reprinted in Subcommittee on Indian Education of the Committee on Labor and Public Welfare, United States Senate, *The Education of American Indians: The Organization Question*, 91 Cong., 1 sess. (Washington, D.C.: Government Printing Office, 1970), vol. 4, pp. 673–816. See also Deborah Shames, ed., *Freedom with Reservation: The Menominee Struggle to Save Their Land and People* (Madison, Wis.: National Committee to Save the Menominee People and Forests, 1972). Congress repealed the termination legislation for the Menominee and restored the tribe to federal trust status in December 1973.

142. Hazel W. Hertzberg, *The Search for an American Indian Identity: Modern Pan-Indian Movements* (Syracuse: Syracuse University Press, 1971), covers organizations prior to 1930, including the Society of American Indians. No history of the National Congress of American Indians exists. Stan Steiner, *The New Indians* (New York: Harper & Row, 1968), is mainly about the National Indian Youth Council. Robert C. Day summarizes briefly the history of Native American activism during the 1960s in "The Emergence of Activism as a Social Movement," in Howard M. Bahr, Bruce Chadwick, and Robert C. Day, eds., *Native Americans Today: Sociological Perspectives* (New York: Harper & Row, 1972), pp. 506–32. Vine Deloria, Jr., *Behind the Trail of Broken Treaties: An Indian Declaration of Independence* (New York: Dell Publishing Co., 1974), presents a brief history of the activities behind the occupation of the BIA building and the "second battle of Wounded Knee" along with the rationale for Indian sovereignty as evolved by Native American activist groups. Another perspective upon the background of modern native political movements is offered in my "Persisting Problems of American Indian Leadership." The next few paragraphs derive from that article with very little alteration of wording.

143. For the theory of the modern reservation and its connection to the federal government and the larger American society, see the articles by Dobyns, Castille, and Jorgensen cited above in note 110.

144. The continuing conflict over native resources is detailed in Kirke Kickingbird and Karen Ducheaux, *One Hundred Million Acres* (New York: Macmillan, 1973); American Friends Service Committee, *Uncommon Controversy: Fishing Rights of the Muckleshoot, Pyallup, and Nisqually Indians* (Seattle: University of Washington Press, 1970); William H. Veeder, "Federal Encroachment on Indian Water Rights and the Impairment of Reservation Development," in Joint Economic Committee of the United States Congress, *Towards Economic Development for Native American Communities* (Washington, D.C.: Government Printing Office, 1969), pp. 449–518.

145. The full citation is William A. Brophy and Sophie D. Aberle *et al.*, *The Indian: America's Unfinished Business* (Norman: University of Oklahoma Press, 1966). Compare this report and Sar A. Levitan and Barbara Hetrick, *Big*

Brother's Indian Programs—With Reservations (New York: McGraw-Hill, 1971), and Alan L. Sorkin, *American Indians and Federal Aid* (Washington, D.C.: The Brookings Institution, 1971), with the Meriam Report for the similarities and differences in the Indian problem and condition as perceived by various commissions and individuals over the last fifty years.

Index

About the Author

Robert F. Berkhofer, Jr.,
is the author of two other books, *Salvation and the Savage:
An Analysis of Protestant Missions and American Indian
Response, 1787–1862* and *A Behavioral Approach to Historical
Analysis.* A professor of American history at the University of
Michigan, he lives in Ann Arbor with his wife and son.

A Note on the Type

This book was set on the Linotype in Janson, a recutting made
direct from type cast from matrices long thought to have been
made by the Dutchman Anton Janson, who was a practicing
type founder in Leipzig during the years 1668–87. However, it
has been conclusively demonstrated that these types are actually
the work of Nicholas Kis (1650–1702), a Hungarian, who most
probably learned his trade from the master Dutch type founder
Dirk Voskens. The type is an excellent example of the influential
and sturdy Dutch types that prevailed in England up to the time
William Caslon developed his own incomparable designs
from them.

The book was composed by American Book–Stratford
Press, Inc., Brattleboro, Vermont; it was printed and bound
by The Haddon Craftsmen, Inc., Scranton, Pennsylvania.

Typography and binding design by Virginia Tan